IT WAS ALL A LIE . . .

I knew exactly where Steve's office was. But I'd only gone inside a couple of times. Sitting at a desk, facing me, was a young woman with dark hair.

She was Steve's mistress.

I lost control, rushed across the room, shoved her out the door, slamming it behind her. I went berserk. There was a baseball bat in the corner—I grabbed it with both hands and started swinging. First the pictures of Steve on the wall. They cracked. Then the trophies on the shelf. They crashed to the floor. The desk, the chairs, the walls—I was doing damage, making lots of noise. But there was no release. No relief. Shock waves of pure anger and confusion rocked me. Steve had gotten rid of me, mentally, years ago . . .

CYNTHIA GARVEY is a former co-host of "A.M. Los Angeles" and "The Morning Show." A frequent lecturer on the devastating effects of child abuse, she now has her own cable TV show, "Motherworks."

ANDY MEISLER has been a TV critic for National Public Radio, and writes for *California* magazine, *The New York Times,* and *TV Guide,* among others.

An Alternate Selection of the Literary Guild and the Doubleday Book Club

THE
SECRET LIFE
OF
CYNDY
GARVEY

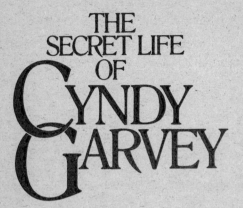

Cynthia Garvey
& Andy Meisler

ST. MARTIN'S PAPERBACKS

For Krisha and Whitney:
"I love you most cause I'm biggest!"
Mom

Insert photo credits:
Photo copyright © 1989 by Harry Langdon
Photo copyright © 1989 by Tony Korody
Photo copyright © 1989 by Erik Stern
Photo copyright © 1989 by Donald Sanders
Photo copyright © 1989 by George Beebe/The Image Bank

Published by arrangement with Doubleday

THE SECRET LIFE OF CYNDY GARVEY

Copyright © 1989 by Cynthia Garvey.

Front cover photo(s) by Morton Beebe/The Image Bank.
Back cover photo by UPI/Bettmann Newsphotos.

Library of Congress Catalog Card Number: 89-32129

ISBN: 0-312-92203-5

Printed in the United States of America

Doubleday hardcover edition/July 1989
St. Martin's Paperbacks edition/May 1990

10 9 8 7 6 5 4 3 2 1

This book could not have been written without the kind help of many friends and colleagues. The authors would like to thank: Gary Bostwick, Bill Davidson, Steve Gelman, Ann Guinn, Mary Ann Kennedy, Laureen Lang, Fran Miller, B. K. Moran, Karen Oblom, Darlene Reid, Bob Roe, Dan Sexton, Chris Truhan, Mark Truhan, and Rosalie Muller Wright.

Special thanks to Shaye Areheart and Herman Gollob, our editors at Doubleday, for their constant support and invaluable advice.

Eternal gratitude to Maureen and Eric Lasher, our agents, for services far beyond the call of duty.

And much love to Kathryn Tschopik, who believed.

"*Nature means children to be children before they become men. If we deviate from this order, we produce a forced fruit, without taste, maturity, or power of lasting; we make young philosophers and old children.*"

JEAN-JACQUES ROUSSEAU

PROLOGUE

This is a story about illusion and reality.

The illusion, which I helped create, was a powerful one. It was: that from 1971 to 1981, a woman named Cyndy Garvey lived a wonderful life. She had a famous, handsome, loving husband. She had a happy family and a glamorous, successful career. She led a public life. A magic life. Hers was a life to be admired or envied.

In reality, Cyndy Garvey did not exist.

She was a phantom. An empty image. A smiling mask that I—Cynthia Garvey—wore in public. In private, in the real world, I was a desperately unhappy woman. My marriage was empty, silent. My real goals had disappeared. Except for my children, my life was a lonely charade.

I kept a public face and a private face. I'd learned to do this as a child: as an abused, unhappy little girl, ashamed of the beatings I received and of the terrible faults my father saw in me. This was my dark, shameful secret. And even as an adult, even as I became "well known," a "public figure," I kept the secret shame hidden.

The real Cynthia Garvey—full of flaws and self-doubt and hope and love and anger—was not to be revealed. I could not afford to lose control. And then, of course, I did. Like many women who've learned to deny the reality of their own lives, I held myself an emotional hostage. The fear and rage did not go away. It just expressed itself, uncontrolled, in various forms of self-destructive behavior. Some of them emotional. Some of them physical. All of them useless, and senseless, and futile.

And so I almost died. I nearly killed myself. I'd been living a lie for so long that I could not face the truth. But then, even in my lowest moments, my love for my children—and through them for life, for reality—pulled me through.

And this is the good part—the real reason I've written this book. For in my despair and helplessness, I finally reached out to people who helped me recover my real identity. Who taught me to untangle the twisted roots of child abuse, who taught me, through the pain of reawakening, to treasure the very things that make me a unique person, to open myself up to the real world. To my own world.

In the last few years, I've reordered my life and my priorities. And most important of all: while getting my life together, I've learned that I am not alone. That for all the publicity, for all the newspaper and magazine accounts, *my* story was a very ordinary one. That there are millions of women like me: abused children who grow into self-abusing adults, denying their real dreams every day.

To them I say: please read this book with an open mind. Please consider my journey. True, it has not been an easy road, or a smooth one. It never is. Occasionally, I still feel the seductive tug of denial. Of fantasy. Of Cyndy.

But then I pull myself back. I refuse to put on the mask. And if I can do it, you can, too.

Cynthia Garvey
January, 1989

CHAPTER 1

"**M**ommy, what are we doing here?"

My eldest daughter, Krisha, seven years old, tugged at my hand. We came to a dead stop in the middle of the Los Angeles Airport arrival terminal; she and her four-year-old sister, Whitney, looked up at me sadly.

"We're here to visit Grandma and Grandpa. Remember?" I lied with a bright smile. I didn't want them to know how devastated I felt, how weary. Their faces grew suspicious, then they looked down. It was no use. They may not have known the truth, but they could sense my sadness.

It was February 15, 1982. The girls and I were in Los Angeles for the final breakup of my marriage, of our family, and of the world my children had known for most of their lives. A few days earlier, the real-estate agent had called and said that the buyers had agreed to meet my price. In the next five days, my husband and I would have to "clean out" almost twelve years of marriage.

That home, that marriage, was nearly gone. In the past. Finished. I was living in New York City then, in a fourteenth-floor apartment, drawing on my savings account and looking for work. I was an unemployed talk-show host, barely a "personality" at all. My husband, Steve Garvey, was living alone, or so I thought, in Los

Angeles. Four months earlier, his team had won the World Series. Eight months earlier, our marriage had sunk so low that I'd asked him if he still loved me. "I don't think so," he'd said. We separated. A few months later I'd discovered that, for my sanity's sake, I couldn't live in the same city with him. Being Mrs. Steve Garvey in Los Angeles was making me ill. So I quit my job, left the show I was co-hosting on a local television station, and took my kids across the country in search of a new start. An escape from the past.

But nobody wanted to hire an unemployed female interviewer. I walked the floor of our apartment late into the night, but I couldn't figure out what had gone wrong.

Every morning, I'd send the girls off to school. Some days, not often, I'd have a meeting at a network or with a station executive. "Cyndy! Thanks for coming," the men in their gray suits would say, looking pleasantly surprised. Delighted! As if I hadn't been phoning for weeks for an appointment. "Yes, yes, you've got some good ideas there." "We're not quite ready to make a commitment." "How's Steve doing?" "He's some ballplayer! Why'd you leave him like that?" "Let's stay in touch, yes, definitely!" Then, I'd go back to the apartment, turn on the television for background noise, and think. I had the Garvey name, but I wasn't *the* Garvey. Without him, it seemed, I had no identity at all.

"Come on guys, let's go." I picked up our luggage, and we headed for the rental car counter. "Sign here, Mrs. Garvey." The girls liked the little shuttle bus; it was brightly painted and it bumped along. In the heavy loop traffic, it took a while just to get to each stop.

The old thoughts came back, whirling through my brain. What had gone wrong? Over the years, Steve's words had turned to stares, our conversations to one-sided arguments. It must have been my fault. Yes. Could there be something . . . wrong with me?

Maybe I was too much for Steve. Maybe I was giving

Steve too little. Was it the work? Was I too public? I'm not public by nature. I'm a private person, so maybe by being public he . . . did that cause me to be away from home too much? But I was only gone from seven in the morning till one in the afternoon. So that couldn't be the reason. Was I too pushy? Well, Steve's the doer. I'm the questioner, the prober. Tell me! I'd pleaded. I'd tried and tried to communicate and he wouldn't talk to me. My questions bounced back. Off a wall. A blank, cold wall.

"Mommy, turn on the radio!" A rental car ride with music was a real treat for two New York City girls used to taxicabs and buses. "Sit still back there," I said, managing another smile. I took the Chevrolet east on Century Boulevard, past billboards for vodka and fancy tape recorders.

I was dressed all wrong, I suddenly realized, in a wool sweater and long skirt, dark colors, structured shoes. New York clothes. This was California, land of sunshine and jogging suits. Except it was winter now and we were in a fog, a light gray fog. The sun was just barely hidden behind a thin film of cloud. This haze, I remembered. I'd seen it nowhere but Los Angeles. I squinted into the glare, the familiar headache beginning to form.

Up onto the San Diego Freeway. How many hundreds of times had I driven this route? But the rental car felt deadened, unfamiliar. Up and over the pass we went; there was a view of the mountains that disappear into the smog each summer. I merged west on the Ventura Freeway, past the shopping malls and tract houses and blank, low-slung office buildings. We rode for thirty minutes; the buildings thinned out to an occasional warehouse. We were going home. No, I caught myself, not any more. The traffic slowed for an accident. The people sat impassively in their cars, windows closed. Is it true? I thought. Had we really lived all the way out here? Where were we? Wherever Steve and I had lived, I'd tried to fit. I'd tried really hard.

I got off at Calabasas, past the kennel and the U-Storage. Left at the light, over the freeway, then left again. Past the stucco gate, and into the "exclusive" development. The streets trailed off into half-built houses; the trees were matchsticks held up by wires. The streets! Park Capri. Park Granada. Park Aurora. Park Sienna. When I'd lived here, the names had sounded merely silly. Now they seemed absurd, obsessive. I stopped at my parents' house to drop off the children for a while. I hadn't seen my parents since I'd left six months ago. Since I'd run away.

"How are you doing, Dad?" I asked, warily.

"Fine," he said, stonefaced. Like many things I had and hadn't done, he disapproved of my leaving Steve. After all, I'd left my home, my perfect family. In his world, good wives didn't do that. Mom hugged the kids and took them inside. I climbed into the car, headed up the slope, and curved around to the left. Left at Park Vicente, go to the end of the cul-de-sac, look for the red roof and the iron gate. We're 4393; it's painted right on the curb.

The house on the hill.

Though Steve was supposed to meet me, there was no car in the driveway. I stood on the doorstep, took a deep breath, and looked around. The last time I'd been here had been a disaster.

It was November, four months earlier. I'd come back to Los Angeles for a small acting job. "Just something to do," my agent had said, "until we find something that's right."

When I drove to the house to check my things, I arrived in the middle of a full-blown party. Parked cars filled up both sides of the street as far back as I could see. The door was opened by a young woman, long dark hair, slightly taller than me. She looked at me, said nothing, and melted back into the crowd. Music was playing. The living room was full of laughing, well-dressed strangers. I recognized nobody. Steve was not in sight.

I felt disoriented, displaced. I pushed through the crowd up to my room, sat down on the bed and tried to pull myself together. We'd hardly ever entertained when we'd lived here together.

A few minutes later, Steve rushed in, wide-eyed. "What are you doing here?" he demanded.

What was I doing here? This had been my home. "Who are all these people? What are they doing here?" Steve said nothing; he just stood there and glared at me. I felt like an intruder. After sitting for a few minutes, I walked quickly down the stairs, looking straight ahead. I rushed out the front door, got into my car, and drove away.

This time, as I drove back toward the house, I tried to make sense of it all.

We'd built our home from the ground up. I was pregnant with Whitney that year. We'd needed more privacy. One day, I'd driven past the hill, then driven up the hill, then found the man who wanted to sell us the lot. On a winter afternoon, I got Steve to come to the real-estate office. I showed him the property layout, the homes we could choose from, and then took him up the hill to show him the view. "Look! This is how far we can see," I said, excited and proud.

"It's fine," said my husband, and that was enough for me.

I worked with the architect and the builder. It took a long time, but we put together a house for a busy family. A *normal* family. There was an office for Steve. His trophy room. A game room for the pool table. A formal dining room and living room for entertaining. But those rooms were rarely, if ever, used. We had no close friends; nor was Steve close to any of his teammates. He rented another office less than a mile away and hardly ever found time to come home. A busy, busy man. Perhaps it was my fault—I'd built a dream house for a different life, but maybe it was only my dream.

Maybe. This time, this last visit, I used my key to open the door.

"Hello?" I said.

The housekeeper, Priscilla Sellery, came in from the back yard. "Hello," she said, in a flat voice. She didn't seem happy to see me. *It's me, Priscilla. Cynthia.* Well, she worked for Steve, not for me any more. A quick tour of the house: it was so neat and clean, it looked unlived-in. A model home.

A moving van pulled up outside; I'd hired five men to help Steve and me move everything out of the house. Then, in a plan that was so sensible and practical it made my insides freeze, we'd move Steve's things into our beach house—the one his business manager had recommended for "investment purposes." I'd make Steve "comfortable," then go back to New York. Anything that was left over—which meant almost everything—was going to the Salvation Army.

"Where do you want us to start?" asked the movers' boss brusquely, sizing me up and then glancing away. For a second, his rudeness startled me. Then it hit me. Okay. I've got it. A Steve Garvey fan.

In a funny way, I didn't blame him for his attitude. What kind of cold bitch, what kind of monster-woman, could fail at this marriage, leave this house, abandon their idea of male perfection? I pointed to the living room furniture, and they moved sluggishly toward it.

In the bedroom, I changed into jeans and a work shirt, tied my hair back with a handkerchief. A car rolled loudly into the driveway. The engine noise stopped and the door slammed.

"Hey, Steve Garvey!"

"How're ya doin', guys?"

"Great series, Steve!"

"Good to see ya, pal."

"Awwwright!!!"

I looked through the doorway. Steve was dressed in pristine white golf pants. A pink shirt. On top of that, a pink sweater.

He looked up at me in the front door, half wary adult, half guilty teenager. He said nothing.

An awful thought. Oh no. This couldn't be happening. "Why are you dressed like that?" I asked, bewildered. "Aren't you going to help me?"

"Hey, I'm entered in the L.A. Open. I look forward to this event. This is the one event each year I look forward to."

"A *golf* tournament?"

"Yeah," said my husband, and got back into the Jaguar. Without another word he started the car, pulled out, and was gone.

And then a strange thing happened: the workmen looked at each other, shocked, and then at me, with pity. It would have to do for the moment. "Hey, guys, let's get going on this job," said the boss, turning to me quizzically, suddenly respectful. Yes, I thought. It's time to get going.

Now the sadness was spiked with anger; the anger drove me to work. Just to get it over with. "The kitchen first, Priscilla," I said. This was *my* room: a typical California sitcom kitchen—pass-through, cream-colored tiles, bar, breakfast area, every gadget ever invented. We started pulling down pots and pans and putting them into boxes. I opened a counter drawer and stared at a pile of newspaper clippings. GARVEY HITS FOUR. DODGERS WIN AGAIN. STEVE G. WINS ALL-STAR VOTE. Oh yes. I'd clipped Steve's articles all through our marriage; the next step was to paste them in the latest scrapbook. Except by the end, when things were really bad, I'd just lost heart.

Like right now. This minute. A wave of nausea swept over me; I rested my head on the counter. Think of the good times, Cynthia: meeting Steve in college, falling in love, the early years together, the girls.

When we'd first moved into this house, I'd cooked Steve elaborate dinners. That was fun; I liked to cook. I was good at it, and most importantly, it meant that my husband was home. That we'd be the kind of family I'd always wanted to belong to.

Steak, vegetables, potatoes, spaghetti, dessert. Lots of those all-important carbohydrates at two-thirty in the afternoon. It was my pleasure; I loved him. I thought that if he got what he needed he would stay healthy, and if he stayed healthy he would be better at what he does, and if he was better at what he does he would be happier, and maybe, just maybe, some of the happiness would rub off on us.

Did it? I'd sit down at the table and we'd talk. No, I'd talk. "Who's pitching tonight?" "Does this guy fool around on the mound?" If it was a pitcher who took forever, then it would be a long game, and I wouldn't see Steve again until well after midnight. "What do you think about redecorating this room?" "About Krisha going to this school or Whitney going to that school?" I'd ask him about the charities he was working for. About his schedule; about arranging some time together during his rare days off when the Dodgers were home. About setting aside a Sunday evening after a Sunday day game. "Let's take the kids to Disneyland." "How about Marineland?" "Let's you and me go to dinner." "Can we stay home together?" *Talk to me, Steve, please.*

He'd look up from his dinner. "Twenty-one Questions," he'd say. That was one of his pet names for me.

Then, when he'd finished his meal, he'd get up, peck me on the cheek, grab his hat—he liked wearing hats in those days—and leave.

He wasn't there the next day, when the movers and I set up the beach house with the things he'd need. Not there when we quit for the afternoon, not there when we started again the next day. "Meet me in the garage, and take what you want for yourselves," I said to the work-men. They were astonished at what they found there: big piles of bats, balls, gloves, caps, jogging suits, sportswear, tennis rackets, shoes. A whole wall of shoes, dozens of pairs of Steve's Size Nine, every style and color, none of them ever out of their boxes. The fruits of our freebie lifestyle: just for being Steve Garvey, Steve got this kind of stuff by the carload. The men looked a little over-whelmed; I guessed they'd never read about this sort of thing in the sports pages. They took armloads of this treasure, then thought of what conceivable use they'd have for it all, and put some back in the charity pile. I left them to eagerly sort it out for themselves.

On Wednesday, I went upstairs to the kids' room. This was harder. Almost too hard. Krisha and Whitney loved their rooms—and yet they hadn't asked to visit them on this trip. Maybe they were handling this better than me. God, I hoped so.

First, Whitney's room. It used to be the nursery; I'd painted it white, with colorful giraffes and elephants on the walls. Very bright things to see when she looked up from her crib. Krisha's room was yellow, with clouds running around the walls. And little people, and birds, even a picture of Duffy the Dog, our cocker spaniel. I picked up the toys and stuffed animals they'd especially wanted to bring back with them. We'd spent all our time together. Which was wonderful—except, where was Daddy? The perfect home. The perfect family. Almost.

Nobody seemed to mind or to notice. Why should they? Every few months, it seemed, the magazine photog-raphers would come around. I'd dress the kids in their Sunday best; the men would drag their lights into the trophy room. Then to the living room, the kitchen, the front step, all of us holding hands. "Give Cyndy a kiss over the chocolate cake!" Fairy-tale shots. I'd ask Steve if he could get them to stop. "Just do this now," he'd say. "This is what we have to do now. Get the girls." And they'd set up more of their little fantasies: I was this woman who met her husband in college and really just lived and died to see him become a major league star. And what was wrong with that, Cyndy? And then the shooting would stop, and Steve would joke with the photographers and give them some bats and balls. And then he'd say he had an appointment, and he'd be gone.

Gone! I sat down on Whitney's bed, and the worst memory of all came back. One Saturday afternoon, while unloading groceries from the car, I looked up to see Whitney, then three, walking down the driveway with her sister on their way to play next door. "Now, stay together, and come back in five minutes," I said. And then, just a few minutes later, Whitney came walking back, her face white as chalk, holding her right arm like a little broken straw. Krisha was frightened. Her sister had climbed a tree, the branch had broken, and she'd fallen five feet to the ground. It was a compound fracture. We could see the bone poking through the skin.

No panic. Steve didn't know where the hospital was, but that was all right, I did. I held Whitney in my arms while I gave him directions. The woman in the emergency room wanted me to fill out some insurance forms first. Ridiculous! I got mad. "We're here. We're going to be here for a while. We'll fill out these papers later. Let's first get my daughter to Dr. Grant." Whitney was trembling. Was she going into shock?

While I was waiting outside the examining room, Steve got up and went out. Was he going to fill out the insurance forms? The next thing I knew, my father was walking toward me. "Where's Steve?" What was my father doing here? How did he know what had happened? Nobody had filled out the insurance forms. Steve had called my father, slipped out without a word, and gone to Dodger Stadium to batting practice. There were three and a half hours to game time. That was too much. Something broke inside me that day, I think.

Suddenly it was all too much again. I left Whitney's

room, went down to the kitchen, and began to cry. What had I done? What had happened to my family? What could I do, too late now, to change things? Change myself? Then I looked up, and there was Priscilla, the housekeeper, standing in front of me. She'd said barely a word to me the whole three days. Now she wanted to tell me something, but she seemed afraid to look at me. What was it?

"Go to the office," she said.

The office. "What office?"

"Go down to Steve's office."

"Steve's office? Why?"

"Just go—you should go," she said, losing her courage and walking away.

Steve's office? And then a terrible thought. An unthinkable connection: in January, when the house was first put on the market, I'd come back here to get everything in order for the real-estate agent. I'd called Steve's office to ask him to help me.

"He's not here, he's out of town," said the man at the answering service.

"Well, where did he go?"

"He's skiing," said the man, in a bored voice.

Skiing? I thought. No, that couldn't be right. Steve didn't ski. He never skied. The baseball club wouldn't let him ski, because he could hurt himself skiing; it was in his contract.

This must be a mistake. "Well, where's his secretary?" I asked. "Let me get in touch with her."

"She's skiing, too," said this stranger, and he hung up.

Wait a minute, I thought. This was *wrong*. Steve's office was for his work for Multiple Sclerosis. It was a charity office, funded by the Multiple Sclerosis Society. His secretary was *from* the Multiple Sclerosis Society. They paid her salary, didn't they? He didn't have a *personal* secretary. I would have known that.

Then I realized I'd never met Steve's secretary.

The implication was obvious, yet I'd ignored it until

that very moment. Why? I was scared by what I'd find, but it was time to find out. I wiped my eyes, walked out the front door, got into the rental car, and drove away.

I knew exactly where Steve's office was. It was maybe five minutes away. But I'd only gone inside a couple of times. In the beginning. I'd had no reason to go in after that. And Steve never talked about what went on there.

The office building was made of wood, muddy brown, very ugly. Steve's office was on the second floor, Room 206. I opened the door. Sitting at a desk, facing me, was a young woman with dark hair, a little taller than me. She was familiar. She was the woman at the party.

She was Steve's mistress. I knew that with a terrible, awful certainty. My head was exploding, bursting. Things were coming together too fast.

"So you were the reason," I said, half to myself, half to her.

She stood up, tried to talk. "But . . . wait . . ."

I lost control. I rushed across the room, pushed her away from the desk. All of a sudden the thought registered that she was bigger than me. Or maybe I was just feeling smaller.

"So you're it!" I said. "So you're his whore! A paid-for charity whore!" And then she was trying to say something, and I was pushing her, shoving her out the door and slamming it behind her. I didn't want to see her any more. I wanted to find out what this office was all about.

First I went to her desk. On it was a diary, one of those big leatherbound five-year planners. I turned the pages and went backward in time. One year, two years, three years. There were her entries. "Stevie and me skiing." "Stevie and me in San Francisco." "Stevie and me pick up his new car." *Stevie!*

I went to the back of the office and sat in Steve's chair. On his desk, where most men have pictures of their wives and children, there was nothing.

In his top drawer were pictures of himself, already autographed. In his bottom drawer were all the articles written about our breakup, about my moving out and going to New York—all the negative articles, all the shots at me, all the supposed reasons I'd left Los Angeles. There was the *Inside Sports* article, published before the breakup, the worst one, the one whose writer we'd sued for libel. The worst article of all.

And underneath was a picture of Steve and his secretary. Smiling.

I looked around. There was a pair of director's chairs with their names on them. And against the wall, God damn him, a couch that folded out into a bed. And a blanket.

My brain was falling to pieces. I went berserk. There was a baseball bat in the corner—I grabbed it with both hands and started swinging.

First the pictures of Steve on the wall. They cracked. Then the trophies on the shelf. They crashed to the floor. The desk, the chair, the walls. I was doing damage, making lots of noise. My hands began to hurt. The bat got heavy. After five minutes, I stopped. I was breathing heavily, my hands bleeding and shaking.

There was no release. No relief. Shock waves of pure anger and confusion rocked me; gradually, though, a single thought filtered through. Steve had stolen my time, three years out of my life. He could have told me he wanted this woman. He could have told me. It would have been bad, it would have changed me. But I could have put it behind me, could have gone on with my life, gone on with my career. Met someone to love and be loved by. Had the third child I'd always wanted. But all that was impossible now. Steve had gotten rid of me, mentally, years ago. He'd set me up to leave me. *I'd been set up.* He'd just thrown me out. Was I crazy then not to notice? Was I crazy now?

I had to get out of that place. Stumbling over the debris, almost tripping, I walked to the door and slammed it behind me.

Outside, on the porch, the sun was still glaring at me

from behind the fog. I walked shakily down the stairs, turned toward the parking lot, and headed to my car.

By concentrating hard, looking straight ahead, I got there. Still shaking, I fumbled for the keys. Then there was a noise, the sound of a door opening and shutting.

I turned around. A man I've never seen before had emerged from the office next door. He must have heard me wrecking the place, but he never tried to stop me, never made a move.

He cupped his hands to his mouth. "No, you're the whore. *You* left Steve!" he yelled. What? This man, this total stranger, knew everything. And he said I was to blame.

Numb now, I got into the car and almost unconsciously, started the engine. I'd tried to play by the rules. But the rules had changed. When? Why?

Set up, set up, I kept thinking. I'll have to play by the new rules now. I put the car in gear and drove away.

CHAPTER 2

At the edge of the parking lot, I braked jerkily to a
stop. The rage I felt literally paralyzed me; for a
few terrifying seconds, I couldn't breathe. I
clutched my chest. My heart hurt. I rocked back and
forth, trying to push back the awful, mocking truth: I'd
been cheated out of a marriage of ten years, ten years I'd
spent mostly alone.

It was pathetic, really. I didn't even know which way
to point the car. Which way *right now,* Cynthia? Toward
my children? They were with my parents, on a trip up the
coast to visit friends. To the old house? It was dark and
empty. To my "home" and non-job? They were three
thousand miles away.

The car took pity on me: it began to drive itself. To the
left, the direction I'd come from. Then left again and
right at the corner. Onto the entrance to the freeway,
away from the city, through the soft green hills.

I was in the far right lane; trucks and cars thundered
past while the events of the past hour began to filter back.
They were like sharp fragments of a nightmare. I gripped
the wheel and held on, gasping for air. Then, suddenly,
the freeway curved left and the traffic stopped: unconsciously, I'd gone straight ahead and gotten off at an exit.

I felt sick to my stomach. This was the route I'd taken
all week—to the beach house, to make sure it was fixed

up just right. For Steve! And now here I was again, as if nothing had happened. I tried to think of my options. But if I had any, I was too dazed, too lost, too stupid to think of them. Disgust and self-hatred flooded through me. When the light turned green I turned left, toward the ocean.

The two-lane road curved upward. To stay on the road, I concentrated on the car ahead of me, keeping the same distance between us, letting it guide me through the turns. The fog thinned. The road went through a dark tunnel; the sudden sunlight at the far end hurt my eyes. The car bumped noisily over the center line; I pulled back to my side and started to descend toward the coastline.

A clump of palm trees, then a glimpse of ocean, then thickening clouds over the Pacific Coast Highway. The house was three miles farther north; I turned hard left onto the private road, past the dilapidated guard booth that was unmanned, as usual. This was our playhouse. Our wonderful tax shelter. It was the ultimate in California privacy. Like all the other houses on the street, 27124 Malibu Cove Colony was invisible from the highway. From the front, a blank, brown, windowless facade. From the ocean, two stories of plate glass; four bedrooms and a deck over the ocean.

I parked the car, let myself in, and stepped through the living room to the sun deck. There was nobody on the beach, no boat on the ocean, no sound except the surf. It was high tide; the waves swirled around the pilings below me.

I stared out at the green-gray ocean all night. The phone didn't ring; no one knocked at the door. I had disappeared. Invisible, I sat on the living room couch facing the water, my thoughts clear.

Yes. Something had been wrong between us for a long time. I had tried to draw him out for so long. To get him to hold me, to pay attention to me. To talk to me.

And now? Why would a man cheat on . . . . no, *give*

up his wife and children without saying a word? Keep a secret for so long? And all the while people were dragging our marriage through the mud. All the while we— no, I—defended it in public, in court.

If only he'd complained to me! If only he'd said he'd wanted someone else, I would have behaved differently. I would not have quit my job; I would have stayed and rearranged my life. Maybe Steve and I would have decided to divorce. Definitely, if he had chosen to stay with her. But now? I was expected to fly back to New York, without saying a word. To pack up. Take the children. And leave Steve and his mistress to live in this nice house. No problem. No mess.

No. I wanted to make sense of this. I wanted the truth. This man had lied to me, had lain in bed next to me and *lied to me.* For three years. Why? And I needed to find out what I'd done wrong. Why hadn't I seen the signs sooner? What had I ignored? What part had I played in this? I couldn't—wouldn't—figure it out from an apartment on Eighty-first Street. Not now. I wouldn't run away this time. I needed to know.

When the sun came up, I stood up, then moved Steve's things from the bedroom to the garage. I still felt stiff and sore, as if I'd been beaten up. I drove to the old house and finished my work with the movers. I told Priscilla, "Your work is finished here. You can go now." Then I drove back to the beach house and dialed Steve's office. "We don't know where he is," said the answering service.

On Saturday I picked up the children. My father had no visible reaction when I told him what had happened; he simply turned and walked away. "What are you going to do now, Cynthia?" asked my mother, embarrassed— whether for me or for my father, I couldn't tell.

"I'm going to stay at the beach house and put the kids into school here," I said.

"All right, Cynthia," said my mother. On the ride to Malibu I told the children the plan.

"Okay, Mommy," said Krisha, sadly. All weekend, I tried to call Steve. All weekend, the answering machine in his office said he couldn't be reached. I didn't leave a message until Sunday afternoon.

"Just tell him I'd like to talk to him," I said. Then I hung up. On Monday I registered the girls in the local school; bought uniforms, arranged for their records to be transferred; made sure my mother could take care of them for three days. I moved like a zombie, in a daze.

On Wednesday I flew to New York to clean out our apartment. My hands were a mass of cuts and bruises from my tirade in Steve's office.

The weather was cold; the city was just as I'd left it. There was very little to move from so temporary a home. Emery Air Freight sent over eight big boxes; I threw in our clothes, the girls' games and books, a few pots and pans. There was room left over in the boxes. I was efficient, a woman in motion.

On the last day, the man I'd begun dating in New York came over and stood among the boxes. He listened to my story with his hands in his pockets. His expression was serious; he wasn't surprised when I told him what Steve had done.

Our relationship, we both knew, wasn't strong enough to support my troubles; I'd have to work this through alone. He didn't want a woman with so much unfinished business. I knew that. He had his own life, his own house, his own world. He wasn't a heel or a white knight. Just the same man he'd been before I'd left a week ago.

But all that was unspoken. "I'm going to stay in Los Angeles" was what I told him.

"I think you should. You have to do what you have to do," he said. I looked at him, a little disappointed. The child in me wanted him to tell me everything would be all right. He didn't. I cried.

I told him I would miss him. He hugged and kissed me and rode out to the airport in my cab. We said goodbye on the sidewalk in front of the terminal. Then he got back in and rode away.

On the plane, right after takeoff, the stewardess suddenly knelt down beside me in the aisle.

"Oh, Cyndy, we're all excited up here in the galley. We really miss you on television."

"Thank you," I said, pulling up the corners of my mouth. Please go away, I thought.

But she wouldn't leave. "You know, I dated your husband," she added, cheerily.

She had my attention now; my head snapped around. "What? When?" I said, looking straight at her for the first time. Staring. She was a fairly good-looking blonde.

I must have scared her. She began to blush and stammer in a singsong voice. "Oh, you know . . . I–I'm based in New York . . . I–I've been stationed here since . . . I meet a lot of athletes . . . Steve and I . . ."

She got up and fled. I'd discovered another one. How many more were there?

I drove back up the coast and moved us into the beach house. I got the children settled in their new school; got their medical records transferred. In a fog, I finished setting up the house. I had the phones turned on; the gas connected. I got workmen in to clean the carpets and the drapes. There were dead water rats in the foundation and in the furnace flues. I hired exterminators to pull them out. I was in a fog. But I felt that, if I kept moving, I would get out of it, somehow. It didn't help that my returning to California seemed to confuse people: in the street, in the stores, acquaintances and strangers—it seemed to make no difference—walked up to me with puzzled expressions on their faces. They'd heard, they said, that I'd left Steve and moved to New York.

"Why are you here?"

"What happened in New York?"

"Are you and Steve back together again? We see him around here, too."

"What's happened to you?"

I didn't know what to say.

Steve finally called me at the end of February. "I have to go to spring training, and I'm coming to get my stuff," he said; I was too shocked to say anything more than agree to a time.

By the time he showed up the next day, I was "ready." The children were in school. I knew I looked awful: I'd lost weight and there were dark circles under my eyes. But I would force him to face me. He owed me that.

His car—a new white Porsche—crunched to a stop outside the house. He let himself in. "Hi, Cyn." His expression was neutral. No, dead. It was frightening.

I knew I had to start right away or I would lose my nerve. Everything came out in a crazy rush.

"Steve, I want us to go into counseling. I want to figure this out. We *must* go. I need to know what happened to us, so I can move on. What did I do wrong? I . . . there are things I have to know. Why did you do this? How could you sleep with that other . . . woman? Then come back and lie down next to me, all those years? Why did you let me get sick? Why did you let the press beat up on me? What did I *do?* I'm the mother of your kids. *Tell me.* Why?"

I was desperate, and Steve was—annoyed! Silent and disapproving. My questions weren't worth an answer. He started moving toward the garage door behind me. To my horror, I found that I was physically repulsed by him; I couldn't help pulling backward as he moved toward me. Feeling sick, I retreated to the other side of the living room, sat down and began to cry.

Steve disappeared into the garage. But he'd have to face me again. Before he'd arrived, fearing something like this would happen, I'd hidden his favorite first-baseman's mitt in another part of the garage, knowing that he wouldn't have the patience to find it. He'd have to ask me. And talk to me. Now, like a bad dream, my pitiful "strategy" began to play itself out. He came out of the garage, put his things down on the floor, and went up-stairs to the bedroom.

A few drops of resolve filtered their way back into me. I followed him up, watched him rummage through the clothes closet. I sat on the bed and pleaded to the back of his neck. "Why did you do it? Who is she? When did you meet her? Where did she come from? *Tell* me!" I noticed that a large picture of me was gone from the wall.

"And where's my picture? Did you bring her here, too?"

He turned around. "Just a few times. She was like my sister," he said.

What? "You don't make love to your sister," I cried.

"We were friends," said Steve. "And after you went away, she was convenient. You know me, Cyn. I don't shop around."

She was convenient. Had my husband, had Steve Gar-vey actually said that? "No! I don't know you," I said, crying again, and fled down the stairs to the kitchen. On the counter were Steve's keys and big leatherbound ap-pointment book. Maybe something in there would tell me the truth. I leafed through it. On the back page was a listing of National League cities. New York. Chicago. Cincinnati. St. Louis. And next to each city there was a woman's name and phone number. Some of the names had stars next to them. It was horrible. Too horrible. Too much of a bad cliché to be true. I had been impolite, looked at something I shouldn't have, and been punished for it. Now I had to be alone with my shame.

I put the book down exactly where I'd found it. I went into the garage and got his glove down from its hiding place. I met him coming down the stairs.

"Go. Get out now," I said, shoving his shoes, his bats, his equipment bag into his arms. I crossed that terrible space between us, grabbed his forearms, and pushed him out the doors. His arms were rigid, like tree branches.

I had one more question, as he piled his things into the

car. "What about the children? What should I tell the children?"

No answer. He was silent as always. He started the car and roared off. And then my husband—a sudden stranger—was gone.

The questions would not go away.

For reasons I didn't really understand—masochism? revenge?—I needed facts, details. How had he gone about it? Why hadn't I known of Steve's other life? I called the phone company and all the credit-card companies, and asked for copies of the three years' worth of bills that had gone directly to our accountant. I was still Mrs. Garvey to them. A celebrity customer. "Of course," said several pleasant voices. "We'll send them out today."

On the credit-card bills were charges for weekend plane trips I'd never been on or been aware of; entries for women's clothing and jewelry stores I'd never been in. I looked up Steve's secretary's name in the phone book. There was a listing for her last name that matched many, many entries on the phone bills.

She lived with her parents. I found this out when I dialed her number. "She's out right now," said an older woman's voice when I asked for her.

"Thank you," I said, and hung up.

She was a waitress. I learned this by accident, from the son of the contractor I'd hired to fix a leak in the roof. I'd hired him before; he came out to give me an estimate.

"What's the matter, Cyndy? You don't look well. What's happened to you. Why are you here?"

He was a sympathetic ear; I told him what had happened and he blushed and turned away. "I know this story," he said. It seemed that his brother-in-law, who now worked for the construction firm, had once managed a coffee shop in the Valley.

She'd worked there. "Yeah, Steve would come there to pick her up," he said. He was embarrassed.

Other people knew the story. A couple from Los Angeles (whom I will call Sam and Virginia Romano), one of the few that Steve and I had socialized with, asked me to see them.

"Come on, Cyndy," said Sam Romano. "You've got to get out. Have dinner with us." Sam was an accountant in his late thirties, in business for himself. Steve had palled around with him, played tennis with him, invited him to ballgames. He'd been sort of an older brother figure to Steve. His wife, Virginia, was a smart, funny woman. We met at a Mexican restaurant not far from their home. I couldn't look at my dinner, much less eat it.

"Did you know?" I asked them. Sam squirmed in the padded plastic booth. "Does anybody know Steve Garvey?" he said.

"But, Sam," I said, "did you *know?*"

I looked into his eyes. With horrible certainty I suddenly realized: of course they had.

He nodded sadly. "We've known almost all along," said Sam. Then his words were a blur: they'd been her friend, *their* friend also, all these years. They'd gone out to eat with them, gone on trips, gone sailing. "There's some obvious affection there, Cyndy," said Sam, as if that would make me feel better.

I put my head on the table. His wife came to the rescue. "She's not like you, Cyndy," said Virginia, putting her hand on my arm. "She can't hold a *candle* to you. She's so ordinary."

I looked at her husband. "Then why didn't you tell me?" I asked, crying now.

Sam thought for a moment, cocked his head and spoke. "I guess we just decided to go with the glitz."

I was beyond anyone's help now, except maybe my own. I called Steve's mistress at her parents' house again, and this time she answered.

"Hello? Who is this?"

"This is Cyndy Garvey. This will not continue. You

will not make money off the Garvey name. I want you out of my husband's office. I want you *gone.*"

She hung up.

I called the director of the Los Angeles Multiple Sclerosis Society. I knew this man; I'd gotten Steve hooked up with his charity years ago. "You know, you have a private business being run out of a charity-funded office," I told him. "I think you should look into this." He said this was a serious matter, and that when Steve was back in town he would call a meeting to discuss it. The meeting was held at his office, just Steve and the director and myself, and it was short: Steve sat in silence and scowled as he was told to separate his personal affairs from his charity work. He said nothing, and left.

I wanted her banished, cast out. In my fevered fantasies, I thought she could be shamed into oblivion. Declared a liability. Damaged goods. A vanquished enemy. No longer an obstacle. Gone!

Through some miracle, I got Steve on the telephone. "Please. I think we should go to counseling now, at least for me," I begged him.

"No, Cyn. I don't love you anymore. Let's leave it at that."

"But I've got to figure out what happened! You let me get beat up publicly. Everyone thinks I'm the bad person. What about the children?"

"You can figure it out yourself," said Steve. Then he hung up.

No. Steve was wrong. I couldn't figure it out. My past was still a blur. For hours and hours I sat and thought about it. It made no sense at all.

The present and future, though, began to harden around me. One day I was shopping with the children; buying them shoes at Robinson's. Shoes with little stars on them. I handed my credit card to the salesclerk; she typed in some numbers, waited, and shook her head.

"You have to go up to the credit office," she said. I was annoyed and mystified. I had been shopping at that store for eight years. My credit was fine.

"Oh hi, Cyndy!" said the credit woman, thrilled to see someone she recognized from television. I smiled back and explained what had happened. She took my card and went into a back office. She came out in a few minutes, still smiling.

"Gee, Cyndy. Your accountants have canceled your credit cards," she said.

"What?"

"They've been canceled." Now she looked exaggeratedly sympathetic.

"Let me have the card back then," I said, frowning. There must have been some mistake. How could they do that? I was getting angry.

"Oh no. We can't do *that.*" She was horrified.

"Then should I—*can* I open up another account?" Despite my sarcasm, the idea seemed to cheer her up. "Do you have a job?" she asked, hopefully. I felt Whitney tug at my arm. She looked like she was going to cry. I turned around, and a half dozen people were in line, listening. "I'll be back," I said, slapping the shoes down on the counter. Then I went home and called the accountant's office. Our money—his baseball money, my ABC money—had gone into a common fund. We had the same bank accounts. The same accountants. If I had no access to our money, how would I live?

The accountant's secretary said he would get back to me. He called several hours later. "You and Steve should not have the same credit cards," he said, as if the notion had just occurred to him.

I asked him why they didn't just cancel Steve's cards. Silence.

"Change Steve's credit card numbers," I said. "I have no job. I can't get new credit. I have two children here. What am I supposed to do? . . . Well?"

"We're going to put you on an allowance, Cyndy," he

said, finally. "We'll pay the mortgage for the beach house, and send you two hundred dollars a week."

"You can't do this," I said, slamming down the phone.

I called our lawyer, the only lawyer I'd ever used. He listened patiently as I explained what had happened.

"You know, Cyndy, I'm Steve's lawyer now. I think you should get other representation." I put down the phone, crying with rage and misery. In the end, I thought, everyone had gone with Steve. And I was alone. They were looking out for Steve now. They had put me in my place.

My place. I was a housewife again, more or less. I had two children, a big house. No husband. But lots of time to put the puzzle pieces together.

In the mornings, I'd get the children dressed and off to school. And then I would clean. Sand from the beach would blow in through cracks in the window frames; I'd vacuum the floors and drapes every day. Scrub all the counter tops. Meticulously iron the children's school clothes. Rearrange the closets. Rearrange the furniture.

Next to the ocean, filled with salt air and fog, the carpets would curl and the damp walls mildew. Outside, the car was covered with a thin film of scum. I scrubbed everything, fighting back the rot. I lost a little bit of the battle every day.

There was no one around to talk to. There never had been; even when we had been together, Steve would park us at the beach house on weekends, eat the lunch I'd cook for him, and go off to the ballpark. On one side of me lived an elderly lady, a recluse. Most of the other houses were empty during the week. On weekends, strangers would sunbathe naked up the beach. One Saturday, a resident I'd never seen before rang my bell and complained. He thought it was improper, he said, for me to hose sand off the girls—without their bathing suits—on the open porch. "Thank you for your suggestion," I said, and closed the door in his face. I ordered two wooden screens to block their view. And ours.

Most afternoons, after the few chores I had left were finished—and perhaps a call to my new lawyer—I'd sit in the living room chair and think. No music on the stereo. No sound except the surf hissing under the living room. I had no appetite and rarely ate. When my bladder began to hurt, I'd get up to empty it and go back to sit in the same spot. There were no answers, really, I'd think, listening to the rhythmic silence. Just the same questions.

"So who cares?" said the waves. "Who cares? Who cares? Who . . . cares?"

When the children came back from school, I'd take them out to play, then give them dinner and put them to bed. I'd try to keep my spirits up in front of them; they were too young to know their mother was . . . ashamed. They were well-behaved, perfect children almost all the time. They were, I thought, keeping me alive.

In the evenings, after I put them to bed, I'd sit some more. Around three or four in the morning, I'd fall asleep. I began to have the same dream almost every night: Steve and his girlfriend, laughing at me. I'd come up behind them, Steve in his Dodger uniform—the big Number Six on his back—and she with her arms around him. I'd try to talk to them and they'd turn around and laugh.

But I could only recognize Steve. The woman, I realized with a shock, had no face. No face at all. She was a complete blank: no mouth, no nose, no eyes. But she was able to laugh. With Steve. At me.

I'd wake up soaked with sweat. To face the next day, exhausted.

I did crazy, desperate things. In late spring, after the season began, I drove to Dodger Stadium and walked into the ticket office.

"Hi, Cyndy!" said the woman who ran the place. I

asked if Steve had left any guest passes under *her* name. "Nope," said the manager after checking her list.

"Well, how about season tickets?"

"Hey, you know where the files are," she said cheerfully. "Why don't you just go over there and look for yourself?"

"Thanks," I said. I found her name and address immediately. I copied down the seat number, left the office, waved to the usher—he knew me, of course—and walked through the turnstile, then through the tunnel to the field boxes.

There she was. She was sitting in a blue Dodger jacket and white shorts, a cup of beer propped between her legs. Next to her, on either side, were two middle-aged people. Her parents, I thought.

I walked down the aisle to her level. It was too perfect! Look straight ahead, and there they were. Look down at the field, and there was Steve at first base. How many games, how many *years* had she been sitting there? When Steve had waved to me in the crowd, was it really me he was waving at?

She saw me, and smirked. Then her mother saw me and, startled, began making shooing motions with her hands. Shoo! Get out of here! Her father, a big man, stood up, facing me, with his arms crossed.

I ignored the parents and glared straight at the woman. "How perfect!" I said. She said nothing, just turned away.

People were beginning to notice us now; to look at me and her and not at the field. What a scene! I thought, giving them a good chance to look at us. I walked back up the stairs and out the stadium exit.

Joe the guard was standing at the players' entrance, as usual. I'd known him for ten years. "Does Steve ever leave here with a dark-haired woman?" I asked him. He looked down at the ground. I asked him again.

"Please, Joe. Tell me."

"Yes, Miss Cyn," he said, finally. He couldn't face me.

I walked out, against the tide of incoming fans, and drove home.

I went through my address book, calling all the people Steve and I had known. All the banquets, all the head tables, all the speeches, all the free tickets, all the smiles. Some were busy, some were out of town, some would get back to me when things slowed down. I ripped their names out: when I was finished, the book was a quarter of its size.

I called my younger brother, Chris, a dentist who lived twenty miles from me. He'd been a high school athlete and idolized Steve; our breakup was painful to him. "Use the anger to push this behind you," he told me. "The highest form of rage is success." We had long, late-night phone conversations, talking in circles past midnight.

I made a friend. Darlene Reid was the mother of a girl in Whitney's class; a woman with a law degree who flew for TWA instead. Once a week I'd put on my dark glasses and go out to lunch with her, pushing the food around my plate to look like I'd eaten something. "Don't stay here, Cynthia," she told me. "It isn't good for you. This is Steve's house. This is Steve's town. Get out!" I nodded, and pushed my plate away.

I tried to keep up a normal life.

"Oh, what beautiful children you have," cooed the woman, the stranger behind me in the supermarket checkout line. "How is your father doing?" she asked them. "Fine," said Krisha and Whitney, bored by her rudeness. She straightened up and smiled at me. "Where's Steve? Why did you leave him?" I looked at her through the sunglasses, tears coming. I flung aside the cart and pulled the children back to the parking lot. I could feel another headache beginning. And I could not sleep.

I wrecked the car one night. I'd taken the girls to dinner at my parents' house; we were coming back to Malibu on a two-lane canyon road. It was raining lightly; a high-way-patrol car pulled out of an unpaved side road to catch a speeder coming the other way.

He pulled out in front of me and his wheels spun on the wet pavement. I couldn't stop. We skidded straight into his passenger side at thirty-five miles per hour. Before we hit, I leaned back in the seat, turned, and threw my arm across the girls seated in the back. They told me later in the hospital that this had saved my life.

The front of the Oldsmobile was completely destroyed. The engine was pushed back towards the passenger compartment; the steering wheel bent upward and dislocated my shoulder. My head hit the side window. The car radio went into my knee. The girls were basically all right, thank God; Whitney came out of it with some scrapes and bruises.

I was unconscious for almost a minute. When I came to, the first thing I saw was the policeman running towards my car. He was shouting at me. "You're clear! You're clear!" he kept yelling. What did he mean by that? I wondered, still dazed but the pain breaking through.

The ambulance took us away before I was able to talk to him. He didn't leave his name. I never found out.

My brother Chris met us at Westlake Hospital and drove us home the next day. For months after that, my shoulder ached. I was further from sleeping than ever. The headaches from the pulled shoulder muscles were unbearable. My brother took pity on me and wrote me a prescription for flurazepam. The pills worked for a while. I fell into a sort of sleep every night and stopped dreaming—of anything.

My new divorce lawyer dropped the case after two months. He was an expert on "goodwill" cases; he felt that, since I'd helped manage Steve's early career, I was entitled to a percentage of any future big contracts he signed. "An interesting case," he said. But Steve, through his lawyer, asked to take the kids for weekends—to his rented house nearby, where he was living with his girl-friend. "No. I don't want them going anywhere with that woman," I told him. He shook his head and asked me to be reasonable. Reasonable? I stared at him.

"I don't want to be part of this fight over the children," he told me over the phone one day. That was not, he said, the kind of thing he enjoyed taking care of. So he was bowing out. He was very sorry, he said; he'd adjust his bill accordingly.

Steve called and asked to see the children without her. "All right," I said. One day he picked the girls up at school in a chauffeur-driven limousine. Another time, when he came to the house, he pulled up in that white Porsche, round and fat like a baseball. He was a single man, living a wonderful life with his mistress and his racing car. I lost control.

I met him on the front steps and, in tears, pulled violently on the front of his shirt. "Stop it!" he said, and twisted my arms behind me. When I stopped struggling he pushed me aside and went in to get the girls. "You can't expect me to let you take the children, after what you've done to us," I shouted after him. I walked around to the back of the house where the children couldn't see me trembling.

The sleeping pills stopped working. I was five, ten, fifteen pounds underweight. Not even thick makeup could hide the dark circles under my eyes. When I went out, people stared at me. I frightened them, I could tell. And why not? I was a strange person. I did strange things, like forgetting where I was going when I drove the girls to school. Or cleaning the kitchen counter six times in a day.

Or finally, desperate to go to sleep, taking the phone off the hook.

My mother, who couldn't reach me that day, got frightened. She came with the police to break down the door. They got inside and woke me up. "Are you all right, Cyndy?" asked one of them. I told them I was fine, and when they left, disgusted, I screamed at my mother.

"I am an adult! I am very tired! I can take a nap when I want to. *I can take care of myself!*" And what if I couldn't? That was nobody's business but my own. She went home. And I was wide awake for another night.

It was in July that it ended. I read in a women's magazine that someone was honoring the elder Mrs. Garvey for being such a wonderful mother, for raising such a wonderful man. Mr. America's Mom! The luncheon honoring them, I read, would be . . . today.

That was it. The worst. I snapped. I drove to Dodger Stadium, drove in against the tide of fans leaving a game. I rode up the elevator, waited for Steve at the entrance to the Stadium Club.

I screamed at him for twenty minutes, and nobody stopped me. I was out of control. Gone berserk. A wild animal.

"You f——! You s——! For all those years I was with you! And now they're going to honor your goddamn mother! Where's your girlfriend, you a——!" It all spilled out, all the rage, all the filth. Broadcasters, team executives, reporters—people I knew!—just stood there and watched, looking at Steve, stone-faced in a corner, then looking at me.

Finally, someone must have given a signal. A couple of frightened-looking security guards came toward me. I cursed them, I cursed everybody. "All right. I'm going now," I said. And they didn't touch me! They didn't see me cry until I sat in my car in the parking lot. They didn't see my body shake when I drove home on the freeway.

The next day, there was a small item in the newspaper about a public "altercation" between the Garveys. What had I done? I tried to figure it out, but my brain wasn't working. I knew why, though; it was because I hadn't slept for so long. I was breaking. I had to get help. If I could just get my strength back, maybe I could.

The next week, I tried very hard to sleep. But it was no use. What if I never got to sleep again? One evening after the children were asleep I got the vial of sleeping pills and took one. No effect. Then another. Then another.

Then, suddenly, there was a gap in my memory. How many pills had I taken? All of a sudden I was shaking and I couldn't stop. I broke out in a drenching sweat. I began to drift in and out of consciousness.

Oh my God, I was going to die. *I didn't want to die.* I just wanted to go to sleep for a while. There were two children in the next room! I managed to stagger to the phone, call the emergency number, give my address.

"I've taken something," I said in a strange, slow, dead voice. I felt like what was left of my heart was breaking apart. "Please come for me," I said. Then I dialed Steve's number. There was no one closer I could think of to call. I told him to come and get the children. Then I hung up and unlocked the front door.

I sat down in my chair and faced the ocean. The next thing I remember, two men dressed exactly the same were carrying me out my door. I couldn't keep my eyes open, but if I listened very carefully I could hear what one of them was saying.

"This skinny chick. I recognize her. Isn't she an actress or something?" he said.

No, I thought as they carried me into the dark night. No. You've made a mistake. "A mistake," I tried to tell him. But somehow I couldn't get his attention.

Oh well, his loss. Too bad. Somebody different, I thought to him anyway, is going with you to the hospital. Not the person you think she is.

Somebody else.

CHAPTER 3

I n fact, I've often been mistaken for another woman.
It's a problem I've struggled with for almost twenty
years. Sometimes I fantasize that someone, somewhere, has stolen my face and voice. She's merged them
with her own personal history and formed an entirely
different "Cyndy Garvey." She's out there on her own,
impersonating me. The world has registered her image,
not mine.

The other Cyndy? She was born in California. Pasa-
dena, most probably. She was a WASP, an all-American
daughter, raised in upper-middle-class affluence and surrounded by friends. She was a cheerleader, a partygoer, a
sorority girl. She became a model, then an actress. It all
came easily to her; she married a famous baseball player,
a hero. And through him, as everybody knows, she became famous herself.

The two of us have very little in common—and the
things we do share I'm not particularly proud of. At
times in my life, I'm ashamed to say, I've tried to become
Cyndy. I thought this would make me and many people
around me happy. I was wrong. This was weak and dishonest and, ultimately, it almost killed me. I want to
banish this other woman. She is, I know now, my worst
enemy.

* * *

I was born on July 16, 1949, in Detroit, Michigan. Though I list Detroit as my hometown on insurance forms, the truth is we didn't have a hometown at all. Detroit was just a convenient starting-off place: every few years during my childhood, between moves, we'd spend a few summer months living there.

We lived with my grandparents. Every evening, my mother and grandmother would work for hours preparing pungent, Old World meals. The same smells would drift from all the other houses in the neighborhood. Every Sunday, we'd dress up and attend Catholic church services conducted in Latin and Slovak, neither of which I understood. The weather was always hot and humid. I remember very little else about living there.

I remember this, though, about my childhood: the same scene, almost a ritual, played out every few years. My father, a blond, stern man, would tell his family—my mother, my two brothers, and me—to wait for him in the dining room. He'd stride in, holding a big map under his arm, and unroll it on the table. Then he'd point to a place.

"Here," he'd say, showing us where we would be moving—immediately. "Take care of it, Anne," he'd tell my mother. Then he'd walk out.

My mother always took care of it. In a military family, sorting and packing was dependents' work—though our father, of course, supervised the entire operation. It was important, we knew, to take the precise minimum of articles necessary to start over. My father believed in traveling light. "No overweight. Everything goes!" he'd say, keeping an eye on Mom as she labeled everything for either the moving van or the trash. My books and sheet music were considered important enough to move. Old toys, old school notebooks, and reports, though, rarely made the cut. When Dad was out of the house, however, Mom usually smuggled some keepsakes into the bottom of a box or suitcase. It was no use, though: she was afraid to unpack them in front of my father. When we got to the new house, she'd hide these boxes in the attic. We never saw their contents again.

On moving day, Dad always woke us before dawn. "Come on! Three hundred miles before breakfast!" he'd say. Then Mark, Chris, and I would pile into the car—one of a succession of big, blue Buicks—and ride away from home: to a white tract house in Fort Worth, Texas. Then a few years later, to a brown tract house in Houston. To a blue ranch house in Topeka, Kansas; a gray and white split-level in Columbus, Ohio; a two-story colonial in Portsmouth, New Hampshire; a brown four-bedroom in Tacoma, Washington.

We'd look out the car's rear window into the darkness as we pulled out of town. We'd wonder: would we ever see the few friends we'd made, the favorite places we'd found there, ever again? "Of course you will, dear," said Mom, smiling bravely back at us. It was nice of her to say that, to keep our hopes up. As the years and moves went by, though, we realized it was more of a wish—a wish she shared with us—than a real possibility. The old house, we knew, was gone forever. At our new home, the big cardboard cartons would be emptied, folded, and stacked up for the next move.

Staying put was not in our father's plans. He belonged to the United States Air Force, and so, automatically, did his family. He was a jet bomber pilot, one of the best of a brave profession, and he was on the move. Moving up, if nothing happened to queer his chances. And we were moving up with him.

The odds, he felt, were not entirely in his favor. Stephen Truhan, my father, was born in Czechoslovakia, in a small town outside of Prague. The men he worked with were native-born Americans. He believed in his adopted country, but he felt he had a lot of catching up to do.

John Truhan, my grandfather, immigrated to this country in 1910—and had the bad luck to make a visit to the Old Country in 1914. He was promptly drafted into the Austro-Hungarian army, forced to fight on the wrong side during World War I, and, his luck turning, survived. He married my grandmother, Mary Besak, in his hometown after the Armistice. Dad was born in 1920; Grandfather took his wife and only child back to the United States in 1924. A slight, gentle man who spoke very little English, he went to work in the steel mills in Farrell, Pennsylvania. Grandmother Truhan, I remember, was a rather large, stern, and forbidding woman. She died of breast cancer when I was seven. She had refused treatment because she was terrified of going into the hospital —of the old school, she believed that anyone going into one had little chance of coming out alive.

Dad, too, spoke no English when he arrived in America. The other children made fun of him for that, calling him a "Hunky" and forcing him, he told us later, to fight every boy in town who was roughly his own age. Things were not much more peaceful for him at home: a razor strop hung prominently on the wall, and was still there when we visited our grandparents in Detroit years later. During the Depression, Grandfather worked as a bartender. "We'd have meals of mashed potatoes—and if I deserved it, I'd get a pat of butter," my father told us. Five cents at the local bakery, he said, would get you a whole red wagonload of broken ice-cream cones. For extra money, he trapped muskrats.

After graduating from high school in 1938, my father sold insurance for a living. He entered the Army in 1942 as an infantryman, transferred to the Air Corps, and made it out of flight training as a second lieutenant. He flew B-24 bombers out of North Africa, surviving thirty-five missions over Europe and returning to the States as a flight instructor. Discharged in 1945, he re-enlisted at the start of the Korean War. He never went to Korea, but he did become a career officer. Not everyone was kept on after the war. He was proud of keeping his commission.

At first he flew B-36s, huge cigar-shaped propeller

planes so big, he told us, that you could leave the cockpit and take a walk inside the wing. Starting in the mid-1950s he flew B-47s, newer jet bombers that refueled in the air and carried atomic bombs around the world. In the early 1960s he was transferred to cargo planes. He retired, a lieutenant colonel, in 1967.

He met my mother in 1946. Anne Hrubik's parents, Helen and Daniel, were also from Czechoslovakia. They, too, spoke Czech. But my mother was born and raised in Detroit; she graduated with honors from high school at the beginning of World War II. She was beautiful once: I knew that. Pictures from that time show her with long, dark, wavy hair, like Rita Hayworth. She had high Slavic cheekbones and perfect olive skin. Her eyes were slightly slanted, almost Tartar. In the old photographs, they sparkle with good humor. They were a striking couple.

After graduation, my mother went to work for an optometrist. "He made me wear eyeglasses with plain glass lenses. I was an advertisement," she told me one day, laughing at her carefree past. Later, she worked as a secretary in a law office; then, as a saleswoman at Saks. One evening, she was in the stands with a girlfriend at a local amateur basketball game; my father, whose parents had moved to Detroit during the war, was playing on one of the teams. They were married that year. My mother quit work, and they moved into the second floor of the Hrubik house on Van Dyke Street.

They had no choice. My father had not yet rejoined the Air Force; he was selling insurance again, and taking some courses at a local engineering college. Grandfather Hrubik, like his wife rather small and foreign-looking, did not get along with my father. What Grandfather did for a living was something of a mystery; in the basement were old casks of wine and a vat for crushing grapes. My older brother Mark, who was born in June, 1947, remembers chickens in the backyard, milk wagons drawn by horses with straw hats, and, in a corner of the basement, mysterious bags full of numbered slips of paper. Another interesting bit of information: one of my great uncles, so the rumors went, was a Communist.

Mark liked to think about those things. He was a quiet, brown-haired child, sensitive and artistic. He was a bit uncoordinated and clumsy as a boy, and preferred reading and listening to records to competing with the local kids in sports. This angered my father very much.

Mark, who later survived being twice wounded in Vietnam, remembers me propped up in my playpen, a skinny blond girl who looked a lot like my younger daughter Whitney, in front of one of the first television sets in the neighborhood. Also, he remembers the fights between my father and his in-laws. They should not talk to his children, Dad told them, in anything other than English. He did not want us learning Czech—a foreign language— from our grandparents.

But there was no danger of that. Before I learned to speak like them—I was never really able to communicate, even when I came back, later, for visits—we had joined the Air Force. And we were living elsewhere. And nowhere. Wherever the Air Force wanted us.

They wanted us wherever my father's planes were based. In Texas, where my younger brother Chris—a little bouncing ball of a boy, nimble and athletic almost from the start—was born, our house was so close to the runway that the dishes shook in the cupboards when the planes took off.

In Kansas, it was very flat: in the summer, the tornadoes danced on the horizon like spinning tops. Sirens blew, and we all hid in the basement or under our school desks. One wonderful morning, though, the sky was clear and my father flew right over our house. He rocked his wings in salute to us! My mother rushed outside, waving back to him, so beautiful and proud. And happy. The happiest I've ever seen her.

When we got to Topeka, my father decided to move us off base. Living "on the economy," it was called, which meant that we lived in ordinary, nonmilitary neighborhoods and went to regular public schools—schools filled with normal kids who lived for years and years in the same place; who made friends in first grade and kept them; who had the same high school math teachers as their older brothers and sisters. I've always wondered why my father did this; in military schools, mixed in with military kids, our frequent moves would have been nothing special. Thrust into the civilian population, we were strangers wherever we went.

We'd usually transfer in the middle of the school term; the teacher would march us to the front of the class and introduce us.

"Cynthia is a military child. Her father is with the Air Force." All the children would stare at me. I'd look down at my shoes, knowing that I'd never be around long enough to join the groups and cliques I could make out just by looking at them. It didn't help that I always tested well and was considered a "bright" kid. Sometimes, to my horror, I'd be held up as an example. "Look at Cynthia," said one teacher. "She's only been here a little while, and already she's gone past most of you." Out of the corner of my eye, I could see the boys in the "dumb" section leering at me. This, I knew, killed any chance I had of making friends. I became "a shy girl." A bookworm.

I liked to go to the library. I liked to stay home in my room, where my bed and dresser and desk, at least, were always the same, and read books about science and biology. I had a wonderful book, made of paper and plastic. I could pull a tab and watch the path of the blood through the veins. I could keep it in my desk drawer, safe. And if I had to leave my room, maybe forever, I could grab it and hide it and take it with me.

As best she could, Mom tried to create some permanency in her children's lives. Wherever we went, she signed us up for the Boy Scouts, the Girl Scouts, and whatever other groups and sports teams she could find. She usually volunteered to work for those organizations; a large part of her day was filled with shuttling us around. When my father wasn't around, she taught me sewing and cooking. I enjoyed that very much. When I was six, she signed me up for something called the National Music Guild: an association of music teachers that used the same teaching methods and standard exams everywhere.

My instrument was a battered old upright piano, lugged from city to city and base to base. Every year, wherever I was, I went to the local headquarters of the Guild to be "rated." I wore a white blouse and a black velvet skirt, shiny black shoes, and a little black tie. Three or five judges, grown-ups I'd never seen before, sat at a long table.

I started with scales, two octaves, followed by A-minor arpeggios and cadences. Then, I sight-read, playing a piece I'd never seen before. I played two pieces I'd prepared, music that proved I was ready to go up to the next level. Finally, hands folded politely in my lap, I answered their questions about music theory. My grade arrived a week later.

I did all right. Proficient, but not inspired. My teachers —men and women, young and old—were sometimes strict, sometimes lenient. One man, I think, didn't like music at all. I felt sorry for him. And me.

And then there was Mrs. Ellis. Mrs. Ellis lived in Columbus, Ohio—where, through some inexplicable Air Force mistake (Had they lost our file? I hoped), I lived all the way from the fourth through eighth grades. Mrs. Ellis was a little old lady with gray hair, cat's-eye glasses on a chain, and a big smile. You had to climb two flights of stairs to get to her room in a big white-frame house. There were always milk and cookies and candy for me. She looked so happy to see me, every week. And I loved her.

Mrs. Ellis matched me up with Andrea Hudson, a civilian girl my own age. Andrea was beautiful, with long blond hair and blue eyes, like Alice in Wonderland. Her mother, a nice woman with a regular house and a regular husband with a regular job, rounded us up for practice and sewed our little recital outfits. I liked going there. Andy was a much better musician than I was; at Mrs. Ellis' recitals we played Bach duets, Andy playing the tough treble parts and me plodding along on the bass. "Why don't you do all four hands?" I kidded her.

In seventh grade, an astonishing thing happened. One of my few girlfriends urged me to try out for the cheerleading squad—and after a few cartwheels and spellouts, I made the team. I simply could not believe it. Me, a cheerleader? Later, back home, I looked in the mirror: I wasn't a "popular" girl, I had no boyfriends. In the past, afraid of being recognized as the new girl, I'd kept my head down. I didn't wear makeup or get my hair done like some of the other girls. I had a turned-up nose and long blond hair. Maybe, though . . .

And then shortly afterward, my father walked in and announced we were moving immediately, following his bombers to New Hampshire. Mrs. Ellis was very sad. "Oh no!" she said, when I brought the news to her. She took my music from me, bent over her desk, and wrote notes in the margin for my parents—and my next instructor, whoever that might be.

"Please watch the arch in her fingers," she wrote to my mother. To whom it may concern: "Don't let Cynthia tuck her chin in." "Tell Cynthia not to stick her tongue out when she plays." She scribbled for a while longer, filling in the space around the notes and clefs, then looked up.

"You've got talent, dear," she said, hugging me. *"Please* don't give it up."

I promised not to. But my next teacher was a fussy young man, and by sixteen I had stopped taking lessons. By age twenty, I had forgotten almost everything. Except Mrs. Ellis. I hoped she remembered me. I still do.

* * *

Somebody—I think it was my brother Mark—once told me that the Air Force put tape recorders in the noses of their planes so they could record the pilots talking to the ground, to their crew, to each other. If I could just get that tape, and listen to my father talk! That would be wonderful.

It puzzled me: he never talked about his work. Was it dangerous refueling six miles up, flying at the speed of sound through clouds and darkness? Was he scared of flying around with atomic bombs? Of someday getting the order to drop them on Russia? Of flying back to find his base, his planes and ground crews, his family blown to bits underneath a mushroom cloud?

I dreamed of asking him. I dreamed of his showing me. I dreamed of somehow finding the magic word, the magic *act,* that would let me break through to his love. I dreamed of his bending down and giving me a hug, of telling me that he loved me. That he was proud of me. That all the work I was doing was just what he wanted. But he never said any of that.

I knew he was brave. The bravest! I knew he was handsome: safe behind my bedroom window, I watched him stride down the driveway in his bright orange flight suit, helmet in hand. Could anyone's father look stronger, more certain of himself than that? I knew that he was very smart: that he'd mastered flying, machines, maps, world politics. On the nights before he'd leave on his missions, he'd spread his huge maps of the world on the kitchen table, pencil in hand, strange rulers and instruments in front of him. Bent over, concentrating fiercely, he planned his flights over mountains, oceans, continents. How did he do it?

Sometimes, when I got an especially good report card, all A's, I'd put it on top of his flight bag in the hall, so he'd be sure to see it before he left. But never, as far as I remember, did he ever compliment me on or even acknowledge that he'd seen my grades.

The real truth, I knew, was in his silence: that I was a bad girl, not smart or brave or pretty enough to be his daughter. Not worthy of his love. And that was the first part of my terrible, guilty secret.

The second part was that I was terrified of my father. We all were, almost all the time—my mother most of all. To the world, he was an officer and a gentleman, a fine man and a good father. To us, he was an angry volcano, liable to explode at any moment. He had high standards for all of us. He hated messiness, lateness, weakness, and sloppy thinking. And we disappointed him greatly.

When I was very young, I remember, he was more tolerant. There were even moments of tenderness: one afternoon, in the back yard, he held my hands from behind me and showed me how to swing a golf club. I can still feel his physical presence. One evening, he taught me the stars and constellations he flew his plane by. "Look up, Cynthia," he said. He pointed out the North Star, the Big Dipper, the Unicorn, the Crab. But that was all of it. Around my seventh birthday, for reasons I'm only now beginning to understand, he became very angry.

In his anger, he was violent. He beat us often—my brother Mark most of all. "You're no good!" he yelled at us. We had let him down.

My first memory of this awful time is of him whipping Mark with his belt: for hours, it seemed, right there in the front hall, holding him by the neck with one big hand and, with his other strong arm, swinging the belt—it made a terrible hissing noise—against my brother's legs, back, and buttocks. I was terrified. My brother screamed and cried. My mother stood off to one side, looking distressed, but did nothing to stop the beating.

What had Mark done? I can't remember. That wasn't important. What was important, I realized sadly, was what, in my father's eyes, he *was:* an awkward kid with glasses, who got C's and D's in school and would rather play with his toy soldiers than compete in basketball and football. That didn't seem so awful a crime; when my father wasn't around, he was sweet and friendly. We liked to sit around in the bedroom, reading books together. I loved my brother very much.

"Dummy! Idiot! Stupid!" my father yelled at him. Just the sight of Mark seemed to make him mad. When he was home, he beat him regularly—sometimes several times a week—for another bad report card, for playing his radio too loud, for "talking back." Most of the time my father beat him with his belt. Occasionally, he cuffed him around the house with his open hand. As Mark grew older, he began to take the beatings differently—staring defiantly at my father rather than crying or pleading. Sometimes the only sound was of my father's hand hitting his flesh. I tried to run away, out of hearing, but the house was too small.

Being a girl protected me from the worst of the beatings. Being a good student deprived him of the most obvious reasons for punishing me. But that, I knew, only hid the obvious truth: that deep down, in his eyes, I was a failure.

I can remember him holding me by the neck and hitting me, hard: that was when I made serious mistakes like shouting to my brother in the house or coming home from school with my shirt outside my skirt. Mostly, though, he'd just grab me by the shoulders, shake me violently for a few seconds—my head flopping back and forth—and shout, "Straighten up!" There was rarely a warning or an explanation. When he was finished, he'd turn on his heel and walk away.

He hit us regularly. There was no way around it. There were unspoken rules to obey, with instant punishment if we broke them. For instance, we'd be hit if we spilled milk at the dinner table. Or used the telephone. Or left our toys out where he could see them.

Worst of all was to get in his way. He hated to be interfered with. That made him very mad. If he was walking inside the house, and came upon an obstacle like a toy or a book, he'd shout with anger and kick it across the room. Several times I saw him kick Buttons, a little dog we owned, a Chihuahua. He, too, knew to keep away from my father. But he'd been in the wrong place at the wrong time; after Dad kicked him in the side, he yelped in pain and slunk under the couch. We learned very early to melt away, back behind a closed door, if we saw our father coming toward us. If we moved too slowly, we'd be cuffed or slapped aside.

My mother never interfered with our punishment. For a while, my younger brother Chris—being so cute and small and bouncy—managed to avoid the worst of my father's anger. I worried, though, about his growing bigger, crossing over to my father's bad side: when I was eleven or twelve, my worst fears were realized. I was in the hall, near the front door. Chris was sitting on the hall stairway, peering down through the banister. To get my attention—"Hi, Cynthia!"—he threw a plastic ball he was holding toward me.

I looked up at the last second. The ball struck me just above my right eye, cutting the skin open. I cried out in pain. As the cut started to bleed, I heard my father rushing toward me. He didn't stop to look at my eye. He ran past me, snatched my brother off the step, and began to hit him. It was a full-scale beating; my father, furious, hit him again and again. Chris howled in pain and terror.

"No! I'm okay! I'm all right!" I shouted at my father. But it had no effect. He kept hitting and hitting Chris, just as hard. Worse, my mother was there, too, looking on, with a sad expression on her face. I begged her, silently: Do something! Stop him! But she did nothing. For a second, a wave of hatred—not for my father, but for my mother, for not protecting us—swept over me. I felt ashamed.

The beatings were painful. But looking back, I realize they weren't the worst part. The worst part was the awful knowledge that he was always *there,* that the sight of us could set him off at any moment. The constant fear was worse than the occasional physical pain. It dictated our every move when he was around. It meant that in the house, when he was home, we were quiet—no playing, no fighting, no running, no shouting. It meant that when he walked through the hallways, we shrank back into doorways, out of his sight. If I had to get to the other side of the house, I planned my route carefully to avoid him. If that wasn't possible, if I had to go past a room he was in, I walked—very quietly—to the doorway, peered around it to make sure he was reading his newspaper or watching television, then sneaked, heart pounding, past him. If I was lucky, he wouldn't see me. If I was lucky, I could escape to my room. To relative safety, and to my books.

Unfortunately, it was impossible to do that all day. Unless my father was away, dinner was always at 1730 hours sharp. Attendance was mandatory. For at least an hour, we had to pass inspection; to sit there under his gaze without setting him off. Mark sat at Dad's right; if he got out of line—slouched, put his elbows on the table, used the wrong tone of voice—Dad would flick out his huge hand and whack Mark on the back of his head. I got hit a few times, also, but not as often as my brother. Being farther away from him helped, I think.

Being wrong, being *stupid,* was dangerous. "Oh, Anne!" my father said, angrily, lifting his dinner plate off the table. He banged it back down. The meat, we knew, belonged at six o'clock, the potatoes at ten o'clock, the vegetables at two o'clock. She had forgotten and gotten it wrong again. "I'm sorry, Stephen," my mother said. She always apologized and took everything back to the kitchen to make things right.

Opinions were dangerous. My brother liked rock-and-roll music; once he asked for money to buy a certain record. "It's cool," he said. My father reacted in a second. Wha-a-a-ck! Sometimes, my mother had an opinion on an election, on raising property taxes, on the local school system. "I think . . ."

"Anne, you don't know what the hell you're talking about!" my father would say, scornfully. My mother looked down and continued eating.

Actually, I don't remember her sitting at the table much at all. Usually she was on her feet, shuttling nervously back and forth between the kitchen and the table, serving my father, mopping up spills before he got angry, chattering about nothing at all, just trying to calm him. As I got older, I began to help her serve and pour. Anything was better than sitting there, just waiting.

I hated dinnertime. By the time I was twelve or so, just the thought of eating with him—just the smell of my mother's cooking—made me frightened. At the table, my hands shook. My stomach hurt. I felt nauseous. The thought of actually eating sickened me; I pushed the food around my plate, to make it look like I'd swallowed some before I could excuse myself and rush back to my room.

I lost weight, got skinnier, but nobody seemed to notice. I sat in my room, tired and hungry now, reading my books and waiting, sadly, to grow up.

I tried to *be* a grown-up. I tried to think grown-up thoughts. Doing that, I thought, would help me to figure out my father. To head off his yelling and hitting. To protect my mother and brothers.

The danger signs were there; I just had to watch for them. If his jaw locked—if he gritted his teeth and his shoulder muscles tensed up—that meant that we had broken a rule, whether we realized what we were doing or not, and that he would explode very soon. Our only hope was to stop whatever we were doing, immediately. *Change the subject. Be quiet. Become invisible.* Mark and I developed a silent language; just a glance across the room or the table was enough to alert him of the emergency.

Some things went without saying. There was no touching my father or his things. No talking in church—no

looking anywhere but straight ahead—or my father
would react.

There was no question of bringing friends to the house;
they would only make noise and annoy my father. Who
knows? Maybe he would beat us up in front of them. I
realized, to my shame, that I could never invite Andrea
into my home. The contrast—The Problem—would be
too evident.

None of the danger and tension that filled my house
was present in Andy's. I studied their household carefully, drinking it all in: when Mr. Hudson came home
from work, for instance, tired though he was, he always
kissed his wife and gave Andy—and sometimes me!—a
hug. Andy's father was never angry or violent; he was a
gentle man. The Hudsons were what I thought a real
family should be like. I envied Andrea.

Once, and only once, I broke my rule and invited three
girls I knew from school over to listen to Beatles records.
For a few minutes, we had fun. I forgot myself and
started to dance to the music with them.

The door to my room flew open, and my father, furious, strode across to the record player and dragged the
needle—with a terrible scratching noise—across the record. Then he pulled the plug out and marched out of the
room.

"Uh, that's my father," I said, embarrassed, but also
secretly relieved that he hadn't hit me—and revealed the
worst of The Secret—while they were there. The girls
looked at each other, gathered up their things, and left.
This was no place for them. We all knew that.

But I still had to live there. I took responsibility for making things as livable as possible. I watched out for my
brothers, for Mark especially. If he left the bathroom
messy in the morning before my father used it—a crime
that would surely get him beaten—I cleaned it up. If he
was playing the radio in his room too loudly, if his bed
was messy, I'd rush down the hall and warn him. "Don't

you know he's here?" I whispered. That was usually enough to get him to stop. As he became a teenager, though, he began to become defiant, to flirt with danger. "Aw, who cares?" he'd say to me, turning the radio up and turning his back. He seemed to be daring Dad to beat him up—and several times, it happened. Mark's attitude terrified me. It seemed crazy, suicidal. I had to watch out for him even harder.

I changed seats with Mark at the dinner table. Now *I* sat at my father's right hand—between Mark and his right arm. He never hit me too hard at the table, anyway. And when he had to reach around me to hit my brother, his blows lost some of their sting.

Whenever conversation took a dangerous turn, or if I saw him narrow his eyes and look closely at any of us, I'd try to distract him. "Can we watch the news now?" I'd say. I knew my father liked the news. The television set was in sight of the table. If I could get him turned around in his chair, if I could get his eyes locked on the screen, we could finish eating and slip away to safety.

We were relatively safe, too, if we were out where strangers could see us. In public my shortcomings, my mother's nervousness, and my father's anger were secrets. Shameful secrets, not to be revealed. In public, in fact, we were a different family. We were the family I always wanted us to be. If only my brothers and I hadn't spoiled things.

"Do you know how lucky you are?" said the smiling grown-up, a civilian man, kneeling down in front of me. I was all dressed up, walking with my family on the way to church. My mother beamed. I dutifully nodded. I knew what the man meant: to the neighborhood adults we never seemed to get to know very well, my father was "a heck of a guy," a strict but fair father with three well-behaved kids, a brave man with an exciting job whom they treated with respect.

It was so confusing. At parties, at the backyard barbecues he sometimes threw for the neighbor-strangers, he'd stand happily in front of the grill, a long fork in one hand and a martini in the other. My mother was the perfect hostess, so pretty, laughing and joking with her guests. The men would argue with him about politics or sports. "No, Steve, it's this way," they'd tell him. Watching from a safe place, the back door or the driveway, I'd wait for the explosion. "Well, maybe you're right," he'd say, nodding and smiling.

That astonished me. I remembered those scenes, saved up those moments in my mind, and played them back and studied them when things got particularly bad. One evening, I remember, my parents took me with them to a country-club dance. They were such a handsome couple! My father in his military uniform, other men shaking his hand and patting him on the back. My mother in her ball gown, her long dark hair flowing around her face.

They danced. My father, so graceful, so manly, gently guided my mother around the dance floor. It was one of the few times I'd actually seen them touch. They never kissed or touched each other at home.

My mother looked lovingly into his eyes. Could I ever, I wondered, get to know this father, this family?

No. It was impossible. One day, when I was thirteen, I realized that. I remember what happened with a sharp, excruciating clarity that hasn't dimmed to this day.

I'd come home in the middle of the day to find my father there, unexpectedly. This happened often; his squadron sometimes arrived back at the base hours, days or even weeks ahead of schedule. This time, he was sitting in his uniform, waiting for me. I was an hour late from a practice session with Andrea. It was noon instead of 11 A.M.

He was furious. His jaw was locked and his face muscles pulsated. "Apologize to your mother!" he said. To mother? Why would she care? She'd known where I was. I'd been only four blocks away. "I'm sorry," I said, with a touch of sarcasm slipping out. Where had that come from? I knew immediately what was going to happen.

He grabbed me by the back of the neck, pulled out his belt and began hitting me with it. He hit me again and again, across my back, across my buttocks, across my legs. It was very painful. His blows were cutting and bruising me. He'd beaten me before, but this was different: I'd begun to develop that year, and I was angry and ashamed in a way I'd never felt before. This was wrong, I suddenly realized. This was bad, evil. *And it wasn't my fault.*

I stood up. "That's enough! That's the end!" I shouted, through the tears. To my surprise, he stopped. His face went completely blank. He left the room.

My mother kneeled down in front of me, her eyes wide open with fright. "Apologize to your father," she begged. I looked at her in a new, grown-up way. Was she out of her mind? I thought. I had nothing to apologize for. I hadn't done anything wrong.

I went into the garage, and, for the only time in my life, saw my father crying. His head was in his hands. I stood across the room from him. "I'm sorry," I said, perfunctorily, and left. I didn't mean it. I hated him. My body hurt. But my hate for him was stronger than the pain.

I went to my room, undressed and looked at my body. There were marks up and down the back of my legs. The next day, I had to go to gym class. People stared at my legs, but nobody asked me for an explanation. I was a stranger, after all.

My father never hit me again. But it was too late. I wasn't interested any more in what he did, or how to please him. He started to avoid me. From then on, he criticized me only through my mother. "Tell your daughter to straighten up," he'd say. From then on, too, every three months or so throughout my teens, I got headaches so severe that I had to stop work, come home from school, and lie down in the dark. I felt as if bombs were exploding inside my head. It was something that my father—although we were not allowed to tell anyone—had also suffered from for years.

Years later, piecing together what little my brothers and I had been told, I learned my father's other secret. His Air Force career had stalled while we were in Columbus. While we were living there, he had been passed over twice for promotion from Captain to Major. One more turndown and he would have been involuntarily retired.

"Your father's going to Washington," Mom told Mark one day around this time. We later learned he'd gone to the Pentagon, gotten hold of his service record, and discovered whatever it was that was holding him back. The Air Force then told him: he'd get his promotion, but he wouldn't be trained to fly the new B-52s. The B-47 was being phased out, but there would still be a plane for him if we moved to Pease Air Force Base in New Hampshire.

Goodbye friends, goodbye school, goodbye Mrs. Ellis. A few years later, when I was sixteen, I was riding in the Buick on the Frank Lodge Expressway near Detroit. I turned to my mother, in the driver's seat next to me.

"Why don't we get out?" I said to her.

"What?"

"Why don't you leave the son of a bitch? Just go?" I think I was as shocked as she was at what I had said.

My mother took her right hand off the big steering wheel, flung it out and back, and slapped me hard across the face.

It was the first and last time my mother ever hit me. I felt sadness, resignation, and anger. I never raised the subject again.

CHAPTER 4

I never asked her, either, what hopes and plans she and my father had for me. Maybe I was afraid to find out. In sixth grade she pulled me out of tap-dancing class, which I loved, and enrolled me in an old-fashioned "charm school." "This is more important," she said. Was it something, I wondered, intended to please my father?

The class, run by a middle-aged woman with dyed eyebrows, was held in a dusty classroom over a stationery store. We walked with books on our heads. We learned to slither along by placing one foot directly ahead of the other. "To give your legs a linear line," she told us. She lectured us on "ladylike deportment," makeup, and the proper girdle for our "individual figures." I don't remember what my grade was. Only that in ten weeks the course was over.

I went back to reading my biology books, and practiced my piano two or three hours every day. Then, just after we moved to New Hampshire, I came home from school one afternoon—and saw my seventh-grade photograph flashed up on the television screen.

". . . one of the local girls who've entered the Miss Teenage Boston Pageant," said the announcer. What??? Mother came up behind me, a look of pure rapture on her face. "You'll love it. It'll be wonderful!" I tried to tell her I didn't want to enter, but she didn't seem to hear me. She just stared, hands clasped, at the television.

Did I want to make my mother unhappy? No. For the next two years she drove me from pageant to pageant; from Miss Teenage This to Junior Miss That. The individual contests blur together; what I remember are dingy auditoriums, lots of adults—and above all, feeling embarrassed and out of place.

Mother enjoyed it all. "Just go out there and be yourself, Cynthia," she told me. "Just show them your essence."

My essence? In bathing suit and high heels, I tottered down runway after runway, trying to keep from falling when I spun around. My legs were long and skinny, my bustline nonexistent.

"Smile at the judges. They want to see *you,"* said all the nervous middle-aged ladies and gentlemen, the contest organizers, who milled around backstage. The judges? Where were they? I couldn't see past the stage lights, and if I squinted or shaded my eyes—well, then, what *would* happen? I couldn't ask my competitors, girls I'd never met before. I pulled my hair back into a ponytail and left my face nearly bare.

"You're a natural. How far do you want to go?" said one official, excitedly, holding me at arm's length before one contest. How far? This was too far, already. I looked around to see a group of the other girls. They were staring daggers.

They must have hated me. One day, the man who was choreographing one of the pageant's production numbers told me that I had a "vamp walk" and "outstanding legs." I was dumbfounded. That was just me, walking, and those were just my legs.

"Your shoulders and hips move together. That's very good, honey," he said. He moved me to the front of the chorus line. "Now, walk up and down for us, Cynthia. See that, girls?" He told me to sit down while the other contestants tried to walk the same way.

My school grades were good, so I got points that way. In the talent category, I played the theme from *Exodus* on the piano. I won once or twice, though I was runner-up many more times than that—perhaps ten times. I worried, when I lost, that my mother would be disappointed, depressed. But no. "Maybe next time," she'd say, smiling bravely. And we'd go on to the next one.

Mother never failed to clip out the beauty contest results —and sometimes, pictures of me—that were printed in the local newspapers.

"There goes 'Queenie,'" said the most popular girl in my new high school. I kept my head down; ducked into an empty classroom to get away from the laughter. I studied harder; the headaches were worse.

But then, in tenth grade, something wonderful happened. On that horrible first day, when I had to walk into homeroom to be introduced, a boy stared at me and whistled. "Who the hell is *that?*" he joked. I looked back at him angrily, but he was smiling admiringly at me. Stanley Shoup was the class greaser, a Fonzie-type before television had invented it. He wore jeans and clean white T-shirts, a leather jacket, and a ducktail. He was two years older than I was, and he drove a Harley-Davidson motorcycle. He spent most of his time in shop classes, he had a "bad reputation," but in reality, he was one of the sweetest people I've ever met. I became "his girl": I was part of a couple. He made me feel less out of place. He took care of me. He made me laugh. My father was away on a long assignment overseas.

Stan took me for long rides in the country, whizzing past farms and astonished cows, me clinging tightly to Stan with my long hair blowing in the breeze. "Cynthia, I really, really like you," said Stan, refusing to go past heavy petting, though I would certainly have followed him. I was starved for affection. Nicely, he seemed to know that, and didn't take advantage. He made me seem special.

My mother liked Stan, and waved us off on our little trips. It seemed she knew how much Stan's attention meant to me. Then, when his squadron returned, my father came back home.

One hot spring day, Stan rode up on his bike without a shirt on.

"You! Get out of here!" said my father. "If you don't wear a shirt and shoes, don't come around here!" He grabbed Stan and nearly pulled him off his motorcycle.

By this time, I was standing in the doorway. Stan turned and looked at me, spun his bike around and roared away. My father turned on his heel and walked past me into the house. He said nothing to me, but I knew that the same thing would happen if Stan came back again. I was powerless. Even though my father wasn't hitting me any more, I was still afraid of his anger. And, just as sad: my mother, who'd been on my side when my father was away, said nothing.

I began to cry. I knew my relationship with Stan was over. I'd still see Stan at school, but that was really the end of us. He went off to college that fall.

At the end of my junior year, Dad was transferred to his final assignment. My brother Mark left home: he refused to come with us, and after a big argument with my father, he moved in with his girlfriend's family.

"That's it, I can't do this any more, Cynthia," he told me, as we were packing up to leave. The next year he enrolled in Ohio University; I didn't see him for years.

It took four days to get the car to Tacoma. This time there was a difference, though: I had my driver's license now, and on the long predawn stretches I took my turn behind the wheel.

In the Rockies, outside of Denver, I turned around in the driver's seat to see my mother, father, and Chris sleeping soundly in the back. I reached for the radio—no, don't touch it, Cynthia. My father had it set on "his" station, and there would be hell to pay if he woke up and found the dial turned.

I gripped the wheel and leaned forward, pressing the gas pedal toward the floor. I switched on the high beams. We hit seventy-five and eighty through the tight mountain curves. I felt in control. When the sun came up, I slowed down. My father stirred and pointed out a roadside restaurant, then motioned me to pull over. Neither of us said a word.

"I'd like to become a doctor—a pediatrician," I told the nice lady in the elegant living room of her house in Tacoma. She sipped her tea, nodded, and said, "You've got the grades for it, dear." Armed with my best dress, a pair of white gloves, and a 3.9 grade-point average, I'd gone to the home of a local graduate of a famous Eastern women's college for my application interview.

I was accepted. The letter also said ("regretfully") that our family income was too high for me to receive a scholarship.

"Well, that's that," said my father. As a backup, I'd applied to a few other schools, one being Michigan State University. As Michigan "residents," my family was eligible for reduced tuition fees. I was admitted into James Madison Honor College, an experimental part of Michigan State University that offered an advanced course of sociology and political science. My secret plan was to satisfy all my liberal arts requirements, transfer into pre-med in my junior year, and earn a scholarship to medical school.

I told no one. I bought a used copy of *Gray's Anatomy*, lugged it to my new school to read each day, and tried to ignore my fellow high school seniors—not hard, because they ignored me. I was again the only military child. They'd been together for four years and had formed all their cliques and friendships—for life?—a long, long time ago.

"Hi. Where did *you* come from?" said an athletic,

sandy-haired boy in the corridor one day. I was astonished. It was Michael Dunbar, a boy I knew was a football player, a class officer, a popular student, and—he
liked me! He looked like Ron Howard. Little Opie grown
up. He had brown hair, freckles, pure Irish features, and
a shy smile. I liked him immediately.

He was wonderful. Michael Dunbar was a kind,
easygoing boy who always seemed to be telling jokes
about himself. Those first few weeks he "bumped into"
me a few more times; he stopped and talked to me, and
broke through my shyness. He called me up and asked
me for a date. And then another, and another. He introduced me to his friends, kidded them into treating me as
their friend. He took me, in his pickup truck, for long
drives in the country. He talked to me about school,
about his friends, about his plans to become a high school
athletic director.

And maybe the nicest thing he did was take me home.

Michael Dunbar had a beautiful home. He lived in a
slightly run-down white house, a little too small, with a
close, warm family that was everything mine wasn't. His
father, Mr. Dunbar, was a construction worker—a
strong, sweet man who obviously loved his wife and children more than life itself. He joked and laughed even
more than Michael. I never heard him raise his voice in
anger. Sometimes, in the middle of dinner, he'd hug Michael or his little sister—or me!—or make a grab for Mrs.
Dunbar, equally nice, who worked in a cafeteria.

"Give me your face!" he'd shout, and reach over the
table to give his wife a big kiss. The rest of us laughed
and applauded. I ate there as often as I dared. Of course,
I never invited Michael to have dinner at my house. That
would have been impossible.

For the last part of our senior year, Michael and I
dated, parked—and one night, in his big old car, we
made love. He was gentle, and agreed to use birth con-

trol. I loved being close to him—to nuzzle my face in his neck, to feel him hold me.

There was talk in school that I'd taken him away from a more popular girl. He was the King of the Prom. I wasn't his Queen, of course—a girl who'd been there four years was named—but he danced only a few moments of the first dance with her. I'd shrunk into the crepe paper at the side of the gym, but he came over and spent the rest of the night with me.

He said we should always be together. I fought back my doubts—how could you count on anything like that? —and said I hoped so, too. He said that he loved me; that he'd follow me. I was seventeen.

After my graduation, my father retired from the Air Force and we moved back to Square One. To Detroit. Both Grandpa Truhan and Grandma Hrubik were still alive, and we moved into the Truhan house, in a run-down neighborhood now predominantly black, to take care of both of them.

That was the summer of '67. The summer of the riots in Detroit. The heat was overwhelming. There was a curfew; National Guard tanks rolled by our house on the way to the black neighborhoods. The riots were only a couple of miles away from us. We saw the pillars of smoke and heard the explosions. My father, who hadn't gotten a job yet, worked in the yard, read the papers, and complained about "the niggers taking over the city."

My grandfather rocked away the days, humming church songs on the front porch. He'd lost whatever English he had; I couldn't speak to him. Mark had already gone away to college. Mother, whom I helped cook and clean for two households that summer, seemed more nervous in Dad's presence than ever. I'm going to college, I thought. I'm getting away from here. Soon.

CHAPTER 5

In September, 1967, my parents dropped me off in East Lansing. My father had told me that he would cover my tuition, but that I would have to get a job to pay my room and board and expenses. That didn't bother me. I was free.

As soon as I was alone, I took a long walk around the huge campus. Michigan State, I realized, was a new world. It was filled with people and possibilities. I was just one of forty-five thousand undergraduates. I was completely anonymous, and that was fine.

It was the height of the 60s; everybody seemed to be improvising, experimenting, working out their lives as they went along. Rock music—the Beatles, Van Morrison, Jefferson Airplane—poured out of the dorm windows. Crew-cut athletes and engineering students walked on the same sidewalks as hippies in bell-bottoms, hiking boots, hand-dyed T-shirts and hair out to there. I saw weirdly dancing Hare Krishnas. Scowling, Afro-wearing black militants. Black Muslims in their tight black suits and bow ties. Orientals. Hispanics. Demonstrations and peace marches seemed to spring up out of thin air. So did the sweet, clinging smell of marijuana. The person in charge of campus housing, it was widely believed, might have been smoking a little too much of it, too.

Case Hall, where I was assigned, was a three-story

coed dorm—split right down the middle between academically oriented students and scholarship athletes. Jocks and nerds were jammed together. Hulking linemen and skinny poetry majors ate in the same attached dining room. The serious students were mainly from middle-class suburbs; most of the athletes were country boys recruited from the Deep South—or, in the case of the black athletes, from the inner city. At one end of the building the stereos blasted out the Rolling Stones and Joni Mitchell. At the other end, they played James Brown and Johnny Cash.

But that was fine with me. I felt a little nervous and shy, true, but also happy. At home. For the first time, I was starting out even with my classmates. *Everybody* was from someplace else. I wasn't quite brave enough, true, to become a hippie, but I turned myself into somebody different from the old Cynthia. I hid my skirts and sweaters in my bottom drawer and bought T-shirts, jeans, mini-skirts, and halter tops. I made new friends. After a few months, I discovered I was in the middle—the middle!—of a group of girls I really liked. And who liked me. There was Hedy, only four-foot-ten with lovely curly hair, a psychology major I became close to. There was Linda, tall and ethereal, with huge, beautiful eyes. There was Tracy, blond and thin, who matched me course for course and job for job.

My roommates were also wonderful. My first was a tall, thin, very intense Jewish girl named Julie who had dark, tight curls. She wore thick wire-rimmed glasses, and never changed out of bell-bottoms and T-shirt. She read philosophy books all night and, when she wasn't studying, wrote endlessly in her journal. "What do you think of this, Cynthia?" she'd ask me, reading me deep, introspective passages I could barely understand. I tried my best to listen sympathetically. I liked her very much.

One night, after dinner, Julie looked up from her textbook. "What's it like, Cynthia?" she asked.

"What's what like?"

"You know. Making love."

I nearly fell off my bunk bed. The little I knew I'd learned with Michael, and I wasn't even too sure about that much. I was afraid to pass on any misinformation. That could warp her life!

I tried to give her only the information that I was absolutely certain of—*Gray's Anatomy* helped there. "But basically," I said, red-faced, "it's wonderful. You'll find that out for yourself, I'm sure."

"Oh yes," she said, turning back to her book. I hope she found a better instructor than me.

My next roommate, Angela, was a black girl—we were both from Detroit, and we hit it off. Angela was a radical: she wore black capes and red berets. Taped above her bed was the famous poster of Huey Newton, rifle in hand, sitting in a wicker chair. But just underneath the surface, Angela was a gentle person, a hardworking student who was studying for a degree in urban planning. "I'm the first person in my family to even think of going to college," she told me one evening.

We danced together to her records in the room. The Temptations, the Supremes, the Four Tops! She joined Omega Psi Phi, the black sorority, and other, more political black student organizations. She was constantly going to demonstrations, meetings, and rallies. Big, handsome black students were always showing up to escort her to them. "Now, don't you be jivin' Cynthia," she said to her dates—in a put-on accent, winking—if they ignored or scowled at me.

"Cynthia ain't coming. But I'm gonna tell her all about it, *later!*"

We weren't flirty or "social" or sorority girls. Most Friday and Saturday nights, we stayed in the dorm and talked or listened to music. On the spur of the moment, we'd go out for ice cream, shopping, to the movies. There was no one to stop me, no one to yell at me.

I even had a boyfriend to talk about. Michael, who'd

managed to get into a junior college about a hundred miles from Michigan State, visited me on weekends. On rare occasions, when we could afford it, we'd rent a motel room. He planned to transfer to Michigan State after his freshman year.

Most of the time, though, I was either studying or working. I blitzed the student job office; on weeknights, I worked at the Kmart on Grand River Avenue. The manager assigned me to the Complaint Window: almost nightly at eight-thirty—until I begged them, laughing, to ease up—my girlfriends would come in and exchange their "defective" records and tapes.

On weekends I worked for the athletic department, showing prospective recruits the campus. "Show 'em a good time, Cynthia," said Duffy Dougherty, the football coach. One of his assistants would slip me some football tickets and cash for expenses.

I was issued a big boatlike Cadillac to drive the "prospects" around. They were very large high school seniors; either extremely shy or almost comically cocky. After the game, I'd take them out to the best restaurant in East Lansing. We'd eat steak and prime ribs. Then, during dessert, I'd give them the pitch: that Michigan State emphasizes "the academic side." That each "student athlete" would be the recipient of "close counseling."

Sometimes, football heroes or not, their mothers would come along for the ride. "Gordie, if all the young ladies here are like Cynthia, this will be a fine place for you to come," said one beehive-haired mother to her son. Hint, hint. Gordie, a hulking lineman, turned beet red. I felt like a tease. After dinner, I knew, we were putting Gordie right to bed in his motel at the Kellogg Center. And I wouldn't be keeping my appointment book clear for his arrival, that was for sure. I already had a boyfriend. And athletes weren't my type.

I didn't mind working. It helped me buy supplies and books, which I devoured. By far my hardest and least interesting job, though, was bussing tables at the Case Hall dining room. It was dirty work. I wore a white dress and a hairnet; I looked like Ruth Buzzi's bag-lady character on "Laugh-In." But after all, it paid the bills.

One afternoon, about halfway through my freshman year, I was late back from class and in a hurry to dump my notes, change, and get to my job. Running from my dorm room to the elevator bank, I tucked my hair into a knot and pulled my hairnet on.

As I rounded the last corner, I heard sounds of "passion" coming from the corridor. A boy, I could see, was passionately kissing his girlfriend. They were in one of the tightest clinches I'd ever seen in public. The girl was small and dark; the boy was medium height but built well. He had slicked-back black hair and was wearing a red button-down cardigan sweater.

I pushed the elevator button and tried to look away. Suddenly, the kissing stopped. "So long," said the guy, sending his girlfriend back down the corridor.

He came over and stood next to me. There were little initials embroidered on his sweater. They said "SPG."

As the elevator arrived he winked at me, and grinned. Too surprised to talk, I just gaped back at him.

"Nice hairdo," he said, as the door closed in front of him. That was the first time I saw Steve Garvey.

I didn't recognize Steve Garvey by sight. But, like most people at Michigan State, I'd heard about him. A sophomore, just a year ahead of me, he was already a baseball and football star. He was "The Garv," a sort of modern-day Jack Armstrong who actually kept his dorm room spotlessly clean. This was considered so amazing that visitors to Case Hall were sometimes led past his open door, just so they could stare at the neatness inside. He owned dozens of golf sweaters in all the colors of the rainbow. It was easy to pick him out in the dining hall; several times that year after our first encounter, he gave me the same wink as he had in the elevator bank.

Well, so what? I certainly wasn't interested in him. The more contact I had with the Case Hall athletes, the less I wanted to do with them. In the corridors, they shoved smaller boys aside on their way to class. At mealtimes, they pushed ahead in line—and even snatched food from the trays of other students. "Hey, wimp! You don't need meat!" they said. They swaggered into study hall, slammed their books down on the table, arranged them in neat little piles, and noisily munched popcorn. On Saturday nights they got drunk and shouted insults at female students passing by their windows.

I had a *nice* boyfriend; we got together whenever I had time to spare. True, that wasn't often: when I wasn't at one of my jobs, I was carrying a twenty-two-unit course load of tough social science courses.

One weekend, Michael decided we should go to a Michigan State–Southern California football game. About all I remember about that day is watching a Michigan State tackler, a man who looked undersized even from the top of the stadium, try to stop O. J. Simpson by grabbing his jersey as he flew past. The jersey tore off in his hand, the player fell flat on his behind, and Simpson ran hundreds of yards—or so it seemed to me—for a touchdown. Who was that poor guy? I looked in Michael's program. It was Steve Garvey. And I was very cold.

The other parts of college, though, were wonderful. It was where I belonged. I realized that each time I returned from a visit home. My father, just as bad-tempered as ever, was in the house all the time now. Mark had enrolled in ROTC at Ohio State. But my mother and Chris were still trapped in Detroit with him. It made me sad.

"Hey, Cynthia! I made it!" said Michael, calling me in Detroit that summer. By working on his grades at his junior college, he'd managed to transfer to Michigan

State. Also, by playing football there, he'd attracted the notice of the Michigan State coaches and earned a non-scholarship spot on the team.

At the beginning of my sophomore year, he moved right into Case Hall. He bounced between the third and fourth teams on the football squad; he wasn't really an athlete. But that didn't bother either of us very much.

At first, it was just like old times: we parked, we went to concerts, we went out with my friends, who all loved him. He was always willing to have fun; compared to me, he hardly studied at all. Once or twice during the really good months, we talked about marriage. "Medical school? Sure! That sounds great to me, Cynthia," he said. But gradually, guiltily, I began to have my doubts. Was I still the high school girl who'd fallen for Michael? I wondered if we were headed in the same direction.

"To medical school?" said my faculty advisor. He leaned back in his chair, looked up at the ceiling, and shook his head. He looked about thirty-five. Glasses, tousled blond hair, corduroy jacket. He had my transcript in front of him.

"You won't make it," he said. "You're a political science student. To get in all your hard science requirements would take four more years."

I froze. James Madison was oriented toward the liberal arts, true. But I'd only been there a year and a half. I had always thought that by grabbing as many science courses as possible, I could make up for it after my sophomore year.

"Uh-uh," he said. Now, panic began to set in.

"But wait a minute. I've got an idea," he said. He reached into a lower drawer of his desk. He thumbed through a course catalogue.

"Oh yeah. Here it is." He read for a few seconds, then looked straight at me for the first time. "There's this brand-new phys ed teaching major. Not the old basketweaving program that the jocks take. This one is hard.

There seems to be a lot of advanced science in it. When you graduate, you'll be in fairly good shape for med school.

"And if you change your mind," he said, peering at me over his glasses, "you can always become a nurse. Or teach gym."

Teach gym? He turned the catalogue around on his desk, and pointed. I saw courses like General Anatomy, Chemistry, Kinesiology, Psychology, and Community Health. Also Team Sports and Safety Education.

"What do you think?" I asked him. He shrugged. "I think you should take it."

"I guess I should," I said.

By the next trimester I was a future doctor disguised as a gym teacher trainee. I rushed around campus from class to class in a baggy green-and-white sweatsuit. The regular physical education majors, mostly stocky girls with pudding-bowl haircuts, looked at me curiously. So did the regular pre-med students. They wore gleaming white lab coats, carried six pens in their shirt pockets, and looked like they hadn't exercised in years.

And yet, the work—the dissections, the experiments, even the statistics course—fascinated me. I'd look at the human body, trace the muscles and nerves and bones, and it all seemed beautiful. Logical.

Many times, when I was lost in my work, my shyness, my differentness, seemed to melt away. I'd like to belong here, I thought. And maybe I really do.

"You've gotta help me get through this, Cynthia," said the football star, smiling toothily at me across the snack bar table. I'd signed up to tutor, for a few dollars an hour, whomever the athletic department sent my way. Most of them just wanted help cramming for a test the next day—and if I *really* wanted to help, to take the test in their place. I never did. A few arrived with copies of their test in advance. "Just circle the right answers, will ya? I'll study those," they'd say.

It was common knowledge that certain professors never flunked the star athletes. There were a number of them registered in Anatomy, a big lecture course held in a hall that seated hundreds. At the final exam, they grouped themselves in the seats behind and above me. The proctor was a tall, pale graduate assistant. He stood behind the podium, glancing at the students and his watch, writing the time remaining on the blackboard.

"Miss Truhan! Come forward!" he said.

I looked up in surprise. I was about halfway through the test. The proctor was leaning over his little microphone, and looking straight at me.

"Bring your test paper with you. Now." Panic!

Everyone was staring. Old feelings swept over me; I had been singled out again. Terrified, I walked down the steps to the front of the class. He took my test paper—and ripped it in half in front of everyone!

"Now, get your things and come with me." I walked as quickly as I could, looking straight ahead, back up to my seat. Then, in the tense silence, I walked all the way down again. He took me to a little room down the hall.

"What did I do?" I asked him. He relaxed a bit. He told me that the athletes behind me were cheating by looking at my paper. He would give me a different test, he said, all by myself, right here in the office.

"But why me? Why didn't you pull *them* out?"

"I—I thought it was the best way to handle the situation," he said, the authority leaking out of him. He was obviously terrified of the athletes. I felt sorry for him. He handed me a new test paper.

"Begin now," he said, and left the room.

I pulled myself together and finished the exam. The news spread quickly through the college. "What did you do, Cynthia?" my friends asked me, concerned, for weeks afterward. "What did you *do?*" The jocks told the story a different way. When they saw me around the dorm they just pointed and laughed.

* * *

Michael and I began to have serious trouble. I was too busy studying, he said, to sustain our relationship. Much more often than I was comfortable with, he wanted me to forget about my work and have fun with him. He himself didn't pay much attention to his courses. Our different priorities, it became painfully obvious, were tearing us apart.

One evening we had a loud argument in front of the library. Michael stalked off. I went inside and sat down at my librarian's desk.

I glanced up. Steve Garvey was standing there, looking at me. He walked over and smiled at me.

"Don't worry. I'm around," he said. Then he patted me on the head, turned around, and left. I was too startled to say anything. I had no idea what he meant. Who was this guy?

"Who do you know in Albuquerque?" asked my father. It was the summer of '69; I was sitting in the backyard of our house in Detroit. My father stared at the envelope in his hand, flipped it over to read the return address again, and handed it to me.

It was mailed from the "Albuquerque Sports Stadium." From Steve Garvey. What? I opened it. "Dear Cindy," it began. Cindy? Nobody called me Cindy. He had a large, careful handwriting, with lots of space between the lines.

"Just a brief hello and a check on how good you're being this summer," I read. There was a page or so about his playing for the Dodger farm team in Albuquerque—"Things are going well for me"—filled mostly with the names of the Southwestern towns the team played in. Then: "Best wishes for a good summer and a hope towards seeing you in the fall. Give my best to Mike and friends!"

"Well, who is it?" said my father.

"Just somebody I know from school," I said. But that

was wrong. I *didn't* know Steve Garvey. That he was playing for the Dodgers (but why in New Mexico?) was news to me. He was checking up on how "good" I'd been? What did he mean by that? Give my best to our friends? What friends?

It was nice of him to write, but I was more confused than ever. Whoever this guy was, it seemed like we had nothing in common.

But for some reason I kept the letter. I folded it up carefully, put it back in its envelope, and put it in my dresser drawer.

"Come *on*, Cynthia," said Michael. It was October, a Saturday night, and he was dragging me out to a post-football-game mixer. Reluctantly, I got into his old car and we drove off campus. The party was in the meeting room of an apartment complex. As soon as we walked through the door, I could see that I shouldn't have gone.

The music was too loud. The place was filled with athletes, many of them drunk from the kegs of beer stacked in the corner. I recognized some of the athletes from Case Hall. Steve Garvey was there with a nursing student from one of my classes.

This was not my type of party. I didn't want to be there. I started to get angry—at myself, at Michael. But we were past working things out. Sensing my anger, Michael just walked away, going off to play pool with a couple of his buddies. I was left alone.

This made me even madder. Now I was fair game for any male in the room. A huge rugby player, very drunk, lurched over and began to drape his free arm over my shoulder. I tried to push him away. It was like fending off a falling tree.

"Aw, c'mon, Cynthia, I've *always* admired you," he slurred. "Let's dance!"

"No!" I spun around, trying to get out of his grasp— and suddenly, there was Steve Garvey, right next to me. And he seemed sober. Maybe he would get me away from my torturer. "Would *you* dance with me?" I asked brusquely. Without a word, he began to dance. The rugby player—outranked—melted back into the crowd.

I just wanted to get out of there. But the record seemed to go on forever. Where was Steve's date during all this time? I wondered. Finally, the music stopped.

"Can I call you?" said Steve.

"I don't think that's a good idea," I said, looking around to see what Michael had made of this. He was still playing pool, oblivious to me.

That was the last straw. I grabbed my coat—a long, blue maxicoat that dragged on the ground—and began to walk home. It was five miles back to campus. It was cold, and beginning to snow lightly. I walked fast. I hate Michigan winters, I thought. I hate Michael. Ahead of me stretched Grand River Avenue, lonely and dark. I had two more years of hard work—and then a fight for a medical school scholarship.

I had to do it all by myself, I thought.

"Do you need a ride?" said a voice on my left. I looked over, still walking. It was Steve Garvey, leaning over his girlfriend to talk to me through his car window. He was in a huge, new Buick Riviera: his girlfriend, a short brunette, looked straight ahead.

"No, thank you. I don't need a ride," I said abruptly.

"Okay. See you around," he said cheerfully.

The girlfriend rolled up her window. The Buick pulled off down the street in a cloud of white smoke.

Suddenly, the anger drained out of me. I was left with the cold, my tiredness, and a two-hour walk. That was dumb, Cynthia, I thought. I trudged back to the dorm. The blowing snow began to stick to the pavement.

CHAPTER 6

Steve Garvey called me the next evening, and I hung up on him. My new roommate, Terry, had been getting obscene phone calls from someone on campus. "Hi, this is Steve," said an unfamiliar voice.

"What do you want? Stop calling!" I said, and slammed down the receiver.

He called right back. "Cynthia, this is Steve. Steve *Garvey.*"

"Oh," I said, embarrassed. "I thought you were someone else."

Steve laughed. "What are you doing back here?" I asked. "I thought you were in Arizona."

"My credits wouldn't transfer," said Steve.

"Well, why did you write me that letter? We don't know each other. And aren't you going out with somebody else?"

Silence. "Do you want to go out?" he asked, finally.

Did I want to go out? I thought about Michael and me. That was over, I knew. I thought about this mysterious man, about how good-looking he was, about taking a chance to make myself less lonely. The decision took only a few seconds.

"Okay. All right," I said. And that was that.

A few nights later, Steve picked me up in the dorm lobby. I was nervous. I was amazed that this person was attracted to me. "You know, I hate this coat," I said, just making conversation while I wrapped myself up.

"Well then—you don't need it," he said, smiling, pulling it off me and handing it to the girl at the front desk. I didn't need it? It was twenty degrees above zero out there. But his big car was parked right outside, and it was already warm. We drove to the movies and he parked close to the entrance. You know, I thought, he was right. I didn't need that draggy coat tonight.

We sat through a double feature: *Romeo and Juliet* and *Barefoot in the Park.* Every now and then, I looked over to the side and checked him out. He looked—well, calm and happy. Handsome, manly. He had on another one of those sweaters, a green one this time. His hair, as always, was slicked back neatly and gleaming. He smelled great.

It was nice to be with him. Relaxing. He took me right home after the movie, said goodnight to me on the front steps, bent over to kiss me, and hesitated.

"It's okay," I said, moving toward him. "It's all right." He kissed me lightly, just once, then walked back to his car. What kind of football player was this? I wondered. The strange part was, I knew I couldn't figure him out. But despite that—maybe even because of that—I was attracted to him.

"I don't play ball here any more," he told me on our second date. He'd signed with the Los Angeles Dodgers baseball team for forty-five thousand dollars, and played for them in their minor league system. Since that made him a professional athlete, he couldn't play baseball or football for Michigan State any longer. Nobody at the University or in the athletics department seemed to mind; they let him stay enrolled in school, and he fitted his physical education requirements around his baseball schedule. The real proof of his status, though, was the faculty-level parking sticker they let him keep on his car. It let him park almost anywhere on campus. Nobody I knew had anything even remotely like that. "You can use it any time you want to," he told me.

Michael and I finally broke up. We both knew it was time we went our separate ways. We'd been together three years.

That winter, Steve and I dated on Saturday nights. I'm going to figure him out, I thought. I'm going to get to the bottom of him, I thought. I didn't, but the attraction remained. We went to concerts, hockey games, more movies—usually just the two of us. (Later, I found out that Friday nights were reserved for the other girl.) On Sunday afternoons, I'd come back to his house and cook dinner for Steve and his roommates. He was a gentleman. He opened doors for me, and "sirred" and "ma'am-ed" every older adult in sight. He smelled nice. But beyond that? That was just out of my reach. The possibilities intrigued me.

He didn't talk much, but gradually, I found out more about him: he was born in Tampa, Florida. Just before he'd been born his father, Joe Garvey, had left the Navy and moved to Tampa, to run a motel there. Steve grew up next door to the motel, he told me, in a house on stilts at the edge of a swamp. He was an only child. His parents— his mother, Mildred, particularly—noticed he was more coordinated than other kids his age, and she began pushing him into sports. At six, he was playing baseball against eight-year-olds. In grade school, he was always by far the best athlete; in high school, he was an all-American. "It's my dream to play baseball in the major leagues," he said. Of his personal life, he'd tell me almost nothing.

I asked him about his old girlfriends.

"My girlfriends? I get a new one each season. One for the baseball season, one for the football season, one for the basketball season," he teased me. I teased him right back: I told him, maybe a little too smugly, that I was the only person on campus who'd never paid to see him play anything. But he just laughed.

It was interesting how he lived. He shared an off-campus apartment with three other athletes, typical happy-go-lucky guys who left empty beer cans and dirty laundry all over the house. In the middle of all this, his room was an island of neatness. His bed was always made, and his clothes were always neatly folded—but he didn't mind the mess his roommates made. "Why not?" I asked him.

"Hey, they're great guys," he said, vaguely. "I'm never here, anyway."

Never here? Where, then? He was hard to figure out. I felt drawn to Steve. Yet I didn't really understand why. He was aloof, distant, like my father. But no, Cynthia, I thought, that was unfair. Unlike my father, he was gentle. He never raised his voice. Didn't that prove that he wasn't like Dad at all?

"I've had my eye on you for a long time," he told me, very early on. I liked that. I liked his quiet strength. His certainty. His sense that he knew where he was going. That he had goals. Like me.

He was strong, solid as a rock. I felt secure and safe in his arms. But there was a shyness about him that surprised me.

It was a challenge to get him to show affection; a smile from him, which I tried to get by telling him a joke or snuggling close to him, meant a lot. He didn't like physical contact in public; at a football game, I remember, I tried to slip my hand into his pocket. Immediately—almost a reflex action—he pulled my hand out and placed it on his arm.

"What are you doing? Are we going to the prom or something?" I said, half jokingly.

"Well, uh . . ." he said, a little flustered.

"No, no," I said. "I want you to hold my hand." And he looked away, but I held on and pulled him closer to me. He didn't protest or snap at me. There was something intriguing, even sexy about this handsome athlete being so shy; when I had the urge to kiss him, I practically had to pull him by the ears toward me. He wasn't much more affectionate in private; although I was ready to, we didn't sleep together until several months into our relationship. He had higher standards than mine, I thought, and I didn't press the point. I was falling in love with him, I knew. But there were loose ends. I wondered how much I really knew about him. There were surprises: he didn't have a checking account, had never written a check in his life, he told me—his mother handled all that for him. He brought his laundry home to Florida, in big duffel bags, for washing. He didn't own a single pair of blue jeans.

One night, around midnight, we were sitting in his apartment watching Johnny Carson on television. The doorbell rang.

"Who's that?" I wondered. It was snowing outside; the temperature wasn't much higher than zero.

Steve got up, went to the door, opened it a crack, and looked out. He murmured something. A little gloved hand holding a small package shot through the opening. Steve took the package, put it on a table, and came back to sit next to me.

"What's that?" I asked, intrigued.

"Oh, nothing."

Playfully, I jumped up and grabbed the package. "Oh, you've got a present," I said, tearing off the fancy wrapping paper. Inside the box was a pair of gold cuff links with his initials, "SPG," engraved on them.

Steve said nothing. I finally wormed it out of him that they were from the nursing student, who, I supposed, was mounting a last-ditch effort to get Steve away from me.

"Why didn't you tell her you're with me?" I said.

"I'm not seeing her any more. She just doesn't get it." Steve said. He stood up and calmly put the cuff links into his dresser drawer.

I gathered up my things for the ride back to the dorm. For some reason I couldn't understand, I was upset that

Steve hadn't straightened things out with the other girl. He had let her waste her time and money.

Soon after that, we began dating on Friday nights, too.

It was around that time that my brother Mark, who had, as I'd feared, been sent to Vietnam, wrote from a hospital there. He'd been wounded in the legs and chest by a North Vietnamese artillery shell. The wounds weren't bad enough to get him sent home. "Don't tell Mom or Dad or Chris about this, okay?" he wrote. I wrote back saying I wouldn't. "Please take care of yourself," I said, and mailed him some books—including *Alive* by Piers Paul Read. It wasn't very subtle, but I was very scared for him.

In December I brought Steve home to Detroit for dinner. I was nervous. I was afraid that if my father blew up, if the family tensions became apparent, Steve would disapprove of me and move on. I was upset to see how my mother had aged during my father's retirement. She was much heavier, and her skin had gone from olive to sallow. She looked unhealthy and very tired. My father, who hadn't found a job that suited him, was building an extra room onto the back of the house to take up his time.

"Hey, I could use some help out here!" yelled my father. That was the first thing we heard after we arrived, his voice carrying through the house as Steve and I stepped through the front door.

Steve hadn't even met him yet. But we went back and saw that my father was struggling to hold up a high wooden beam. Without a word, Steve mounted a stepladder and held up the beam. Dad grunted in approval and started to hammer the beam in place.

I looked at the two of them. They looked good together. A phrase popped into my head. My voice, clear as a bell, saying, "This is going to work."

Around my parents, Steve was ultra-polite. He called them "sir" and "ma'am" at every opportunity. He charmed my mother, who scurried around him during dinner, serving him plates and plates of food. My brother Chris, who was a star on his high school baseball team, clearly adored Steve. My father, a golf and baseball fan, talked to him for hours.

Chris just sat there, wide-eyed. So did I. I felt a strong feeling of . . . relief? Yes, that was it. I knew that I didn't have to work at getting Steve accepted. Finally, after all these years, I had pleased my father. Somehow. He didn't say anything rude to Steve, or shoot me a warning glance.

No! As Steve told him about his baseball plans, he listened eagerly. He was actually touching Steve—squeezing his shoulder, shaking his hand! I'd *never* seen him do that before. For the first time in a long time, I felt safe around my father. It was a good, almost giddy, feeling.

Imagine: this young man—who wanted me—had won over my family. With his all-American good looks and polite manners, he was unmistakably *right*. My body relaxed. I could let down my guard, at least for a while. At least this choice, this part of me, was all right.

"Stevie was always a good little boy," said Mildred Garvey to me. I nodded and smiled my best smile.

Steve had taken me down to Tampa over the Christmas vacation. We were sitting around the dinner table listening to the Garvey family history. Mildred, his mother, chain-smoked nervously.

"Steve is so terrific. Why aren't there more little Garveys?" I chirped.

The labor pains from bearing Steve were so tremendous, Mildred told me, that she decided then and there to have only one child.

She proudly showed me his bedroom, which was tiny, connected to his parents' by a common bathroom, and absolutely overflowing with trophies, plaques, and framed photographs. It was a shrine, really.

She asked me very little about myself, but I filled in the silences by asking lots of questions about them. Mildred was an accountant for the state of Florida. Joe, she said, had quit the motel business and joined Greyhound as a bus driver. Most of the year he drove regular routes, but during spring training he was assigned to drive the Dodger team bus at their training camp at Vero Beach. When Steve was growing up, he said, he'd taken him to spring training each February.

"They ask for me every year," said Joe, a sweet, soft-spoken man who stood about six foot three. The Dodger players, he said, smiling, called him "Bussy." I didn't think that was so great, but I liked him very much. Obviously, his son's signing with the team was like a fairy tale come true.

Just as obviously, Mildred ran the Garvey household. She was clearly the boss. Sometimes she'd get into a bad mood and sit, silent and glowering, at the kitchen table. When she started chain-smoking and drinking lots of cups of black coffee, it seemed best to stay away from her.

"Does she like me?" I asked Steve, a little nervously, when we were alone.

"Sure she does," he said, as if the answer was obvious. We were curled up on the floor, on pillows, watching Johnny Carson as usual.

"Tomorrow I'll take you to Busch Gardens," said Steve. "And when we get married, we'll go . . ."

"Wait! What do you mean 'When we get married'?" I said, sharply. I was startled. The subject of marriage had never come up before. I thought, Be very careful now, Cynthia. I liked Steve a lot, but I wasn't absolutely sure that I loved him. On the other hand, I still wanted to be with him. Had I just insulted him? I grabbed his hand and looked at him anxiously.

To my relief, Steve just smiled. "You would be good in my life," he said.

But what life was that? "You'll be on the road all the time. I'll hardly see you at all," I said.

"Oh no. I'll come back to visit," he said. And I left it at that. He looked so sweet and sincere that I grabbed onto him. Under the hard muscles, I could feel him softening slightly. He smelled so fresh. I felt so secure.

Maybe I could get through to the soft part of him, I thought. Maybe.

Steve left for the Dodgers' rookie camp in January. "Take care of things," he said, as we kissed goodbye at the airport. "Yes," I said, grabbing him around the waist. I still felt a distance from him, though. He was so determined. So different.

This was the last half of Steve's fourth year in college. He was way short of the credits he needed to graduate. Even though he was playing ball full-time, he'd worked out an arrangement with the university to graduate that June. He'd earn the easy version of the phys ed degree by taking "correspondence" courses. What this meant was that every semester I had to register him for his classes. Most of the time, the computer kicked his name out as "not registered," and I had to knock on doors, beg and plead to gray-haired lady registrars, to get him re-entered. I met with his academic advisor to make sure he was taking the right courses he needed to graduate. When Steve was too tired, I wrote his term papers for him.

He needed me. I missed him very much. Still, there were constant reminders of him. He'd left me the keys to the Riviera with the magic parking sticker. As I drove around campus, peering over the steering wheel of that huge car, I was instantly recognizable.

The word was out. I was Steve Garvey's steady girlfriend: "Garv's girl." Now the football players didn't laugh at me or try to pick me up. No more jokes, no more jostling. I was a new person: they treated me as a sort of stand-in for Steve. And they loved Steve.

"Hey, Cynthia! How's Steve?" they yelled.

"How's The Garv?"

"Say hello to The Garv for me!"

Since I was The Garv's girl, nobody else asked me out. I probably wouldn't have accepted, anyway. Or would I? I wondered. I wasn't engaged to Steve. What, exactly, was my obligation to him? In the evenings, after I finished studying, I'd go to the intramural swimming pool and swim laps for an hour. Then I'd shower, dry off, and go back home to think about Steve.

The best part was that Steve was thinking about me, too. I hadn't really expected that. When we were together, he was anything but romantic. When we were apart, as we would be for practically the next two years, he was just the opposite.

He wrote me two or three times a week, usually on Dodger stationery, in his wide-spaced, arrow-straight script. His words were passionate, uninhibited. He wrote that he loved me very much. He wrote of his loneliness, of how much he missed me, of his plans and dreams, and how big a part I was of them.

I wrote back, trying to justify his faith in me. I'd tell him what was happening in my classes, and he'd tell me about competing at third base for a spot on the Dodgers; trying to catch the eye of the Dodger management. He must have had what they were looking for: after spring training, he was assigned to the Dodgers' Triple A farm team—their highest—in Spokane, Washington. "Sweetheart," he wrote me from there, "try to be understanding of our situation and the fullness of my love for you. We will be the man and wife we can't wait to be and experience the oneness that keeps us so close."

This was a side of Steve I'd never seen in person. It was a wonderful, romantic side. But—man and wife? We'd still been going together for less than a year, and we'd been physically together far less than that. Maybe, I wondered, the relationship worked best when we were apart.

Maybe he liked me where I was: his faithful girlfriend, far away.

No. It was wrong of me to think that, I decided. And then Steve erased the doubts.

"When the school year is over, come out to Spokane for the summer," said Steve, one night over the phone. "Great!" I said. At long last, a chance to spend some time with him, see whether we could live together. The plan was for me to move in with Steve and his roommates, and to get a job to occupy me while his club was on the road.

I met Steve at the Spokane airport on a sunny June afternoon; I'd flown in from Michigan, and his team, the Spokane Indians, was coming back from a road trip.

"This is Cynthia," he said proudly to his teammates. They immediately lined up to file past me and shake my hand.

They looked me up and down, and smiled a little too widely. "Nice to meet you," said one. Then he turned his head toward Steve and muttered, "Eight and a half."

"Heard a lot about you," said another. Then, "Eight."

"Hiya, Cindy. Nine."

"Hi. Seven and a half."

And so on, all the way down the line. "What were those numbers for?" I asked Steve, when we were seated together on the team bus.

"Oh well," he blushed.

"What?"

"They were, uh, grading you. From one to ten."

"Oh *wonderful,"* I said, sarcastically. "I hope I met their expectations."

The world of minor league baseball certainly had its surprises. The Indians in 1970 were managed by Tommy Lasorda, a happy-go-lucky guy who'd been in the Dodger organization forever and who talked a mile a minute. "Hey, Garv! Hang on to this one!" he said when Steve introduced us. His teammates included future Dodger players Charlie Hough, Geoff Zahn, Bobby Valentine, Davey Lopes, Tom Paciorek, and Bill Russell. The team played in a tiny stadium near downtown Spokane. I saw what they meant by "minor" league: the Indians sold mimeographed programs, and held gala events like "Elks Lodge Night" and "Safety School Patrol Night." Players actually married their girlfriends, under crossed bats, at home plate before the game. It was a carnival. A jumble of sounds and noises. But even amid the confusion and silliness, Steve stood out.

It was the first time I'd seen him in his baseball uniform. The effect was breathtaking. In his red-and-white stretch pants and shirt, he was even more handsome than ever. His legs stood out like tree trunks. His arms were massive, muscled. With his high cheekbones, his features seemed chiseled onto his face. He was a beautiful man who did wonderful things.

Yes, and he loved doing what he did. In the dugout during the game, he always sat right next to the coaches. He wants to learn all he can from them, I thought.

In the field, playing third base, he looked strong and graceful—not like some of the other players, who seemed nervous, eager to impress, and desperate to succeed. At the plate, bat held high, he stood almost straight up, like a soldier. He looked calm, almost detached. He didn't spit or scratch like most of the other guys. His uniform was almost always spotless. When he hit the ball— *c-r-a-a-a-ck!* an amazing sound—the ball usually rocketed into the outfield.

The crowd cheered him. "Garv! Garv! Garv!" they shouted. They went wild. And he was *my* boyfriend. He was nuts about *me.* I could hardly believe my good fortune.

After the game, groups of young girls pressed forward to the railing to get his autograph.

"Hey, Steve!"

"This way, Steve!"

"Over here, Steve!"

I looked on, happy for his popularity, proud of his success. There was no reason to be jealous. He was blushing. Blushing and signing.

It was an exciting, happy-go-lucky time. Steve and I lived in a decrepit duplex near the waterfront which we shared with Bill Buckner. "Billy Bucks" was the team's first baseman. Steve played across the diamond at third. There was a strong undercurrent of competition between them: at night, when they came home from the game, they added up their statistics and announced them to each other. "Three hits, no errors, two rbi's." "A game-winning homer, no errors." "Four hard-hit balls." "No strikeouts."

I liked Billy immediately. He lived and played with a passion. Steve liked Billy, I felt, because he was what Steve couldn't be—a free spirit. Billy was a wild man—when he struck out, he slammed his bat down on home plate. One time, tagged out trying to stretch a single into a double, he kicked second base so hard he broke his toe. He was absolutely driven to make a success of himself. One night, after Billy told me how his father had committed suicide when he was sixteen, I thought I understood why.

Steve and Billy owned a car, a junky red convertible that rarely started without a push. They hatched a scheme to sell the car to the Indians' public relations man, and somehow—with a new battery and Steve's honest face—they managed to unload it on him.

And yet. I got the feeling that no matter how well Steve was doing he really wasn't a full-fledged member of the team. He was different from his teammates, and not in ways they particularly appreciated. In the mornings, I'd go down and watch the players work out. Tommy Lasorda had appointed Steve to lead the running drills. That was no favor to Steve: off he'd run, bright-eyed and bushy-tailed, while the other players grumbled and lagged behind him. "C'mon! Let's go! Move it!" said

Steve. When Tommy wasn't around, the other players shouted insults and curses at him. Once, another player hung back a whole lap around the field and deliberately tripped Steve as he went by. Steve just stared at him curiously for a second, then leaped to his feet and kept running.

On off days or after day games, Billy met his girlfriend Jan and went out to eat—and drink—with the other players and their dates.

We never went. Nobody even asked us, which puzzled me. "Oh, they know I don't drink or do that kind of stuff," said Steve. Most evenings, I stayed home and cooked. He seemed perfectly happy to stay home and watch television with me. We talked about the future. And then one day, not more than a couple of weeks after I arrived in Spokane, the future arrived.

"They want me down there!" said Steve, coming home from the game one night. He was literally shaking with excitement.

"Who? Where?"

"The big club!" The Dodgers! I hugged him. This was what he had been working for! A couple of Dodgers had been called up for Army Reserve duty, he said, and they wanted him to fly down to Los Angeles right away.

"It's just for ten days," said Steve. Was I going with him? I asked. "No. You stay here. In the house. I'll be back then."

The next day, he was gone. And I was left with Bill Buckner. Billy had just broken up with Jan. He was alone, too. One night I cooked a steak dinner and put it in the oven for him. He came home from a night game at 12:30 A.M. I was already in bed.

He'd done badly that night. I heard the oven door slam and—

BAM!! CRASH!! There was a tremendous noise from the living room. I put on my bathrobe and, terrified, went to take a look. Billy was so mad that he'd taken out the steak and flung it, plate and all. There was a big stain on the wall and broken china on the floor. When I realized what had happened, I went back to my bedroom and locked the door. The next day, Billy calmly cleaned up his mess himself. But I'd had enough. I called Steve and asked him when he was coming back.

"I'm not coming back," said Steve, excitedly. "They want me to stay down here. I'm going on the road trip with the Dodgers."

Yes, that was great. But what about me? "Do you want me to come with you?" I asked.

A pause. "Well, yeah. Sure." said Steve, finally. "Come to Los Angeles before you go back to school." Funny, I thought. It almost sounded as if he didn't want me with him. But I packed up, gave Billy a goodbye peck on the cheek, and flew down to Los Angeles.

I'd never been to California before. The taxi ride from the airport seemed to take hours; the buildings along the freeway were small and shabby. I rode past factories and warehouses. This was glamorous Hollywood? Steve was staying at the Biltmore, a huge old hotel in downtown Los Angeles—a part I'd never seen on television. He seemed happy to see me and, the next day, took me out to Dodger Stadium for a practice before a night game.

Dodger Stadium, also in the middle of the old part of Los Angeles, sat in a hole on a hillside. The stadium was huge and very clean, painted in pastel colors, all swooping lines and angles, like a big '50s drive-in. "C'mon. I want to introduce you to some people," said Steve. He took me down into the basement of the stadium, to Al Campanis' office. Campanis, Steve explained, was the general manager—the man who really ran the Dodgers. Who was in charge of Steve's future.

Al Campanis was a short, round man, sitting behind his desk in a big chair. He was smoking the biggest cigar I'd ever seen.

"Uh, Mr. Campanis," said Steve. "This is Cynthia Truhan. The girl I've been telling you about."

Mr. Campanis took a long look at me, took the cigar out of his mouth, then turned to Steve.

"So, when're you kids gettin' married?" he said, in a tough New York accent.

Oh my God. We really had no plans to get married. It was a question we'd—I'd—been avoiding. But this man wasn't joking. And he could obviously make or break Steve's career. A wrong answer—whatever that might be —would be disastrous. Steve looked terrified. He glanced at me, smiled nervously, then turned back to Campanis.

"Uh, well, we . . . as soon as we . . . the problem is, we don't know any jewelry stores in Los Angeles," he said, improvising madly. It was the best he could do.

Campanis dismissed Steve's excuse with a wave of his hand. "Just a minute," he said, looking up a number on his Rolodex and dialing the phone.

"Hey, it's Al," he said. "Yeah. Yeah. Hey, listen. I got two kids here who need an engagement ring. Yeah. Yeah. This afternoon? Okay, thanks."

"It's all set. No problem," said Campanis to Steve. The next few hours were just a blur. Before we knew it, we were in a cab headed for the L.A. Jewelry Mart. Campanis' friend the jeweler was fawning over us, talking to Steve about the Dodgers, selling us a diamond ring for a ridiculously low price.

I was so stunned that I didn't even question what was happening. Steve handed me a ticket, for the "family section" above third base. I walked through the tunnel and, looking carefully at the ticket number, found my seat.

"Hey! What're you doin' here? Who do you belong to?" a fancily dressed black woman, sitting next to me, asked angrily. She was, I learned later, Willie Crawford's wife, Dee.

"I—I'm Steve Garvey's girlfriend. Here's my ticket," I said, holding it out to her. She snorted and turned away. Nobody talked to me, at least not until Steve came to bat for the first time.

I stood up and clapped. And then, for some reason, the organist began playing a hearts-and-flowers tune.

"Look up there," somebody told me, and pointed. On the message board, in big letters, it said:

THE DODGERS ARE HAPPY TO ANNOUNCE
THE ENGAGEMENT
OF
CYNTHIA ANNE TRUHAN
OF
GROSSE POINTE WOODS, MICHIGAN
TO
STEVEN PATRICK GARVEY

What? Was this Steve's idea? Wasn't this something we should have decided in private? I looked down at him, and he was staring at the ground, embarrassed, dragging his bat behind him. This must have been Mr. Campanis' idea. The players in the dugout were making fun of him.

"Way to go, lover boy!"

"Hit a homer for her!"

"Go up there and give her a kiss!"

All around the stadium, the fans were giving Steve a good-natured round of applause. Thousands and thousands of people, all congratulating me on my engagement. Could it be, then, that I really *was* engaged? "It must be," was the thought that ran through my numbed brain.

I was twenty years old.

CHAPTER 7

I was amazed. Absolutely overwhelmed. Never in my wildest fantasies had I imagined anything like this happening. *Did* things like this happen? I slumped back in my seat and tried to sort things out. The way things were going, I thought, Steve and I were bound to get engaged sooner or later. And now we were. Or should we? Were we?

The doubts pushed their way to the front: I'd never actually agreed to marry Steve, and wasn't that the way it was supposed to work? I worried about Steve's sincerity, his silences, the way of life he planned for us. But what were those vague fears compared to thousands of cheering people? I loved him. It had been announced. We were engaged, officially.

The ballgame ended. None of the other wives or girlfriends said anything to me, but I made my way through the tunnel, down the ramps to the Dodgers' dressing room. I waited in the hallway for Steve to emerge. There were dozens of people milling around, but I knew none of them.

"Who are you waiting for?" said a security guard, suspiciously.

"I'm waiting for Steve. Steve Garvey."

"Oh yeah? Oh! You're Cynthia, right? The *fiancée.*"

"That's right. I'm Cynthia Truhan," I said, nervously.

"Well," he said, "why don't you wait with the rest of the wives?"

He motioned me into a small, windowless room. I looked around; there were a few battered old couches pushed against the bare concrete walls. Seated on them, in little groups, were the same women I'd seen in the stands. None of them said a word to me. I was too shy to approach them.

Then Steve came in. Immediately, a small crowd gathered around him.

"Oh, hi, Steve!"

"Hey, congratulations!"

"Where'd you meet her?"

"When's the wedding?"

Steve didn't introduce me; he just grabbed me by the hand and led me out.

"How'd you like that?" he said. "Your name up in lights."

What could I tell him? There was no doubt about it, I suddenly realized: a part of me was excited, too. "On the *scoreboard*—is that the way they do things here?" I asked. Here as in Hollywood, I thought.

We drove back to the hotel. Two days later, Steve and the Dodgers were gone on a road trip. I flew back to Detroit for the rest of the summer vacation. A week later, Steve mailed me a big photograph of the scoreboard with our names on it. Just like I remembered; I was really his fiancée.

The main thing I was afraid of was my father's reaction. Would the news set him off? Send him into a rage at me? I was a Catholic girl who'd been living in a hotel room with a baseball player, after all. I was so terrified of my father that when I met him at the airport, I covered my engagement ring with my right hand.

"So I hear you're engaged," said my father, flatly. Driving me home from Detroit Metropolitan, he looked straight ahead through the windshield. I relaxed a little bit. I was relieved to see he wasn't angry.

My mother, on the other hand, was ecstatic. "Oh, how wonderful!" she said, hugging me and gazing at my diamond. "Steve is such a lovely boy. You're so lucky, Cynthia." But something about her reaction was strange. She seemed *too* happy. In a daze, almost; as if she were trying to escape from the unpleasantness of her real world through some fairy-tale notion of our engagement. Again and again, she asked me the same questions about Steve and our plans, and smiled too widely as I gave her the same answers. I asked her if there was anything wrong. "No, no!" she said. But suddenly I noticed she was looking much older. Her hair was grayer and wispier. Her body was thicker. Scariest of all, her movements were stiff and jerky.

That fall, back at Michigan State, I moved into an off-campus apartment, signed up for seventeen units and kept Steve's phantom academic career going. Since this was his fifth year, it was even harder to keep him registered. Sometimes it even became necessary to pretend he was really on campus. I practiced signing his name—a skill that came in handy later. I copied his big scrawl off his letters, until I could safely forge it on his registration forms. At the end of the school year, when even Steve couldn't get out of coming back briefly for his final exams, I sat in for him on a couple of tough ones: freshman English, which he'd never taken, and a teaching skills evaluation test.

It was worth it. Steve did well with the Dodgers that year. He got into thirty-four games for them, playing third base and batting .269. And once again, the longer he was away from me, the more ardent his letters became. I read them over and over; I fell more in love with the Steve who was writing them. The possibility—the probability!—that I could live with *this* man excited me. I formed a plan. I would become a pediatrician. He would admire me for that. At night, after I finished work, I would go to the stadium to watch him play.

And most important: if I loved Steve, if I really worked hard, I could bring the gentle side—the letter side—out of him. That would be my other job.

Of course, I couldn't do that until we were really living together full-time. When I had him to myself. When we really got to know each other. That would be a while. But it was worth the wait, no question.

"Tell me about your headaches. What are they like?" asked Steve. It was the winter of 1970; he was calling me from Fort Jackson, an Army base in Columbia, South Carolina. Like a lot of other ballplayers during the Vietnam era, he was fulfilling his military obligation by taking six months of basic training and then going into the Reserves. Every August, he'd leave his team for three weeks to go off for military training.

It seemed wrong to him that he should have to go through with this. It wasn't likely that he'd be sent to Vietnam, but just the possibility scared both of us. If he could get out of the Army for medical reasons, he'd be able to go to the Dodgers' training camp in the spring. I felt funny about all of this. I knew it was wrong.

I described my migraines: how I saw bright spots and twinkling lights; how my fingers felt numb, my tongue swelled up, and, during particularly bad ones, I felt sick to my stomach and threw up. "Okay," said Steve, "I'll tell them that. I'll try it." He entered basic training at the end of November. By the middle of December he'd been named "barracks orderly" of his platoon. "The Drill Sergeant chose me to be his aide and carry out his orders!" he wrote. That certainly sounded like something that would happen to Steve. He sent a picture of himself, in full-dress uniform, to my father.

"He cuts a fine figure," said my father to me. For the first time in my life, he actually asked me questions—

about Steve. "How's he doing down there?" he said. "Uh, just fine," I said.

Steve was doing fine. He'd somehow gotten several letters from his doctors in Florida, all confirming his "problem." He sat outside the base neurologist's office for three days, on the bottom of the appointment list, waiting to see the doctor and describe "his" symptoms. But when he did get to tell his story, they believed it. By Christmas he was declared unfit for duty and given a medical discharge. A miracle! He called Al Campanis with the good news. Then he wrote to me.

"Now, aren't we going to have fun come December 22nd—yeah, Ma'am!" said his letter. "Dinners, shows, places to go, people to see, love, affection, kisses, hugs, and a thousand other things we always enjoy!" I wrote him back, telling him how happy I was that he'd escaped the military.

There was a problem, though. The real story, if it got out, would certainly send my father into a rage. I lied to him that they'd found something wrong, a murmur, with Steve's heart.

Another secret to keep. I made Steve's plane reservations; he'd be home with me in Detroit for the holidays.

But there was no holiday that year. Before Christmas, my father went into the hospital for an emergency hernia operation. When I got home, about a week before Christmas Day, my father had been gone for several days. It was ten o'clock on a windy, freezing cold evening when I rang the doorbell. My mother opened the door and stared at me.

"Merry Christmas, Mom!" I said, moving to hug her. I recoiled. Her hair was in a tangled mess. She was in her nightgown; her bathrobe, stained with food, was half on and half off. She looked at me—no, through me—and began rambling in a dull monotone.

"Your brother's on drugs," she said.

What? "Mom, I—"

"Your brother's on drugs. I know your brother's on drugs. There are people trying to kill me. I have to check downstairs. *I have to check downstairs.*" Her eyes opened wide with fright and she started to move toward the basement stairs. I grabbed her arm and steered her into the living room, where my brother Chris was watching television. The fear was beginning to sink in. What was going on here? I sat Mom down on the couch. Hugging herself, she began to rock back and forth.

"What's wrong with Mom?" I asked my brother. Poor Chris. He was fifteen years old and very scared. He kept looking at the television, as if by acting normally he could keep things under control.

"She's been acting real strange," he said, fighting the panic. He told me that the day before he'd had to leave school and drive her home. Mom, in her nightgown, had shown up at his high school, wandering through the halls and trying to find someone to tell that her son was on drugs.

Chris, I knew, was a straight-arrow athlete. For his friends to see our mother like that! The shame must have been awful. Crushing. "She'll be okay," I said, leading her upstairs. I wasn't sure what to do, but I knew I had to do something. The only sure thing was that it was up to me. I was the only one left.

"You should be a good daughter," said my father, from his bed at Cottage Hospital during visiting hours the next day. My stomach churned; I knew what he was going to say next. "You should drop out of college for a while and help your mother." Yes, there it was. For a few moments, I actually considered abandoning college.

No! "Don't worry," I said coldly. "I'll take care of her."

I tried. But in a way, I knew, my father was right. I *was* selfish: I was thinking of myself as well as Mom; afraid that Steve—proper, fastidious Steve—would be shocked, repulsed, turned off by my mother's condition. He'd just go away; he'd spend the great future with someone else. And then where would I be? My mother was wandering around the house with a flashlight, muttering that people were poisoning her. When I put her to bed that night the frustration was too much. I did a horrible thing; I grabbed her by the shoulders and shook her.

"Please don't blow this for me. Please!" I yelled at her, out of control, myself, for a moment. She looked back at me blankly and shrank down into her pillow. I was ashamed of myself immediately. I still am.

Steve arrived at the airport a couple of days before Christmas. He was in his Army uniform, happy to see me and absolutely ecstatic about getting out of the service. We drove home.

"Listen, I've got something to tell you," I said, after he'd told me his news. "My mother's not well. I don't know what to do about it." I gave him a watered-down version of events. He listened carefully, then lapsed into silence.

That night, I slept next to my mother to keep her from wandering. The next day, Steve watched football games on television and visited friends. I tried to keep Mom in bed and out of sight. In the afternoon he told me he was leaving for Florida the next day. "I want to drive down and see Millie and Joe," he said.

For a moment or two, I panicked. Oh God, I thought. *Don't leave. Stay and help me.* But in a moment or two I fought the feeling back. Maybe this was for the best. Of course it was. It would be better for the future that Steve didn't see this. This was a problem from the past. My problem, not his. Let him go now, Cynthia. Don't force him to see things that would make him leave for good. "Okay," I said, as calmly as possible. He left early in the morning. I hoped he'd still be there for me when this was over.

On Christmas Eve, the darkest part of the nightmare began. Chris had the flu. I'd just cooked him a big spaghetti dinner, which he proceeded to throw up. I'd gotten him into bed and he was telling me about his basketball exploits. Then I heard my mother, who was supposed to be in her bedroom, rummaging around the den. "Just a second," I said to Chris, sighed, and went out to round her up.

My mother had a book of matches in her hand. She had set the drapes on fire. She was watching, fascinated, as bright little flames flashed and sparkled along the bottom edge.

For a second, I was hypnotized by the flames, also. Then: we're all going to die!

"Mom! What are you doing!" I shouted. "Stop! Stop it!"

I grabbed her and flung her out of the room. There was a big pillow on the couch; I used it to beat out the flames. I got a pot of water and poured it on the fabric until it stopped smoldering. Then I just stood there, trembling. My mother watched me from the doorway, blankly. She was somewhere else. The look on her face was the most frightening thing of all.

The tremors began to die down. All right, I thought. Let's think calmly now. My mother is very sick. Too sick for me to take care of now. I got her dressed, put her in the car, and drove her to the emergency room at Detroit General Hospital. I described what had happened to the doctor and he admitted her immediately. "Come back tomorrow," he said, after I'd signed all the forms. They'd put her in the hospital's psychiatric ward.

"What's wrong with her?" I asked the nurse on duty the next day. "Has she seen an internist? Have you given her a physical? A blood test? A brain scan?"

"Well, the psychiatrist will see her soon," said the nurse. "Soon" was several days later. "Your mother has had a nervous breakdown. She's gone over the edge," said the psychiatrist, with a strange cheerfulness. He was a thin, fortyish, even-featured man in a white coat. During her physical examination, he said, after I'd pressed him, they'd found a small bump on the back of her head, but in his opinion it wasn't the cause of my mother's illness. Yes, she was very sick. No, they didn't know how long her treatment would be. At that instant, with a small flash of insight, I saw myself as he saw me: a frightened twenty-year-old girl with a little bit of medical knowledge, struggling to tell him, The Doctor, that I could even try to understand my mother's treatment.

He smiled a little too broadly and patted me on the arm. "Don't worry. Leave it to us," he said. I could visit my mother, he said, for fifteen minutes three times a week.

At the end of the Christmas break I drove back to Michigan State, explained the situation to my instructors, and with their reluctant approval set up a crazy, inside-out schedule. I didn't drop any courses; I simply turned my weekends into weekdays. I drove from Detroit to East Lansing to school on Friday mornings, met privately with my teachers each Friday afternoon, then stayed in my room, doing my coursework, through Sunday evening. Then I drove home. During the week I stayed in Detroit, visiting my mother and taking care of my father while he recuperated at home.

My father never visited my mother at Detroit General; Chris was too young to get in. Steve called me on the phone every few days, but we never talked about my mother. That was his decision. Or was it mine?

Each visiting day, I waited for her to be brought out into the day room: a depressing place complete with worn couches, a television set that was always on, and the same kind of wire-cage nurse's station they used in *One Flew Over The Cuckoo's Nest.* The day room was filled with patients of every race, sex, and age: they all wore gray, open-backed hospital gowns and bathrobes. Some sat silently, some rocked back and forth, some cried, some screamed, some attacked themselves or other patients. Everyone smoked; the room smelled strongly of a weird combination of disinfectant and cigarettes. When one of the patients got violent or tried to walk out the front door, which was often, a huge black guard grabbed the patient by the wrists until he or she calmed down.

My mother was not violent. Nor did she get better. Every time I saw her, she seemed to be buried deeper in her new world. By sneaking a look through the cage at her chart, I saw that they had her on a combination of tranquilizers and antidepressants. The drugs stopped her rambling; as the weeks passed, her tongue got thick in her mouth. She could barely talk. At home she sometimes sneaked a cigarette when my father wasn't watching; in the hospital, she chain-smoked an unending supply. "How are you feeling, Mom?" I'd ask. She'd smile sadly. After exactly fifteen minutes, the nurse would come and take her back to her room.

I'd wait to catch her psychiatrist on the fly. From time to time, he whizzed through the day room on the way to another part of the ward.

"Is my mother getting better?" I asked him. He held his clipboard in front of him and smiled that same smile.

"She's doing just fine, Cynthia, just fine!"

"But sometimes she doesn't even recognize me!"

"Well, it's going to take a while. Then she'll come back."

"But you've got her drugged. She's all drugged up. She's—"

But then, somehow, he managed—always—to sidestep me, pat me on the arm, and rush off. I hugged myself and dug my nails into my palms in frustration. I couldn't antagonize this man; he had my mother's life in his hands. And he knew what was best. Didn't he? I took a last look at the back of his coat and drove home through the snow.

By February I knew all the nurses on the day shift. Mom was completely unable to talk; she tried to write me notes but her scrawl was unreadable.

One day, one of the nurses, a short, friendly-looking woman, pulled me aside and told me my mother had "lost control" the night before. "They put her in a strait-jacket and a padded room," she said sadly.

"Oh my God," I said. My sweet, gentle mother. In a straitjacket.

Suddenly I was completely, searingly certain: if I didn't get my mother out of there, she'd die or spend the rest of her life there. I felt surprisingly clear-headed. I walked back to my mother's room. She was sitting on a chair; on her bed were unfastened arm and leg restraints. They were made of leather. They looked strong enough to hold down an elephant. My mother looked too frail to walk out into the hallway on her own.

"Let's go, Mom," I said. I helped her out of the chair and put my long coat over her shoulders. She leaned on my arm. I led her past the nurses' station.

"Where are you going?" exclaimed one of the nurses.

I turned and faced her. "This is enough! We're going home," I said.

"*You* can't take her home," she said. Beside her, another nurse punched some numbers on a telephone. I heard bells, buzzers, a commotion in the distance.

"If you don't let my mother out of here," I said, my voice starting to shake, "I'll cause a scene. A big scene." And then, as if by magic, the psychiatrist was by my side.

"What's the problem here?" he said.

"I'm taking her out of here. She's much worse. You're not doing her any good."

And then, to my amazement, The Smile was gone! He was furious. "You have to realize," he said angrily, "that if you take her now you're fully and totally responsible. This is A.M.A."

"What?"

"Against medical advice."

Against medical advice. I took his clipboard. It was my mother's chart. I signed in big letters across the top: "Cynthia Truhan—A.M.A." I handed it back to him. He looked even angrier.

Now we had to get out the door. But my confidence

was draining away. The big guard was right where he always was, his arms crossed and his face impassive.

I looked him straight in the eye. "We're going home now," I said. And he just stepped aside and opened the door! I led my mother, who was only wearing paper slippers, across the street to the car. "Almost there, almost there," I kept saying in the car, over the whir of the heater fan. When I put her to bed, she slept around the clock. When she woke up the next day, I came in and saw her looking out the window. "You're home now," I said to her, sitting on the bed and grabbing her hand. "You're not going back." For the first time, she began to cry.

A few days later I took her to a local internist. He gave her a complete physical work-up. We talked about the blow to the back of her head; during her hospitalization, Chris had remembered an incident, just before I arrived, when Mom had hurt herself, trying to lift a big, boxy air conditioner out of its window frame; it had slipped and hit her head.

It was this new doctor's opinion that the blow, combined with the stress she'd been under, pushed her into a breakdown. He prescribed some new, weaker medication and gave me a strict diet for her to follow.

I cooked and cleaned and took care of her. Gradually, over the next few weeks, Mom got better. She slept many hours a day. Her color improved. Her speech became almost completely coherent. Eventually, she felt well enough to sit in the living room.

By March I was able to spend more time at school. "Look," I said to my father, "I want to graduate. You're home with her. I want you to take care of her. I know you can do it without yelling at her. But I'm going to come home every weekend now, and I'm going to check up every night." For those calls, my father put on his jolly Officers' Club voice. "Hey, Cynthia! Everything's fine! Things are just great here!" They weren't, but at least they were getting better. As for Steve, he never asked about my situation at home and I was too tired and ashamed to bring it up. I felt totally alone.

When I got back to school full time, Steve was off playing ball. In late spring, he invited me to join him in St. Louis. The Dodgers would be there to play the Cardinals, he said, and we would have a couple of days together.

My plane landed late in the evening. I got to the Chase Park Plaza Hotel at eleven-thirty, checked in, and met Steve in the lobby. I kissed him. He seemed, as always, a bit embarrassed. My shy boyfriend, I thought happily. "I'm starved," I said, heading toward a little restaurant–bar off the lobby. It was, at that hour, the only eating place open.

I took maybe two steps before Steve caught up with me. He grabbed my shirt collar and yanked me to a stop. I looked up, startled, to see what the joke was. There was none.

"You can't go in there," he said flatly.

"Why not?" I said, in surprise.

"You just can't."

"Why?"

"There are some ballplayers in there."

"So?" I still didn't understand.

Steve looked off toward the far wall. "They're in there with people who, uh, aren't their wives."

This is ridiculous, I thought. I was very hungry. And tired. "But that's their problem, isn't it?" I said. "And I'm not going to tell on them."

"Never mind. You just can't go in there," he said, his jaw set.

Now I was getting mad. "Well, forget you," I said, pulling away and marching to the elevator. Still hungry, I lay in my bed and thought the situation over. What kind of double standard was this, where the innocent couples, not the adulterers, had to tiptoe around? Still, I thought, Steve was struggling that year to make the team. He was playing only part-time at third base and not hitting all that well. He must have been scared of getting the veteran players mad at him. It was a good thing Steve was different from his teammates. Tomorrow, I thought drowsily, we would work it out.

We never really did. He was friendly and smiling the next morning, as if the night before had never happened. The players he introduced me to in the lobby looked, in their flowered shirts, pointy collars, and silly-looking golf pants, less like cheating husbands than overgrown, naughty boys. Steve and I had a fine time sightseeing and shopping that day. Later in the season we met in Chicago, and at Steve's suggestion we ate outside the hotel in nice restaurants. The problem was solved.

Steve made it back to East Lansing for our graduation. I did what I came here for, I thought during the ceremony. And as a bonus, I got Steve out with his degree.

That summer, I took a student-teaching job in Detroit while Steve struggled with the Dodgers. The episode with my mother was never discussed. We talked a lot about Steve's frustration; about trying to catch the attention of the manager, Walt Alston; about his fears that he would be sent back to the minor leagues; that he would blow his one chance to get into the only profession he'd ever aspired to. He also talked a lot about baseball; rules, strategy, everything. I learned quickly.

I could see now that he was struggling. At the end of the season, in which the Dodgers finished second in their division, Steve's batting average was very low. I felt he needed my support more than ever. Without talking it over with Steve, I decided to stay with him through the winter season and, when we got to Los Angeles, apply to medical school at UCLA.

We were married October 29, 1971, in St. Joan of Arc's Church in Detroit. All went well; my mother looked better than I'd seen her since before her illness. I was very proud of her. I loved her very much. Even my father looked moderately pleased.

Some of my school friends were there; there was no

one from the Dodgers. Two priests—one speaking English, one Slovak—conducted the ceremony. As I walked up the aisle past her, I turned to my mother and, pulling a flower from my bouquet, handed it to her. She was crying and smiling at the same time. It was wonderful.

The next few moments are burned into my memory. I looked up. Steve and my father were standing at the altar. Two tall, strong men. They were almost identical. The same man! The resemblance was as striking as if I were seeing them together for the first time.

My father took my hand, and patted it. His touch was strange, electrifying. When was the last time he'd held my hand? My mind was numb; I couldn't remember.

My father, tears in his eyes, placed my hand in Steve's. As I turned to face the priests, a thought filtered through the haze: I've finally made him happy. Maybe it all came out right, after all.

CHAPTER 8

"Hey, Mr. G!" I shouted. "Nice buns!"

My husband, pedaling effortlessly ahead of me up Fiji Way, looked back over his shoulder. Steve grinned slyly, stopped his new three-speed at the side of the road, and waited for me to catch up. He glanced around to see if anyone else was watching. Then he put his hand on his hip, thrust his rear end at me, and struck a "seductive" pose. I laughed.

"What a tease!" I kidded him, braking to a stop. I got off my bike, grabbed his behind, and punched him play-fully on the arm. It was true. He was the best-looking man I'd ever seen. In his tight white shorts and clean white tennis shirt he was incredibly sexy—at least to me. I loved him. He was my husband. We were far from De-troit; finally alone together. And the future for both of us seemed unlimited. Right then and there, deliberately, I closed my eyes and committed that moment to memory. Fifteen years later, the image—and the feeling of pure, exhilarating freedom—is as strong as ever.

It was January, 1972. We were living in Playa Del Rey, a beach town just south of Santa Monica. It was our first real home together; after two uncomfortable months staying with my parents in Detroit, we'd driven cross-country to California.

It had been a wonderful trip. The best. We had no

money to speak of, the weather and the roads were miserable, but each hour with Steve took me farther from Detroit, from my father, from the grind of college. For six days we pushed our way through the Mid- and Southwest; we stayed in dingy hotels wherever we happened to stop for the night. So what? I thought. It was a thrilling adventure. *I had made it out.*

The highways were the same ones I'd traveled with my family—but this time, things were different. No more hiding, afraid to make a sound, in the back seat. No more tension. No more yelling. No more predawn departures and sixteen-hour rides.

This time I was up front, with the handsome man I loved—my husband!—sitting next to me. "You know the way, you drive," said Steve, handing me the keys on the first day. The thought that he trusted me, that he let me be in control, that he loved me enough to let me take care of things, made my love for him even greater.

Every morning, at breakfast at some dingy roadside cafe, I unfolded the map and planned our route. "We're here. By dinnertime, I'd like us to be *here.*"

"Sounds good to me, Cyn," he said. Just like that! I did most of the driving, pushing us along at seventy, seventy-five, eighty. "Heavy Foot," he called me, smiling across at me. I kept the car heater going; Steve sat there in his shirtsleeves, his bare feet propped up on the dashboard. I snuck a peek at him every once in a while. When I caught his eye, he reached over and gave my hair, which I'd pulled back into a ponytail, a playful pull. He sat there peeling oranges and eating them, staring serenely out the windshield, reading *The Sporting News,* listening to the radio. He didn't talk much, but he didn't seem to mind my asking him questions. There was no reason to keep quiet. No topic I had to avoid. No way to annoy him at all!

I asked him about baseball; about the fine print in the newspaper he seemed to be studying so intently. He explained the box scores to me. I asked him what kind of big leaguer he wanted to become. He told me about Gil Hodges, a former Dodger who was now a manager. He admired Gil Hodges very much. "He was a gentleman ballplayer. A straight arrow," said Steve. I pumped him some more, hungry for conversation. He talked about his dream of becoming the Dodgers' third baseman, the first successful player at that position they'd had for years.

I was so proud of him. On the long silent stretches, I thought about my plans for becoming a doctor, of our hopes meshing wonderfully.

I pointed the car west and went even faster. We seemed to be flying—speeding along in a wonderful, cozy bubble. Finally, in Arizona, we were pulled over by a highway patrolman.

The policeman walked up, leaned down to my window, and said curtly, "Where do you think you're heading?"

I was so happy, so loosened up from the trip, that the thought of getting a ticket didn't bother me at all. I began to joke with him.

"Oh, Officer, we've got to get to L.A.! My husband's just signed with the Dodgers. We've got to play some baseball!" I said, kiddingly.

Oops, I thought, giddily. We're in trouble now. But, to my surprise, the man's stern expression softened.

"Really?" he said.

He took off his sunglasses and peered past me into the car. Steve's baseball bats and blue Dodger equipment bag were lying on the back seat.

Steve leaned over me, shrugged his shoulders, and grinned sheepishly at the patrolman. "Steve Garvey. Nice to meet you," he said. They shook hands. And then, to my astonishment, the patrolman let me off with just a warning.

I drove off toward Los Angeles, staying at sixty-five for a few miles. Steve leaned back, as relaxed as before. He had no doubts, his expression seemed to say, that there were more pleasant surprises ahead.

* * *

There were. California—at least the part we'd wound up in—was like no place I'd ever seen before. When we got into Los Angeles, we checked into a hotel called the Jamaica Bay Inn in Playa Del Rey. We began looking for an apartment nearby. Why go any farther? I thought. We had found paradise.

I was amazed by the weather in Los Angeles. While Michigan was still covered with snow, the houses here—all white, beige, and pink, and built to keep the weather in, not out—sparkled under blue skies. It was a foreign, exotic place to me. We put on our bathing suits and went to the beach on Christmas Day! It was always seventy degrees, exactly: the people were all young, like us, and rode bikes just like the pair I bought for us one day. "And it's only ten minutes from the airport," said Steve, thinking of his travel schedule.

It was less a neighborhood where people lived than a big amusement park for grown-ups. Almost everyone in Playa Del Rey, I learned, was single. There were no children, no other married couples that I could find. The town was next to Marina Del Rey, *the* swinging section of Los Angeles. The area's social life centered on the dozens of fern-filled bars in the area. Even the local Boys Supermarket was a hot pickup place: one afternoon, a character with a mustache, bell-bottoms, and flowered shirt tried to pick me up in the parking lot. Well so what? I thought. I could handle guys like that. I'd found my man, worth ten of those idiots.

We rented a one-bedroom apartment, at 8200 Redlands Street, for four hundred dollars a month. The hallways were dark, and none of the other tenants seemed to be home during the day. On the advice of one of the other ballplayers, we went out and filled it with rented furniture. The furniture was not the prettiest. But it filled the rooms. For a little while, at least, it would be good enough. It was our first home together.

The important thing was that I was with Steve. That I

had him. During those first few weeks, we spent most of our time together. We took long walks, long bike rides. We ate out at grungy Mexican restaurants over on Sunset Boulevard. We went dancing, to the beach. Just the two of us, usually. Who else did we need? Who else was there? After all, we knew hardly anyone out here. The other young Dodgers? Some of them lived nearby, but Steve explained that most of the guys just liked to go out with their girlfriends and get drunk. "I'd rather stay home with you, Cyn," said Steve.

That was fine with me. I wasn't alone. I was with Steve. And I did meet some of the Dodger veterans and their wives. Joe and Lee Moeller. He was a Dodger pitcher; they were in their thirties. Also, Jimmy and Jeannie Lefebvre. They lived across the street from us, in a huge apartment with floor-to-ceiling windows. He was another longtime Dodger, an infielder. She had two kids; she was nice, and liked to invite me along for movies and walks in a nearby park.

One day, I asked her what it was like when she'd been the young wife of a young baseball player. *"Nobody's* as young as you are," laughed Jeannie. We were sitting on a park bench, watching her kids play.

She told me about being a baseball wife in the early sixties, when Jimmy was just "breaking in."

"The wives still wore white gloves to the stadium," she said, rolling her eyes at the thought of it. "We gave each other little teas, little dinners. We went to fashion shows. It was like a whole social club type of thing."

It sounded a lot like my parents' Officers' Club gatherings. I told her so. "Oh, but it's almost all different now," she said, with a wave of her hand. From the little smile on her face, I couldn't tell whether she missed the old days or not.

"What's that you're looking at, Steve? Here, let me see." We'd stopped to eat at a coffee shop one evening, and Steve had pulled a little piece of colored cardboard out of his pocket. He was studying it intently. I looked over his shoulder. It was the Dodgers' 1972 schedule.

"What do those little squares mean?" I asked.

Steve looked up, smiled at my question, and explained. The light blue squares, he said, were home games. The dark blue squares were away games. Road games. The white squares were open dates. "But not really days off," said Steve. "A lot of them are travel days."

Travel days? While Steve ate, I counted squares. It didn't take long to figure the amount of time Steve would be gone that summer. Two weeks out of every month! I'd had no idea. Somehow it had never occurred to me that baseball players were away from home that much.

I'd been dumb. Naive. For just a second, thinking of all the time I'd be alone, I panicked. It was just like my lonely growing up—but wait a minute, Cynthia. This was different. The schedule ended in September. That was when medical school started; he'd have the whole winter free. He'd be home for me when I needed him.

Yes, I'd be lonely at first, but it would work out in the end. I smiled across at my husband, and handed him back the schedule. I'd have him all to myself after all, until the season started.

"I don't think you should come with me to Florida just yet," said Steve. That made sense, I agreed. The Dodgers, he'd said, didn't like their young players being "distracted" during spring training. He was going three weeks early to get the jump on the veterans. I'd meet him there when he was settled in. I packed his bags for him and drove him to the airport. "See you in a little while," he said. And then he waved goodbye from the plane window.

I missed Steve already. Back in the apartment, the empty packing cartons lay scattered around. For a few moments, they reminded me of my mother and those moving days not so long ago.

But this was different, I thought. I was free now! An

adult, with a hard-working husband and a marriage to support. We had very little money; much of Steve's bonus had gone to pay his tuition; the rest had been invested in Florida real estate for him by his parents. I went to the local school district and presented my teaching credential; I was told they'd be glad to take me on as a substitute.

The paperwork, they said, would take a little while. Each morning, to pass the time, I got into the car and explored another part of Los Angeles. The weather remained perfect. Usually, I just pointed the nose of the car into the giant maze of freeways. I got hopelessly lost enough times to eventually figure them out. I went to Disneyland. Hollywood. Farmer's Market. Santa Monica. I took long walks on the beach. Los Angeles was so spread out—so diverse. There was a different city in every direction.

One trip, though, had a definite purpose. I called UCLA and made an appointment with the dean in charge of medical school admissions. I drove to Westwood, in a trial run, several days beforehand, just to make sure I would get there in time.

"If you do all right on the Medical School Admissions Test, I don't see any problem," said the dean, after studying my college transcript. My strange course load had worked, after all! I signed up for a practice test, and even bought a few first-year medical texts from the college bookstore. When Steve called me from Florida—he called every few days, though he was too busy to write—I told him what I had done.

"That's nice, Cyn," he said. He told me he was hitting the ball very well. "That's great. Keep it up!" I said.

I flew out to Florida to join Steve for the last week of spring training. Dodgertown, in Vero Beach, was a huge outdoor complex that, at first glance, looked like a country club. Officials drove around in golf carts. The grass was very green and perfectly mowed, except that there were baseball diamonds mixed in with the tennis courts and golf courses. Dodgertown was filled with what looked like hundreds of young baseball players, all wearing Dodger uniforms. All of them, I soon realized, were competing for jobs in the "organization."

There was a definite pecking order. The lowest-rated minor leaguers practiced on their own diamonds, as did the high minor leaguers struggling to make the Dodgers. Steve, I was proud to learn, practiced with the major leaguers—the *real* Dodgers—in a little stadium, not just a practice field.

My first full day there, I had breakfast with Steve, straightened up our motel room, then took a seat in the grandstand to watch Steve play.

Other Dodger wives, whom I hadn't yet met, were sitting in the seats below me. Steve, one of the youngest players on the field, was in the batting cage, hitting ball after ball for clean hits. Every fifth or sixth hit was a home run. Fantastic! I stood up and clapped.

"Hurray, Steve Garvey!" I shouted.

Then, lower down, I saw the women look up and watch Steve, too. Their voices drifted up toward me.

"Who's that?" said one.

"Steve Garvey," said another.

"Hummph," said the first woman. "It looks like he'll make the big club this year. *He* came up awful fast."

I swelled with pride. Soon batting practice was over. The players began to disperse. The wives picked up their things and began to leave, too. Where were they all going? I wondered. I walked quickly out of the stadium, following them.

"Excuse me," I said to the woman closest to me. "What happens now?"

She turned and faced me. "Who are you?" said one of the wives, who looked to be in her late twenties.

"I'm Cynthia Garvey," I said.

"Oh yeah," she said. "You're Steve Garvey's girl. He'll probably be playing for us this summer."

"Yes! That'll be great!" I said. "But can you tell me—"

Suddenly, a surprising thing happened. *All* the women turned—and began firing questions at me.

"Where do you come from?" said one.

"I'm from Detroit. I—"

"How much time have you spent in the minors?"

The minors? "Well, hardly any. Steve and I met—"

"You haven't been *down?* Well, what have you been doing the last few years?"

"I've been in college. I just graduated, and we were married—"

I never finished. At the word "college," the first woman looked at me strangely and turned her back.

"She hasn't put in her time," she said to the others. They walked away. Stunned, I hung back and followed them from a distance to the next practice area.

"It's strange, Mrs. Garvey. I don't know when I should kiss a boy. If I like him, I mean." The serious-looking brown-haired girl, and five or six of her fourteen-year-old classmates, were gathered around my desk. Spring training had ended. Steve had indeed made the team. I was back in Los Angeles, substitute teaching.

"When do you think?" I said.

"Um, after the first date? Maybe the second?"

I nodded my head, smiled, and told her that sounded about right.

The class ended shortly after that. I was filling in for the health education teacher at a local junior high school. Because of my degree, this was the kind of assignment the school district usually called me for.

The call would come early in the morning, two or three days a week. I taught health and sex ed all the way from seventh to twelfth grade. I loved the work. Teaching was fun. I seemed to be good at it. Maybe, I thought, because I was just six or seven years older than the students, they opened up to me.

There were a few giggles, but not too many, when I

made my colored-chalk drawings of the reproductive system. But since I was a sub, I didn't really have to stick to the syllabus.

"Does anyone have any questions? Write them on a piece of paper, and pass them up to me," I said. The kids leaned over, shielding their writing from snoopers. They folded their questions into tiny squares. For the rest of the period, I answered as many as possible.

Can you get pregnant the first time you do it? When you have your period? In a swimming pool? What's an orgasm? Is it the same as "coming"? How long can you carry a condom in your pocket before it gets weird?

I was as straightforward as I could be, and afterward, talked to the ones who stayed behind. Mostly I chatted with the girl students. A surprising number had the same question, and it wasn't really about sex at all: they felt they were smarter, more mature, than their boyfriends, and it worried them.

"It's nothing to worry about," I said. "Boys develop slower than girls. Who knows?" I joked. "Maybe they'll even catch up to you some someday."

One of the principals offered me a full-time teaching contract, but I thanked him and turned him down. After all, I hoped to be in medical school by the fall. Meanwhile, with the regular baseball season starting, I wanted to be with Steve as much as I could.

I loved spending precious time at home with him. And the best way to spend it with him, I figured, was to help him. To support him. Steve was fighting for his job, for his dream, that year. Making it easier for my husband was what I was supposed to do.

Our routine rarely varied. When the Dodgers were in town, Steve got up at ten-thirty in the morning and puttered around the apartment while I did the chores. I laid out his clothes for the day, making sure everything matched. I cleaned the house, did the shopping, paid our bills and did the accounts. Then, when I was finished, we'd have a few hours alone together.

Sometimes, we'd go for a walk or a ride. Or we'd stay home and relax, no tension or nervousness at all. That was fine with me. That was more than fine.

Steve read the newspaper or watched television. If he looked receptive, calm, I'd start a conversation. There was so much I wanted to know about this guy! And now that I had him with me, I could ask him about—everything. Anything!

"Tell me about your old girlfriends, Steve."

Steve would look up from his newspaper.

"Oh," he'd say with a grin, "I switched 'em with every season."

He didn't seem to mind my asking. But no matter how I teased, no matter how playfully I asked, I could never get him to describe them to me. I had better luck on some other topics; after much friendly cajoling, I got him to talk about his childhood.

"I grew up in a house on stilts. I was the only kid on the block," said Steve, one day. When he was a little boy, he told me, he practiced hitting baseballs by smashing grapefruits off a tree with a broom handle. He did it so well, he said, that his parents lied about his age and enrolled him in the Little League when he was only six.

At six! I knew from growing up with Mark and Chris that that was two years ahead of schedule. "Oh, I was a husky little kid," said Steve, "I could handle it.

"My parents could see," he said proudly, "that I had great hand-eye coordination." He did so well that he was always the best player on his team. That pleased his parents very much. "Still," he admitted, "it was lonely sometimes. I really would have liked a brother or sister."

When he was eight or nine, his maternal grandmother moved into their house. Mrs. Winkler was an invalid, and since both of Steve's parents worked, it was Steve's job to take care of her after school.

"Oh sure. I took her to the bathroom. I helped her

take her bath," said Steve, very reluctantly. "My father installed a red light on the porch. My grandmother had a switch for it near her bed. When it went on, she needed help. If I wasn't around when the light flashed, that meant I'd really get it from my parents later."

I told him I thought that was a terrible, terrible responsibility for a little boy. My saying that seemed to surprise him.

"Oh, but I really loved her," he said.

"And I love you," I said. My heart went out to that little kid. And to my husband. Steve grinned, and pointed to his watch. It was almost two o'clock. Time for dinner for baseball players. My big league baseball player.

At three o'clock, I'd drive Steve to the ballpark for batting practice. I'd drive back home, finish up whatever needed to be done, and make it back to the ballpark by seven. I parked in the players' lot, got out my ticket, and walked up the ramp to the Family Section: Section 105, behind home plate, where the Dodger management assigned the wives and children. All the free tickets they gave us had specific seat numbers stamped on them. The wives of the starting players sat in the first four rows. The starting pitcher's wife always had seat 1-A. Scattered behind them were the spouses of the coaches and substitutes and rookies. When a player's status on the team changed, I soon learned, so, mysteriously and automatically, did his ticket numbers.

Everyone in the Family Section, I could see, *belonged* to somebody. Each was somebody's wife, somebody's child, somebody's girlfriend. The wives of the established players wore necklaces with their husbands' uniform number—in gold, and studded with diamonds—around their necks. The black wives talked almost exclusively to each other; so did the wives of the white veterans.

It was just like high school; once again, I felt like the new girl, the intruder. I never managed to break through my shyness and join any of the groups.

So I did what came naturally and seemed comfortable: I brought books with me to the stadium, and tried to make myself as inconspicuous as possible. To pass the time between innings, I read. There were usually empty seats to the left and right of me.

Sometimes I tried to strike up a conversation with one of the wives or girlfriends of a rookie or a substitute, but their concentration on the game was much higher than mine. Many kept the score of the game with elaborate diagrams and symbols. A couple of months into the season, I noticed that the pitchers' wives wrote comments in red ink in the margins of their scorecards. They usually did this after an opposing team's batter got a hit off their husband. When I worked up the courage, I leaned forward in my seat to make out what they were writing. They were excuses! No, they were *explanations*: "Third baseman out of position"; "bad hop on infield dirt"; "bad call by first-base umpire."

On the other hand, when a Dodger got a hit or pulled off a good fielding play, it was expected that all the wives cheer loudly—that player's wife often looked around the section to make sure. Sometimes, my nose in my book, I missed a good play or pitch, forgot to applaud, and was glared at. I shrank down into my seat, trying hard to become invisible.

When the game ended, the women all trooped down to the Waiting Room. The couches, I learned, were reserved for the veterans' wives, who sat in the same spot after every game. Depending on whether the team had won or lost, whether their man had done badly or well, the women were either bubbling with laughter or plunged into gloom.

I usually stood against the wall near the door. Just waiting. Or sometimes, I went back out to the empty box seats to watch something beautiful: after all the fans had filed out, the field went dark. The stadium was plunged into near-darkness; interesting shadows stretched across the huge, quiet stadium. Then sprinklers came on, the air grew fresher, and I inhaled the lovely smell of the tenderly maintained grass. What was I getting into? I wondered, sometimes. The baseball world was far more structured and complex than I had expected.

After about thirty minutes the players would begin to emerge from the dressing room. A knot of fans stood there, waiting for the players. When Steve came out, his hair still wet and shining, he'd sign autographs all the way to the car. "Hey! Our new third baseman!" they yelled after him.

We'd drive home on the nearly empty streets. I'd ask Steve questions about the game; after sitting in silence all night, I'd be starved for conversation. "What happened in the fifth inning?" "Why did they take out the pitcher?" "Is their third baseman a good player?" He'd patiently answer me. We'd be home and in bed by 1 A.M.

Not every night. One day, before we left home, Steve asked me to wait for him in the parking lot after the game. When I arrived, at midnight, he was standing with the manager, Walter Alston.

I blinked. Walter Alston! Walter Alston, Steve had told me, had been managing the Dodgers for many years. He was a very famous man. As far as the players were concerned, a very powerful man.

He was aloof. Someone to be wary of. He was grayhaired and distinguished-looking. To my twenty-two-year-old eyes, in fact, he looked very old. Much too old, I thought one day while watching him in the dugout, to be wearing a baseball uniform designed for young men and boys.

Now, though, Mr. Alston was wearing slacks and a sport coat. Steve, standing next to him, had a strange, slightly frightened expression on his face.

"We're going for a little ride," said Steve. It was obvious from the way he looked at me that I was not to ask any questions.

But what was going on? Steve wasn't part of Walter

Alston's inner circle. If anything, he was in the manager's doghouse. Steve was hitting fairly well, but he was making a lot of errors at third base. He was, he'd told me worriedly several times, in danger of being benched—or worse, being sent back down to the minor leagues. "That would be the end," he said.

Mr. Alston got into the front seat next to Steve. I sat in the back. Was he going to break some kind of bad news to us? I tensed, and leaned forward to listen to their conversation. Steve headed out onto the Hollywood Freeway and began nervously talking to his manager. He told Mr. Alston how hard he was working to improve his fielding, and how sorry he was to let the team down.

"Just hang in there, son," said Mr. Alston distractedly. He didn't seem to be listening all that closely. He pointed to the right; Steve got off the freeway at Sunset and headed up into the hills.

Mr. Alston told Steve when and where to turn. We pulled into the driveway of a white, medium-sized house. Walt and Lela Alston, I knew, lived in a big house in the suburbs, miles and miles from Hollywood.

"Thanks a lot, Garv," said Mr. Alston, getting out of the car and walking up the front steps. Steve backed up, turned the car around, and headed back down toward Sunset.

Could this be . . . ? The tension was gone, replaced by pure astonishment.

"Where are we? Who lives here?" I asked Steve.

"A friend of his," he said, staring straight ahead.

"A friend who isn't his wife?"

Suddenly, Steve turned all the way around and glared back at me.

"This is not to be discussed."

"But why . . ."

"This is *not* to be discussed!"

We drove home in silence. But that was just the beginning. We made the same ride with Alston, who, I later learned, didn't drive, about a dozen times that year; on our third trip, the door to the house opened and an attractive blond woman in her forties came out.

"This is ——," said Alston.

"Nice to meet you," I said.

"Thanks a lot, Garv," said the manager, closing the car door behind him. Steve still wouldn't talk about it. But I wondered, all that year, why Alston had entrusted him with his secret. Was it because Steve was a straight arrow? Not a gossip? Not close to a lot of the other players?

I was glad Steve wasn't like the others. But I worried, anyway. If this was the manager, the leader, didn't he make the rules? And what, exactly, were they?

I trusted Steve, of course. Before he left on each road trip, I slipped little love notes into his suitcase. I also thought, while I was at it, that I would broaden his mind. Make him a better person for when his playing days were over. I bought books for him to read, books I thought he would enjoy. Not too artistic. No novels. Books about history. Biographies. I slipped those into his suitcase, too. Almost always, though, the books would come back the same way they went in—unopened. Though neither Steve nor I ever mentioned the books—or the love notes, for that matter—this disappointed me. Until, one day, I put Jim Bouton's *Ball Four*—a funny bestseller about baseball—underneath his clothes. Contact. When I pulled it out of his dirty shirts, it looked like it had been read. Maybe I was getting through?

I rented a piano, which I put in the apartment and practiced when Steve was on the road. I haunted the local library, taking out as many books as I could. On a cloudy Saturday afternoon, I took the MSAT practice test at UCLA. It wasn't as difficult as I'd feared. I also, purely accidentally, stumbled into my first job in "show business." One day, on one of my solitary sightseeing trips, I stopped for a cup of coffee at the Dorothy Chandler Pavilion in downtown Los Angeles. There was a cafeteria in the basement for tourists.

"Can I join you?" asked a paunchy middle-aged man in a business suit. On his lapel was a convention badge. EXHIBITOR said the blue ribbon trailing beneath it. His name was HENRY.

"Sure," I said, warily, not really wanting to share my table. But Henry, in town for—surprise—a convention, began to talk about himself. He was a distributor of photographic accessories, he said, on a break from his booth in the Convention Center. Los Angeles was a nice town, but nobody walked anywhere. Business was a little slow. "And you?"

I told him what Steve and I were doing in California.

He sat up straight and looked me up and down in surprise. "Really? No kidding!" he said. This is very silly, I thought. It was if I had told him that I was Betty Crocker. Or Amelia Earhart's illegitimate daughter. Or Miss America.

"Listen," he said, excitedly, "would you like to help me?"

Help him? "How?"

He smiled and shook his head at my naïveté. "By helping out in the booth, honey!" All I had to do, he said, was put on some nice clothes and demonstrate his products for potential buyers. "Say hello to them. Talk with them. Make them feel at home," he said. For five days' work, he would give me two thousand dollars.

"You're kidding!" I said. Two thousand dollars was a lot of money for us. We could use it, badly. It wasn't fair to tease me like that. He smiled and shook his head. He gave me his card, wrote down the booth number, and told me to meet him the next day at 8 A.M.

I put on my best suit, blouse, and high heels, drove to the Convention Center, and sure enough, there was Henry. He gave me my own badge—this one was battery-powered, with little imitation flashbulbs twinkling around the edge. He showed me how to put together the tripods, filters, and flash attachments he was selling. Then he set up an easel with a sign on it:

MEET
CYNTHIA GARVEY
WIFE OF
L.A. DODGER
BASEBALL PLAYER
9 A.M. TO 6 P.M.

Henry stepped back and beamed at it. "Don't forget to be friendly!" he said, as the convention doors opened. In a few minutes, the place was swarming with buyers from camera stores all over the country.

They all looked very much like my new boss. "Which player is she married to?" they asked him.

"Steve Garvey."

"Who?"

"The third baseman, dummy."

"Oh yeah. Yeah. Right."

I gave them all my little spiel about the equipment, set the self-timer on the Polaroid, and rushed around in front of the camera to pose for pictures with them.

At the end of the convention, my mouth was aching from all the smiling and my feet were killing me. But Henry, true to his word, handed me twenty new hundred-dollar bills. "Great job," he said.

"Hey, nice," said Steve, when I told him about it at the airport. "Is this guy coming back next year?" I laughed at him. Cynthia Garvey, convention model! What a joke. My toes were still numb. The whole thing embarrassed me. But we could use the money.

In those early days, before Steve began playing regularly, it was surprising and exciting to see a story about my husband in the newspaper. Needless to say, I clipped them all out. They sometimes even mentioned me; a few months into the season, I noticed a picture of him with the caption, "Recently married to the lovely Cindi."

What a funny mistake! Cindi? Nobody ever called me that. The "i" on the end, I thought, made me sound like a Grosse Pointe sorority girl, the kind that signed her name with a little heart instead of a dot. I laughed. "Look what they called me here, Steve," I said. "Cindi. C-I-N-D-*I*."

I stuck my hand on my hip, put on my best airhead face, and said in a singsong voice: "Cindi, Mindi, Bindi, Muffy, Fluffy!"

Steve looked up from his sports section and grinned. But he didn't say anything.

At the end of the summer, my MSAT practice scores came back: if what the dean at UCLA had said was right, they were good enough to give me a real chance of getting into medical school that winter.

"Look at this," I said to Steve, excitedly, as I showed him my filled-out application forms for the real MSAT.

He glanced at them, then looked up, puzzled. "But what about Santo Domingo?" he asked. Santo Domingo?

"Al Campanis wants me to play in Santo Domingo this winter. I have to. And you're supposed to come with me. All the wives go down there."

That was the first I'd heard about this. I wasn't even sure, I realized, that I knew where Santo Domingo was. "Why didn't you tell me before?" I asked, astonished. "I thought you knew," he said. And that was all he had to say. I sat in the corner of the living room and thought it over.

I was confused. Filled with doubt, guilt, and a frightening surge of anger. But anger was dangerous; I fought it down. It was obvious that Steve was so pressured, so nervous about keeping his place on the Dodgers, that he had forgotten about my plans. Was that fair?

No. But on the other hand, Steve's big chance—his only chance; there was no second chance—was happening right now. He was making his big push. Wouldn't leaving him on his own in the middle of it all be abandoning him?

Would he be disappointed in me? Would he . . . turn somewhere else for encouragement? An unpleasant image flooded into my head: the baseball groupies, the young girls in jeans and tube tops, who hung out around the stadium before and after games. I'd noticed them from the start.

And here was Steve, saying he needed *me*. His wife.

Right then and there, I made my decision. It was surprisingly easy, surprisingly fast. I could always postpone starting medical school. There was always another semester, another year for me. Wasn't there? The next day, I put the application papers in my dresser drawer. I've got lots of time, I told myself.

CHAPTER 9

"**H**ey! How're you two loners doin' over there? Are you all right?" asked the woman on my right.

I looked across the aisle of the old propeller airliner and saw a smiling, dark-haired woman. She had a toddler on her lap. Her husband, a craggy-faced ballplayer, was sitting next to her. "Just fine," I said, giving her the best smile I could summon up.

Steve and I—along with about a dozen Dodger players and their wives—were headed for Santo Domingo, the capital of the Dominican Republic. Most of what I knew about this Caribbean country—which, I soon realized, was almost nothing—I knew from grammar school geography lessons. The rest I'd learned from Steve: the Dodgers had a "working agreement" with a team down there called the Licey ("Lee-SAY") Tigers; every year, Al Campanis sent down his most promising players to play alongside the Latin American regulars. Other major league teams had similar arrangements with Dominican League clubs. Tommy Lasorda, who'd managed Steve at Spokane, was flying down with us to run the Tigers.

Steve would earn $2000 a month playing winter ball. That was a lot of money for us. Only a few days after the end of the season, we'd flown to Miami to meet the other

Americans assigned to our team. I knew only a few of the ballplayers. Their wives, just like before, were cool to me.

Not Mary Ann Grabarkewitz, though. "C'mon, honey. Sit over here with us," she said, in a wonderful Texas accent. She was wearing a cheerfully colored maternity blouse and slacks. As the plane lurched and dipped over the ocean, she turned slightly green but still managed to tell me about herself. She'd married Billy Grabarkewitz when she was eighteen; they'd spent three years in the minor leagues before he was called up to the big club. Both Billy and Mary Ann were a few years older than we were. Little Vaughn was three; their second baby was due in five months.

Billy was a third baseman, like Steve. He was famous among the Dodgers for being injured almost all the time, and in an amazing number of ways. The other players liked Billy. As we sat with them, they came over to kid him.

"Hey, Grabby, how're ya feelin'?"

"How's your knee doin' *this* hour?"

"Watch out! Don't hit your head on the ceiling! You've almost made it to the first game!"

Billy took it all good-naturedly, sassing them back about their own supposed shortcomings. Steve sat back in his seat, basking in this friendly, very manly type of banter. But he said nothing. And none of the other players said anything to him.

After changing planes in Miami we landed again, this time in Haiti. We all rushed out, looked at the grass knickknacks in the souvenir store, and stared at the fields of sugar cane growing right up to the runway. Then we reboarded. The old plane revved itself up and made the short hop—across the greenest forest I'd ever seen—to Santo Domingo. It was almost dusk. Everyone looked very tired. Somebody wheeled up some rickety stairs and opened the door.

Even at that hour, the heat and humidity were staggering. We filed out, just wanting to get to our hotel and take a shower. We walked into a scene from a low-budget movie: outside the little adobe terminal, which was surrounded by palm trees, soldiers with helmets and machine guns stood guard. Somebody who looked like he was an officer herded us down the stairs and into a little circle on the asphalt. Somebody else dumped our baggage down beside us. The plane, whose engines had never stopped turning, taxied away.

To my surprise, there was a small crowd of Dominicans waiting patiently to greet us. A mariachi band began playing. A man in a business suit and a sash, who I guessed—correctly, it turned out—was the mayor, started making a speech. *"Bienvenido!"* he said, and that was about all I understood. For what seemed like hours, but was probably only about thirty minutes, he gave us his best welcoming address, in Spanish. Then, after shaking the mayor's hand, Tommy Lasorda stepped forward and gave his answering speech. *"Gracias, gracias, señores y señoras!"* said Tommy, who began to speak in a kind of pidgin Spanish. It was not an especially short speech. The women, myself included, began to sweat through our makeup. The men, fidgeting and shifting from one foot to the other, looked even more uncomfortable.

I started studying the faces in the crowd. Most of the people looked poor, although there was a smattering of well-dressed businessmen and their wives.

Most of them were hanging on Tommy's every word. One poorly dressed woman, though, was staring—right at me! And then at Steve, standing there beside the stairway. Her eyes locked onto mine. She seemed to be studying my face. Then Steve's. Then mine. I felt uncomfortable. *Different.* I was suddenly very conscious of my brand-new American jeans and shirt, my long blond hair. What could she be thinking?

Back and forth went the woman's gaze. She looked puzzled about something. Then suddenly, as if a light bulb had gone on in her head, her eyes widened in amazement, she smiled triumphantly, and pointed at the two of us.

"¡Mira! ¡Mira! Ken y Barbie!" she shouted.

Her accent was so strong that, for a second, the names didn't register for a second. *Ken y Barbie.* Ken and Barbie! Then, everybody in the Dodgers' party got it—and then *they* were staring at us. Everyone laughed. So did I. ¡Ken y Barbie! Imagine!

"Hey, Steve, we're famous," I joked. He grinned at me. Eventually, a rickety brown school bus drove up, and they took us away.

"Can we go home now?" joked Mary Ann, a few days later. I laughed along. What else was there to do?

For now, "home" was the Hotel Embajador—not the best hotel in town, but the best we could afford. It was where the American players and their wives stayed; a four-story pile of stucco just a short walk from the Tigers' ballpark. We soon learned the Embajador's little peculiarities: when the electricity was working, which was sometimes, the hotel was air-conditioned and had working elevators. When it wasn't—which was often—it was either sweltering or plunged into darkness. After Mary Ann got stuck in the elevator for several hours one day, I learned to take the stairs. One evening, before the Tigers played one of their night games, the stadium lights were turned on—and at the same moment, the hotel was plunged into darkness.

The swimming pool was always empty. But that was for the best, since the green scum was never cleaned from the bottom, either. A little old man patrolled the corridors at all hours, trying, for some reason, to clean the concrete floors with a hand-powered carpet sweeper.

In some ways, though, it wasn't very much different from our life in Los Angeles. The Licey Tigers played their games at night; after he finished practicing with the team early in the mornings, Steve and I spent lots of time together, usually in our gray-walled little hotel room.

First I did the chores, which included squashing cock-roaches and chasing mice. Steve, who hated bugs and cringed at the sight of them, watched in amazed admiration—sometimes even calling in other people to watch me—when I went on my daily cockroach patrol.

I did our laundry in the bathtub. One day, early on, Steve came in and caught me stirring the dirty clothes with one of his golf clubs. He just threw back his head and laughed. It was good to see him happy; without the television or sports pages to distract him, he seemed quieter, harder to draw out than in Los Angeles.

"What is this: Twenty-one Questions?" he asked me, one morning. That was the first time I heard my nick-name.

But I could understand what was happening to him. That winter, I think, I began to grasp the politics of base-ball. The way the Los Angeles Dodgers' system worked. What Steve was really up against. What I had to help him get through.

"You, Garv! Just keep hitting and we'll find a place for you," said Tommy Lasorda, munching on one of the lo-cal pizzas—about the only thing made in town that even faintly resembled American food.

Almost every afternoon, Tommy held court in his top-floor hotel suite, talking to his American players about his plans for them. Tommy would always ask Steve to bring me along. I'd sit in a corner and read the American newspapers and magazines—it was important, he said, for him to keep up with the sports news—that he some-how managed to obtain. While I read, they talked about their plans. It was known that Tommy would be manag-ing the Dodgers after Walt Alston retired. And that the young players in the Dominican would be the nucleus of Tommy's team. Steve was Tommy's third baseman. He was counting on Steve.

"They're watching me. This is where I prove myself," said Steve, gathering up his equipment to go over to the stadium. He was as nervous as I'd ever seen him. The

Dodgers, he'd explained, had gone through dozens of young players in the last few years, searching for a good third baseman. Now, they were looking at him. The only problem was, Steve wasn't good enough to play third.

He could hit. That was no problem. But he simply could not make the long throw from third to first. Not with any consistency. "When I hurt my right shoulder playing football in college, the muscles got stretched out," he told me, reluctantly, one morning in the room. The Dodgers didn't know this; he had to make them think that he would improve with practice.

He didn't. Some mornings Mary Ann and I would take a couple of books, sit in the stands behind first base, and watch the Tigers work out. I loved to watch Steve hit: the ball flew off his bat, with a wonderful, sharp crack, to every part of the field. But when the ball was hit to him at third base, my heart leapt up. "Oh no!" I'd say. Mary Ann and I watched sadly as, more often than not, the ball would fly into the stands, or over the first baseman's head into right field. This happened day after day. After a while, all we could do was make a joke out of it. "Duck! Watch out!" we yelled after each error. Steve looked up at us and smiled sheepishly. I knew he was being torn up inside. But what could he do? What could I do?

"Don't argue with anybody in a military uniform. Don't wear short shorts. Travel in groups. And *don't* go into the slums," said the man from the U.S. embassy.

Like all the other men who worked in the low, gray embassy building, he wore black pants, short hair, a white short-sleeved shirt, and a name tag. He was very nice. He gave us a card that allowed us to buy lunch at the embassy cafeteria. And he taught all the wives a Spanish phrase: *"Mi esposo está un pelotero."* That means: "My husband is a ballplayer." Usually, but not always, that phrase stopped the Dominican men from shouting obscene comments when they saw us walking on the street. Nobody said anything to the soldiers, who raced through the streets in their jeeps. On the jeeps were machine guns, which they pointed, grinning, at people on the street as they drove by.

Unaccompanied women had a ten o'clock curfew. After that, we were told, the police assumed that all females on the street were prostitutes and dealt with them "appropriately." Many nights I heard the crackle of machine-gun fire outside my window. The soldiers were either drunk or just bored; the next morning, houses and street signs would be riddled with fresh bullet holes.

We weren't in Spokane, that was for sure. After we were settled in, Mary Ann and I looked for a nursery school for Vaughn. The embassy gave us a list of possible schools; we hired a taxi and rode around the island to investigate. Although the few rich people lived in beautiful mansions on the hills, all the people who took care of children in their homes lived in the flatlands. And, like most of the people on the island, they were very poor. All of the "schools" were just tin shacks, with chickens, pigs, and nearly naked children running around in dirt-covered front yards. Many of the children had open sores. They begged us for money. Afterward, whenever we went into town, we made sure we had a supply of spare coins and Band-Aids, bandages and ointment cribbed from the team's supply.

Mary Ann, who by no stretch of the imagination had had a rich upbringing back in Texas, was as appalled as I was. She just looked at me and shook her head. We talked about it on the way back to the hotel. If this was an adventure—an exciting Caribbean vacation—it was a different kind than we'd seen advertised.

They played baseball differently here, too. For the Dominicans, the game wasn't a "pastime." It was an escape. An obsession.

The stadium on game nights was a madhouse. The fans, all men, all dressed in cheap pants and white shirts, let out their frustrations on the players. Inside the

ballpark, at least, the worst of them were like wild animals. They drank beer—*cerveza*—nonstop. They yelled
and cursed at the opposing team and fought with the
opposing fans. Soldiers walked up and down the aisles,
breaking up fights with blackjacks and rifle butts. The
men lit fires in the stands. They gambled noisily with
each other on every pitch. They threw rocks and empty
beer bottles at the players—and each other. A wire mesh
screen separated the playing field from the seats, but
there was no protection for the wives, who sat together
behind home plate.

One particularly scary night, Steve made four errors at
third base. His throws were sailing into the stands, one
after another. The crowd—*everybody*—hissed at him. It
sounded like a giant snake, getting ready to attack. It was
terrifying.

The fans stood and shook their fists at my husband.
They shouted for his substitute, a native player. *"¡Quer-
emos el Dominicano!"* "We want the Dominican!" I
didn't know what was worse: the crowd's threats, or the
sight of Steve, still out there at third base, his shoulders
slumped, staring at the ground. But I knew now what I
had to do.

"Come on, Steve, let's get out of here. Let's *do* something," I said.

The mornings after his bad games, Steve sat silent and
stone-faced in the room. I had to draw him out, get his
mind off his problems. I had to be his cheerleader.

We'd walk it off. I'd grab his hand and pull him along
with me on walks through the Old City. Go to the embassy for a grilled-cheese sandwich. We'd go out for a
pizza; shop for trinkets. I became Chatty Cathy, talking
nonstop about anything but baseball.

"You know, I miss the seasons, I really do. I even miss
the cold."

"I wonder how our friends back in Michigan are doing?" I'd read letters from them, tell him about the letters I'd written.

"I got seven cockroaches when you were away last night."

"This sure is a strange island, isn't it?"

Sometimes I did silly things, like skipping down the street or running rings around him. I bought him funny straw hats; taught him to dance the merengue to the music from the radio. Gradually, he'd loosen up. He wouldn't say much, but I knew he was relaxing. I loved him for that. He'd grin, lift his head a bit, and we'd go back to the glamorous Embajador.

Then he would have another bad game, and it would start all over again. Another walk. Another talk. One day, we passed a Dominican wedding; festive music playing, all the family and friends dressed in their very best.

A guest stared at us as we walked past.

"¡Ay! ¡La esposa y el esposo!"

He rushed up to us, pulled us inside, escorted us to the wedding cake, and pointed proudly to the plastic bride and groom on top. The little bride figure had long blond hair. The groom was dark-haired, but light-skinned.

"¡Está usted!" he said.

Suddenly, we were surrounded by laughing, applauding Dominicans.

"Yep, I guess it is," I laughed. I turned to Steve. He was smiling, too. That was a good sign.

Unfortunately, I couldn't seem to make contact with the other wives. Most of them seemed to be genuinely miserable and to resent my trying to be upbeat.

Time moved slowly in Santo Domingo. The heat was numbing. There was one movie theater. It showed European films with Spanish subtitles. Most days, we sat and sunned ourselves next to the empty pool. Or we played Yahtzee, a kind of poker game played with dice instead of cards: the players were usually Steve, myself, Mary Ann, Grabby, or Doug Rau, a young pitcher who was single.

For hours, we'd slam the dice on the card table and write down our scores. Running out of special Yahtzee pads was a big crisis; we'd grab anybody flying to the States and make them swear they'd bring some back for us.

Most of the players liked to drink. Because of the heat and—I assume—the pressure, they liked to drink a lot. On the bus rides home from road games they'd knock off six-packs of beer and reel up to their rooms.

All except Steve, of course. He didn't drink. He'd step off the bus cold sober, a tight look of disapproval on his face.

In turn, the other players would look contemptuously at him. It was a tense and distressing scene. I felt it was something he could avoid. "You don't have to get drunk," I said to Steve one evening. "But couldn't you just drink a beer or two? They'll like you better." He just frowned and shook his head. Subject dismissed.

After home games, the players ate—and drank pitchers of beer—in the local pizza place. When they were drunk, which was nearly every night, the players swore nonstop. Steve would lean over to Tommy Lasorda and say, "There are children around. I don't approve of this." Tommy would just look up from his meal, pat Steve on the arm, and shrug.

One night, Steve stood up at the table and made this announcement to everyone. Steve Yeager, our catcher, looked up at Steve with an expression of pure disgust.

"F—— a——," he said, and rushed at Steve. My husband stood his ground, and they grappled a bit before the other players pulled them apart. I was terrified. If Steve was hurt in a fight, his entire career could be over.

"Why did you say that? Why are you doing this?" I asked him. But when we got upstairs he refused to talk about it. It was as if it had never happened.

It was frustrating. The team's dislike for Steve spilled over to the wives. And to me. Few of the women my age would have anything to do with me. They never invited me to their lunches at the embassy. Sometimes, they even moved their chairs away from me when I sat near them by the pool.

Thank God for Mary Ann Grabarkewitz. Like most of the other wives, she married young and stood by her husband while he worked his way up through the minor leagues. But in other ways she was different. She read books, looked at parts of the newspaper other than the sports pages—and would talk to me.

We'd laugh and joke. And sometimes, talk about serious things. She told me about the terrible time when Bill broke his ankle, badly, while he was in the minors. How worried they were that he'd never play baseball again. How worried she was *now* that her husband, not a superstar, would be cut off, shut out, fired in the prime of his career.

"How will we live in Los Angeles? It's such a wild town. What will we do with our lives when the guys retire?" asked Mary Ann one day, looking depressed.

In my naïveté—my selfishness, too—I really didn't know what she was talking about. After all, I thought, Steve will be a star. He'll be with the Dodgers for years and years. He's much too straight-arrow to ever cheat on me. I'd never be one of those wives who lived only through her husband. I was going to be a doctor, wasn't I?

"Oh, why bother worrying about those things now?" I told her, with a little laugh. Whatever came up, I assured her, we could handle it.

I could handle it. A college friend sent me down some medical textbooks, and I sat in the hotel lobby for hours, reading.

One day, word flashed through the hotel that a well-known National League player had murdered his Dominican mistress in a motel room the night before. It was on the Spanish-language radio, and then—nothing. No more news reports, no trial. Officials from his U.S. team flew down, fixed everything, and took the player back to the

States with them. But what about the woman? Nobody seemed to know.

As the season went on and his errors added up, Steve seemed to pull away. He confided in me less and less. Some days, we barely talked at all. It was as if, just by being there, I was distracting him from more important things. Our lovemaking, never really frequent, became almost nonexistent.

In the dark, even with Steve beside me, I was lonely. One night, I snuggled up to him in bed and whispered something affectionate in his ear. "Calm down," said Steve. Calm down?

"Oh, Steve cares about you very much," said Mary Ann the next day, squeezing my arm in sympathy. "He's just worried about making the team." She smiled at me and told me to cheer up. How wonderful of her; she was getting more and more pregnant—and more uncomfortable in the heat and humidity—by the day.

There was a month to go in the winter season. Luckily, Billy Grabarkewitz broke his thumb in a game a few days later, and Grabby, Mary Ann and Vaughn packed to fly back to Miami.

"I'm jealous," I told Grabby, his hand in a cast, at the airport. I gave him, and then Mary Ann, a kiss.

Over the next two seasons, as it happened, Steve beat out Grabby for an infield spot on the Dodgers. Mary Ann lived down in Orange County—along with other veteran Dodger families like the Claude Osteens and the Jim Lefebvres—about an hour's drive from where we settled in Los Angeles. Although we talked on the telephone occasionally, and saw each other at the ballpark, we were never again as close as we were in Santo Domingo.

In spring training of 1973, Billy Grabarkewitz hurt his arm in practice. He was put on the injured reserve list and traded to another team.

Mary Ann called me with the news that summer. I began to cry at the thought of losing her.

Billy was traded a few more times, and his baseball career ended in 1975. Mary Ann and Billy were divorced in 1977; she's now the vice-president of a real estate firm in San Antonio.

Mary Ann and I lost touch with each other. A few months ago, though, I talked with her again, and it was as if we had last talked only yesterday. She remembered, too, our farewell phone call.

"I couldn't understand why you sounded so lonely," she said. "I thought you had lots of other friends, somewhere."

CHAPTER 10

We had missed the off-season completely. By the time we came back from the Caribbean, Steve was due at spring training. It felt almost like being in the Air Force again; Steve heading out to far-off assignments, me lagging behind, taking care of the details. The way things were going, I realized, I would have a hard time trying to get into school that fall.

It seemed the right time to move out of the gloomy apartment on Redlands. We looked at an apartment at 8740 Tuscany, just a few blocks away. It was a beige-colored, three-story stucco building with a tiny pool wedged next to the parking area. Our third-story apartment with two bedrooms and a wooden-fenced balcony rented for six hundred dollars a month. I handed over the first and last months' rent on the spot. I was getting very good at packing and unpacking; I moved all our things over in one afternoon.

Apartment 302 was light and airy. Our new neighbors, as far as I could tell, were all either cops—male—or stewardesses—female. We were the only married couple in the building. Every weekday at 5 P.M., whoever was off duty would gather at poolside for "Happy Hour." Since I wasn't much of a drinker, I tried to stay away from the pool during those times—or, if I got too lonely with Steve on the road, I'd nurse one drink until things broke up at dinnertime.

Everyone loved the idea of Steve living next to them. They'd shout from poolside when he walked by on his way in or out.

"Hey! There's Steve Garvey."

"That's his wife."

"He's on the Dodgers."

"He lives here!"

"Have a drink with us!"

Steve would smile and shake his head. Steve never told them that he never drank. Or that his life as a Dodger was less than perfect.

The fact was, Steve's career was very much in danger that season. Because of his errors, a young player named Ron Cey had won the third baseman's job from him. Steve was benched. He was reduced to pinch-hitting—coming in late in the game to substitute for a pitcher or a weak hitter—and occasionally playing the outfield.

"I don't have a position, Cyn," he'd tell me, holding his head in his hands. I could see he felt it all slipping away from him. There were rumors, reported in the papers, that he would be traded to the Montreal Expos. He was pinch-hitting well, but that didn't make him feel any better. "They're showcasing me," he said. They were showing the other clubs around the league how well he could hit—in order to get more for him in a trade.

It was painful to watch him at the ballpark. With nothing to do, he paced the dugout. He carried a lead pipe, used for warmup swings. When he couldn't take it any more, he slammed the pipe into the dugout railing. I heard that terrible sound all the way up in the stands.

He was eating himself up. At home, he was even quieter than ever. In his misery, he seemed to be drawing farther into himself. Before the games he sat, stonefaced, in the living room, saying nothing.

I was miserable, too. My heart went out to my husband. What could I do? I loved this man so much—and he was suffering. I tried everything I could; all the old tricks, and some new ones. In the mornings, making sure to smile and talk cheerfully, I pulled him out of the house for walks and bicycle rides. I began to turn down more substitute-teaching assignments so I could stay home and keep him company. I made him teach me to play tennis —and my awkward attempts sometimes got him to laugh. It made him feel good, I thought, because he was good at tennis. In charge of teaching me. In control of the game.

Then I had a fantastic idea. I'd be his secret fan club.

At that time, Steve got only a handful of fan letters each week—mostly from children. "I never get any *good* ones," he said to me one night. So when he was on the road, I sat down at home and wrote him anonymous, sexy letters.

"You're my favorite ballplayer," I scribbled, disguising my handwriting.

"You're the best-looking guy out there."

"I watch you from the stands—just you, Steve!—every day."

"You look so *sexy* in that tight-fitting uniform!"

I didn't sign the love notes, but I drenched them in perfume and kissed lipstick marks on them. I drove around Los Angeles and mailed them from different boxes.

He brought them home. He showed some of them to me with a sheepish grin; they seemed to cheer him up a little. I tried to kid him, get his mind off his worries.

"Hey! Who is this lady? I'm jealous," I said. "What kind of a person would write a letter like this? Hah! This address looks phony to me, Steve."

He never caught on that it was me who was writing them. Or if he did, he didn't tell me.

What was worse, he just sank deeper into his depression. The season dragged on. I stopped going to all the games; I knew he didn't want me to see him fail.

"Don't bother, Cyn," he said, when I asked him if he wanted me to drive him to the stadium. "Don't bother."

Steve had just lost a game for the Dodgers. He'd thrown the ball away. It was on television; I'd watched him at home.

The phone rang. "Hey, Garvey! You——! Why don't you go—— yourself!" rasped a beery male voice.

I slammed down the phone. It rang again, right away. Another man. "Hey, Garvey! Get off the field! And get an arm!" Click.

Dazed, I set the receiver down on the table. It was no mystery how the caller had gotten our phone number; Steve was listed in the book just like everyone else. I told him what had happened when he came home that night. "Don't tell anybody. Just get us an unlisted number," he said. Then he sat down in his chair, silent.

But somehow, even though I changed our phone number, the calls kept coming. There were several regular callers, all of them more or less obscene. Sometimes they'd hang up when I announced who I was. Most of the time they just kept cursing.

A few calls came through when Steve was home. I could tell what was going on.

"Hello?" Steve would say; then even I, standing across the room, could hear the filth pouring out of the telephone. Steve wouldn't hang up. He'd simply stand there, absolutely rigid, his face getting grimmer and grimmer as he listened. He'd say nothing, listening until the caller ran out of steam. Then he'd hang up the phone gently.

He was punishing himself for his mistakes! It was heartbreaking. Nobody—least of all my husband—should have to go through this.

"Is there anything for me to do . . . ?" I asked. He shook his head. Mixed in with the sadness was confusion, disappointment. When he needed me most, my husband was shutting me out. I just had to try harder.

* * *

I moved us again, this time to a place nearby called Cross Creek Village. This was a complex of about a dozen three-story buildings. It was a week or so before I could find my way around the winding pathways between the apartment blocks; each building—ours was Building C— had a big dark brown initial painted on its brown walls. Almost every balcony, I seem to recall, had one of those crystal wind chimes hanging noisily from it. The rent at Cross Creek was higher than at our last place, but it had a bigger pool and some private tennis courts: the better to keep Steve distracted.

I played tennis with Steve whenever I could. For a while, he'd laugh with me as I tried to remember my lessons and hit the ball at least one time out of three. Yet, in his depression, Steve would rarely ask me to play. I'd have to drag him onto the court.

Afterward, we'd barbecue an early dinner. I'd try to draw Steve out about his frustrations.

"No, I don't want to talk about it," he'd say. He'd prod the meat on the grill and look away from me.

And then, one day, Steve lost his wedding ring.

We were in the apartment when I noticed it wasn't on his finger. "Where is it, Steve?" I asked.

"Oh, it's in my locker," he said. I knew that the players took off their rings before the game. I also knew that some of the married players took off their wedding rings when they went on road trips. "Getting rid of the gold," it was called. Those players had nothing to do with Steve, I knew. But a few days later, the ring was still gone.

"It's in my golf bag," he said.

"Well, could you put it back on? It's important to me, Steve," I said.

Later that week, when I was pulling out of our parking space, I heard a crunch under my left rear tire. I stopped, got out and kneeled down. I'd run over Steve's wedding ring; it was twisted and flattened. Steve must have dropped it from his bag. Maybe today. Maybe weeks ago.

A streak of pure fear ran through me. This was a sign. A symbol. I was losing my husband. But why? The obvious reason—another woman—didn't make sense.

No. It wasn't that. It was just that in his misery, he was pulling away from me. I wasn't giving him what he needed. I *must be doing something very wrong.*

Things couldn't go on like this. Could they? I thought of all that Steve meant to me and realized, to my horror, that I wasn't sure. And then, in late June, everything changed.

CHAPTER 11

Everything.

One Sunday, between games of a doubleheader, I stood in my kitchen and called the Dodger clubhouse. I was worried about Steve; he hadn't played in the first game, and I knew he'd be depressed. I hoped a call from me would cheer him up.

Walt Alston answered the phone. "How are you doing, Cynthia?" he said.

"I'm fine," I said. And then, without thinking—and with a recklessness that still puzzles me after all these years—I broke all the rules. "But Steve's not doing well at all, Walt," I said. "You know what I mean?"

Dead silence at the other end. I felt a sting of fear. Had I insulted Walt Alston, driven Steve even farther into the doghouse?

"Wa–a–a–l," said the manager, finally, "there's no opening here. I can't find a place for our boy to play."

He almost sounded apologetic. That kept my courage up. Maybe . . . ? The idea, which I hadn't even discussed with Steve, popped into my mind.

"Well, why not put Steve at first base?" I said.

More silence.

"He played some in the minor leagues, Walt. He won't have to throw. Billy Buckner isn't playing well, either."

Oh my God, I realized. What had I done? I, a mere

wife, had told Walter Alston how to manage his team! Had I ruined everything for Steve? The silence was even longer this time.

"Hmm," said Alston, finally. "Maybe we'll give it a go." *Maybe we'll give it a go?*

"Here's Steve now. 'Bye," said Walt.

"What did you say to him? What the hell did you say to him?" said Steve. I told him. Over the phone line, I could hear him draw in his breath. And that was all.

For the second game of that doubleheader, Alston moved Steve to first base—and he stayed there. His real baseball career began that day.

For many years, Steve made it clear to me that the story of his switch was not to be told to anyone. Then, like other parts of our life together, he turned it into a funny story; told it many times to reporters and banquet audiences.

By that time, of course, he was secure in his stardom.

It all seemed to turn around in a second. At first base, Steve could concentrate on hitting without worrying about his long throws. His true abilities came out; he won a spot in the Dodgers' starting lineup. The newspaper reporters grabbed on to him: the articles on Steve came out faster than I could clip and paste them. GARVEY'S BLAZING BAT EARNS HIM JOB; GARVEY HAPPY IN L.A.; PERSEVERANCE IS KEY TO RISE OF STEVE GARVEY.

The articles were all positive, and often very funny. "Baseball takes many twists and turns," wrote one reporter:

> . . . most of which test the character and composure of the players, but few were bestowed the ignominy of indifference that was Steve Garvey's plight in the spring of 1973 at Vero Beach.
>
> 1972 had to be a nightmare for the rugged youngster from Tampa, Fla., whose father annually bussed the Dodgers through Spring and young Steve, as a teenager

would help his dad with the players' luggage. So, Garvey had tremendous pride as a Dodger but his erratic throws from the hot corner last season deleted from his performance at the plate and the brass decided Steve's best shot was to play the outfield. Where he languished in a miserable April, May and June.

"I was a lost soul the first part of the season," Garvey recalls. "Never have I played utility, in college or in the minors, and it just isn't my style. But the club was playing well, and in first place, so all I could do was stay in shape, get in as much hitting as possible, and await my opportunity . . . Believe me, just playing regularly is more than worth learning a new position . . . I'm living again!"

The stories all read pretty much like that one. Sometimes, there was even a paragraph or two "about" me:

Steve's biggest booster is his beautiful wife, Cindy, once bat girl for the Detroit Tigers. The two were married Oct. 29, 1971. Cindy staunchly stood by Steve in the dark days of '72 and early '73, contending that her hubby would prove himself.

Garvey is now simply proving to the Dodgers his wife's faith was well warranted. And in the pennant race ahead, it may well be Steve's bat that will carry the club to important victories.

The bat girl part wasn't really true, of course. And for some peculiar reason, *all* the reporters kept calling me "Cindy." But all the hype and flattery seemed harmless. The most important part was that Steve had truly come alive.

Each morning, he bounced out of bed and left for the ballpark even earlier. He started a ritual that he practiced as long as we were together. When he came home from the ballpark, he grabbed a pencil and wrote down his hits

—"2 for 5,"; "1 for 4, home run")—on that day's square of the kitchen calendar. *And he talked to me.*

Mostly, we talked about baseball. Now that he was doing well, that was what he wanted to talk about. To keep him talking, I paid more attention to his playing when I sat in the stands. I studied him from my seat. I made sure I remembered exactly what he'd done in the game.

"Did you see that tonight, Cyn?"

"Oh yes, Steve. Three hits. You were *wonderful,*" I said, playfully. Steve grinned.

I even gave him suggestions—and, to my surprise, he took them seriously. "You know," I said, "you're always getting two strikes against you," I said. "They're throwing you bad balls, way outside. Why don't you stop swinging at the first pitch?"

I noticed that he never bunted, that he rarely hit balls to right field. I told him; he listened carefully and changed his habits. *He was paying attention to me.*

He beamed at me when I noticed something that could help him. "You're my camera in the stands," said Steve. I was delighted. He asked me, "Am I too close to home plate? Am I swinging at bad balls?" I was delighted. His success, I felt, was bringing us closer together.

The games were easier to go to. Afterward, Steve wouldn't hang around any more with the other players. He'd burst out of the locker room, full of energy. He stood up straight. He began a habit of kissing every woman in sight—wives, team secretaries, little girls, passersby. Finally, he'd give me a kiss and we'd leave together.

He wouldn't say anything until we were alone.

"Did you see? I hung in there today. *Two* three-two counts." That meant he'd waited patiently for a good pitch.

"Oh yeah. *Wonderful.*" But he could see that I was proud of him. We talked about it all the way home.

* * *

It was strange, though. After all those months of pressure —of keeping Steve going—were over, I sometimes felt more tired than ever before. There was a feeling of empti- ness, of anticlimax. To my surprise, I kept putting off the paperwork for taking the MSAT.

It just seemed like . . . so much work. More time away from Steve.

"Oh, I don't know, Steve," I said one afternoon. "Maybe it's too late for me. I've been out of school al- most two years now. Everybody in my class will be younger than me. They'll be all speeded up and ready to go. What do you think?"

Steve looked up from his paper. He hadn't been listen- ing.

"Oh never mind," I said. "Just thinking aloud."

"Hey, Steve. What would you think if I made some extra money, um, modeling."

He looked up from the television set. "You're kid- ding," he said.

"No, I mean it."

"Sounds great, Cyn!" he said. To my surprise, he looked genuinely interested.

A few days earlier, a peculiar thing had happened at Dodger Stadium. I was sitting in a field box before the game, watching the celebrity softball contest the Dodgers put on every year. A pack of photographers was standing on the field, taking pictures of the actors and actresses as they had fun trying to play ball.

They were a different group from the regular sports photographers. One of them, between shots, began to turn around and stare at me. I stared back. He was about thirty-five, wearing jeans and a workshirt, and he squinted at me solemnly. Eventually he came over and introduced himself.

I told him who I was. "Have you ever done any model- ing work?" he said.

"God no," I said.

"Well, you should, y'know," he said, very seriously. "You're a natural. They're looking for people like you these days. All-American blondes. You know what I mean. California types."

That was the silliest thing I'd heard in a long time. "But I'm not from California. I'm from Detroit," I said.

He didn't seem to hear me. He was writing a name and phone number on a piece of paper.

"I want you to call this woman. She's the best agent in L.A." How weird! He pushed the paper into my hand and walked back onto the field.

I called the number and made an appointment with Nina Blanchard. She ran her own modeling agency. Her office was in Hollywood. "Bring a photograph of yourself," she said. All I could find was a blurry Instamatic print somebody had taken.

The picture was so amateurish, I was embarrassed to show it to her. But that was all I had. Nina Blanchard was a brisk, businesslike, expensively dressed woman. Not like the man in Detroit at all.

She looked at the snapshot. Then up at me. Back to the photo. Me again.

"Yes," she said, matter-of-factly.

"You're kidding!" I said. She frowned at me, annoyed, as if I was asking for flattery. "No," she said. This was business.

She told me that I'd have to spend five hundred dollars getting professional photos taken. "Sure. No problem," said Steve, when I asked him if he thought it was worth it. When I had my portfolio—and a black-and-white, eight-by-ten head shot that read CYNTHIA GARVEY—she sent me out on "look-sees." These were casting calls that ad agencies held for models. Once or twice a week, I'd show up to sit in the hall with a dozen or so blond women who looked almost exactly like me.

It reminded me of my beauty pageant days. Yet it was different; I felt oddly detached from the whole process, as though I were watching another, possibly younger version of myself. In a movie, maybe. A documentary.

"Is Cynthia Garvey here?"

I'd go into a room and face five or six ad men, all dressed in open-necked shirts and gold chains, all sitting together on a couch. One of them would read from a clipboard.

"I see you're married, Cynthia. What does your husband do?"

"He's a baseball player."

"Oh, really?" He looked up, mildly interested. "Which one?"

"Steve Garvey."

"Oh. Really." Most of the ad people didn't recognize his name. They all asked me to turn around and walk across the room. A couple of times they asked me to pull up my skirt so they could see my legs. It was all very businesslike: "Just above the knees, please."

Another time, for a liquor ad, they asked me to pose in a bathing suit alongside a brunette and a redhead. They wanted to shoot us from behind, with our long hair falling across our shoulders.

"Thanks very much, girls. Leave your phone numbers with the secretary."

I only did a couple of assignments, but Nina told me not to worry. "They're looking for people just like you," she said.

Somehow, my plan to go to medical school faded further and further back. Months before, I'd set my mind on enrolling in the session that began January 15. I never even filled out the registration forms.

"I've made it, Cyn," said Steve, smiling at me. It was a sunny day in September. We were sitting on the steps in front of the apartment building; he was as happy as I'd seen him. I was happy for him.

"I've made it. They're not showcasing me any more." The Dodgers, he said, wanted to send him to Santo Domingo again. But this time, just to hone his skills at first base. Not to prove himself.

"We'll have a better time this winter," he said. But Steve, I thought. Medical school.

"I really want you to come with me," said Steve, earnestly. "You know, I really love it that you'll be with me there." I melted. This was the first time in a long time that he'd said he needed me.

But he *did* need me. This proved it. I held on to his words—and somehow, the thought of medical school seemed frivolous, selfish. Our marriage was real. It was happening *now*. My part in it was important. Becoming a doctor would take years—years working just for myself. What were these plans, my wishful thinking, against the reality, the needs of the present? For a long second, I thought about it.

And I gave up without a fight. It was my choice, and mine alone. I loved this man. I wanted to be with him. "Okay, Steve," I said. "We'll go."

CHAPTER 12

"Why don't we go look for a house?" I asked Steve, before we left for the Caribbean. After all, I said, his job looked more secure now. With his salary from Santo Domingo—and anything I earned modeling, as a bonus—we'd be able to scrape up a decent down payment.

Billy Buckner had gotten married and bought a house in a suburb called Woodland Hills. "Let's go visit them this afternoon," I said to Steve, a few days after the regular season ended.

Billy and Jan showed us around the neighborhood. It was quiet and clean; a family place. I had an optimistic plan: we'd move a few houses down from the Buckners. Steve and Billy would be close friends and neighbors; Jan and I and some of the other wives would get to be close friends, too. We bought a house—a brown tri-level on Paul Revere Drive—and arranged to move in when we came back from Santo Domingo.

If I couldn't be a doctor, I thought, I'd be a normal suburban housewife. We'd raise a family. We'd be more like the other Dodgers. That would be good for Steve and me in the long run. Wouldn't it?

I could definitely see it that winter in Santo Domingo: Steve's status with the Dodgers had soared. His pinch-hitting days were over. He was their first baseman. A starter! It was an exciting, gratifying time for my husband. I was very happy for him.

Tommy Lasorda looked happy with him, too. During that second trip to the Dominican Republic, as I remember it, he always seemed to be standing next to Steve. Gradually, we were being drawn into his inner circle. No other player was as close to him.

"C'mon over here, Garv," he'd yell, and introduce him to one of the Dominican dignitaries he was friendly with.

He'd throw an arm around Steve's shoulder and pull him playfully towards him. *"Mi primer basero,"* he said, proudly. His first baseman.

More and more often, Tommy included us in his dinners with the local businessmen and politicians. Steve and I sat quietly, listening to Tommy talk baseball in Spanish. Relays of dark-skinned servants—our hosts were always light-skinned, European-looking—brought out course after course. I'd try to smile politely at the men smiling broadly at me. The Dominican women, all stunningly dressed, said nothing.

Two or three times a week, Tommy invited us out to eat with him and the other coaches. "Watch this, Garv," he said one night. He'd ordered a big steak and eaten half of it; he winked at us as he called the waiter over.

"This is terrible. A terrible steak. *Es malo. ¡Muy malo!"* he said.

The waiter, wringing his hands in fear, whisked Tommy's steak away. The restaurant manager came out, bowing and scraping and spewing apologies in Spanish at a mile a minute. Tommy sat sternly with his arms folded. In no time at all, an even bigger steak was set down before him. He cut off a piece, tasted it, and nodded. Great celebration!

"See? Works every time," said Tommy, eyes twinkling, after the manager had bowed himself back to the kitchen. Steve laughed.

* * *

Steve was having a great time. I could see it; the tension of last year was gone. That was wonderful; the problem was that we had even less contact than before with the other families. Steve didn't seem to mind his lack of friends on the team; his days were full. Without anyone to talk to, though, mine were endless.

Mary Ann and Billy weren't down with us that winter. In their spare time, the men would leave the Embajador and go off on all-male golfing expeditions organized by the club. Steve went along contentedly, if silently, with them.

That left me with the other wives. None of their husbands, I saw, had the inside track with Tommy that Steve had. Most were fighting just to stay in the Dodger organization.

As usual, the women pointedly ignored me at the hotel swimming pool. One day I worked up the courage to ask if I could join them for lunch. "Oh, we're not going anywhere," said one of them. Later I went to the embassy to eat alone; I saw them all sitting together at a far table.

That was too blatant, too painful. And, truth to tell, I wasn't feeling too well in the tropical heat. That night, I told Steve what had happened.

"Look, I think I'd better go home for awhile," I said. But silently I begged Steve to stop me. Tell me that you want me to stay, Steve, I thought. That you'll help me work things out with the others. That you'll help me get them to like us.

Steve thought it over for a few seconds.

"Do what you want, Cyn," he said. "Do what you have to do." I packed up and left the next day.

I flew to Detroit, where I visited my parents. It was there I confirmed what I'd already suspected—that I was pregnant. It was marvelous news. I'd always wanted children —I'd always assumed Steve did, too—and now, with our new house, we could have a real family. I also realized that I'd never become a doctor. But that was just a dream, wasn't it?

I kept the news to myself until the last week of winter ball. Then, I flew down to Santo Domingo to surprise Steve. I was unpacking my suitcase when he came into the room.

I turned, and smiled, and pointed to my stomach.

"So that's it, huh?" he said. No jumping up and down, but he seemed pleased.

"When's it due?" he asked.

That was the best part. "Mid-October," I said, happily. The baseball season was over then. "At least you'll be around."

Steve didn't say anything. But the timing, I thought, was perfect. This was the best thing that I—and only I—could do for him.

"Congratulations," said Nina Blanchard. Truth to tell, I hadn't been too excited about becoming a model. I felt guilty about that; she'd put a lot of effort into getting me started. And now I was pregnant. But she took it in stride. "Don't worry. You just come back to us when you're ready." Then she wished me well.

We moved into the brown-and-white house. It cost fifty-two thousand dollars altogether, which was just a little more than we were able to pay. It was the same as every fourth house on our street: three bedrooms, a den, nice kitchen, smallish backyard. A few Dodger families—the Buckners, the Ron Ceys, the Steve Yeagers, the Dusty Bakers—lived nearby. All the rest of our neighbors were older couples, in their thirties and forties, with children.

They were nice women, and they invited me over to their houses a few times, but we had little in common. All they wanted to talk about was Steve and his career. "You're home alone a lot, aren't you?" they asked. Steve's life, with his road trips and night games, was strange, exotic, completely out of synch with all the other men in the neighborhood. I felt different. An oddity. An outsider again.

It was odd, I thought. Standing at my window, looking out at the neighborhood, I hardly ever saw anyone using the front door. The California houses were blank, expressionless, towards the front. They opened up to the back, out of sight.

In the mornings, all the garage doors would open and the men would drive away to work. In the afternoons, the wives would drive their kids from lesson to lesson in their big brown station wagons. In between, the women—dressed in warmup suits and tennis shoes—would drive in and out as they did their chores; to go to the health club or jogging or to the tennis court. They'd drive over to each others' houses for coffee.

I spent most of my time alone that season. When Steve was gone, I decorated the house, adding a new floor, or new deck, or some new furniture to surprise him every time a road trip ended. In the evenings, to fill the long hours, I went to the local community center to take courses in first aid and CPR. "It'll come in handy," I told Steve.

Sadly, the friendships with our Dodger neighbors never materialized. In the beginning of that season, Billy and the other players picked Steve up at the house and they drove to and from the ballpark together. Then suddenly they stopped coming.

I asked him why. "I'd rather drive to the ballpark myself," he said. From what I gathered in the Waiting Room that year, the other players resented his lingering in the locker room, giving interview after interview to reporters, and holding them up. So they went their separate ways.

Steve didn't seem to mind. He was as happy as I'd ever seen him that year. By early spring, he was among the league leaders in batting. He couldn't wait to come home and write down his hits on the kitchen calendar. His fielding at first base was perfectly fine. He was hitting home runs, winning games. After the games were over, he was so besieged by reporters that he was usually the last player to dress. At home, I took messages from newspaper people all day long. There seemed to be an article about him every day. They were mostly like this one:

Until Steve Garvey stole his thunder, Tom Seaver was busy convincing a Dodger Stadium crowd of 27,283 Wednesday night that he definitely deserved the distinction of being baseball's highest paid pitcher.

Seaver, the former University of Southern California star who has been the ace of the New York Mets' staff for eight years now, limited the Dodgers to but three hits and struck out a stunning 16 batters in 12 brilliant innings of work.

But in the end, Garvey stole the show.

"I felt just satisfied getting the bat on the ball," grinned Garvey after his solo home run in the sixth inning set the stage for his bases-loaded single with one out in the bottom of the 14th—yes, 14th—inning to give the Dodgers a rugged 2–1 victory over the Mets that completed an 8–1 home stand.

"That last run batted in will stay with me a long time," Garvey said. "Something like that makes you feel we can go all the way this year.

"I just thank God I was able to do it."

"What's all this about God, Steve?" I teased him, holding up the article. "Since when have *you* gotten religious?"

He grinned slyly. A joke, just between us. But what was the harm? I was, of course, happy for his success. And the coming baby, I felt, would bring us closer together. He seemed to enjoy the idea that I was pregnant. We shopped together for baby furniture. He often patted my stomach, and told me that he was hoping for a girl. "If it's a boy," he said, "I won't be around the house to spend enough time with him."

* * *

As Steve became a well-known Dodger, our world began to change. At a local restaurant one evening, we were standing in line for a table, as usual. There were several couples ahead of us. The maître d' rushed over. "Mr. Garvey! Steve! It's an honor to see you. Come on! I'll seat you right away."

The other couples turned and stared at us.

"Oh no!" I whispered to Steve.

"Gee, no thanks. We'll wait our turn," he said.

"No, come on. It's all right," said the maître d'.

"Well . . ." said Steve, looking at my, by then, slightly expanded stomach. And, to my horror, the man began whisking us to the front of the line.

I braced myself for abuse from the other people in line. But they didn't seem to mind! They smiled at Steve as he went by, and he stuck out his hand and worked his way down the line. "Hey, nice to see you."

"Great game the other night, Steve!"

"Thanks a lot."

"Keep up the good work!"

"I'll try. Have a nice dinner." And then suddenly we were seated at the best table in the house. The restaurant owner came out to sit and talk with us. Somehow, the check—like hundreds of checks to follow—just never came.

People and companies began to send us things for free. During the day, trucks pulled up and disgorged boxes and boxes of clothes and sporting goods. "Sign here," the drivers said. Dozens of baseball shoes, bats, gloves. Running shoes and jogging suits for both me and Steve. Tennis racquets. One afternoon, I took inventory in the garage, and discovered we owned *fifty-five* tennis racquets. Every couple of weeks, Steve brought home a box of prime steaks—a big Dodger fan was also a meat wholesaler. It was hard to eat them fast enough.

On an off day early that season, Steve drove up to the

house in a huge, chrome-covered, mustard-gold Oldsmobile sedan.

I went out to the driveway and stared at it. The interior was splashed with shiny knobs and fake wood. It was, I realized, almost laughing out loud, one of the ugliest cars I'd ever seen.

"What's this?" I said.

"That's our new car," said Steve.

"You bought *that?*"

"No, silly. I get it free for a season if I do some radio spots. Just for the local Olds and Cadillac dealers."

I looked at our tired old Buick, thought of the convenience of having two cars. Suddenly, the Oldsmobile didn't look quite so bad.

"Well, that makes sense, I guess." A free car. Imagine that.

There were a few new obligations that went along with Steve's "fame." Almost every day, Steve brought home a box of balls to autograph for the Dodgers. It was in his contract; they sold these balls, and gave them away to friends and business contacts. My old college forging skills came in handy; after a few minutes' practice, I could sign Steve's name again just as well as he could. We spent hours together, just signing his name. The only sound was the "scritch-scritch" of our felt-tips. "Hey, Garvey, get with it. My autograph is better than yours," I joked. Steve thought that was a riot.

He loved the fact that he was now getting lots of fan mail at the ballpark. He brought all of it home, every week, in a big green duffel bag. He read every letter, and separated them into three piles: the letters from children and incoherent adults were answered, by the Dodgers' secretary, with an autographed picture and a pre-printed note of thanks. The literate grown-ups got an autographed photo and a short personal note. The letters typed on corporate letterheads, from admiring executives or businessmen proposing endorsement deals, got long personal replies. "Call me!" he scrawled across the bottom. And he wrote down our home number.

Many of them called for Steve when he was gone, and I dutifully took down their messages for him.

Considering that I spent so much time alone, the loss of privacy was very peculiar: we lived on a main street in Woodland Hills, and after a while, though our phone number was unlisted, our address became well known. Unfamiliar cars crept past slowly, the people inside peering out for a look at Steve. We became a regular stop on the Woodland Hills school bus route: at three-thirty, the kids piled out and knocked on the door.

"Can Steve come out and sign autographs?" they begged. If the team was home, and if he hadn't left for the ballpark, Steve would stand in the front yard and autograph bats, balls, gloves, baseball cards—whatever the kids thrust at him.

When Steve wasn't home, I'd have to explain to the crowd of disappointed children.

"Steve's gone to the ballpark. You'll have to come back another time."

"But can we wait for him here?"

"No. Steve just left. You'll just have to come earlier."

"But we can't come earlier. They just let us out of school!"

"Sorry, you guys. Try again tomorrow."

If I was lucky, I could keep Steve at home until the school bus arrived. As the season went on, though, and the days got hotter, Steve left earlier for the ballpark. My pregnancy made me tired, so I timed my naps so that I'd be awake when school let out.

"Sorry, kids. I'm really sorry."

They'd come back the next day, anyway.

It was amazing. Everybody, it seemed, knew Steve. When we were out shopping or eating or just taking a walk, complete strangers came up and talked to us. Some of them walked right over and patted my stomach.

"When's it due?" they asked Steve.

"After the season," said Steve. I tried to keep a smile on my face. It was hard, though; although the people were nice, this combination of the personal and impersonal confused me. How, exactly, do you talk about personal things with a total stranger? Neither the fans nor Steve seemed to worry about it. It was almost a ritual; their questions, and Steve's answers, were always the same.

"Are you hoping for a boy or a girl?"

"Doesn't matter. As long as it's healthy."

"Come on, Steve. We've got to go," I'd say.

Steve would smile and shrug. That was usually when they asked Steve for his autograph. He'd sign with a flourish.

"Yours, too," they'd say sometimes, handing me the pen and paper. The first time that happened, I was startled. My autograph? Why *my* autograph?

C-y-n—, I wrote, and suddenly stopped. Cynthia? They didn't know me as Cynthia. In the newspapers, I was always "Cindy." How could I write my real name without confusing them? Maybe even making them mad?

C-y-n-d-y, I finished up. Cyndy Garvey. A made-up name. A compromise.

"Gotta go now," said Steve. Then we'd shake hands, and walk away, and never see them again.

It was a hot, early-summer day. But inside the hairdressers', it was nice and cool. The women talked to each other over the whir of the hair dryers. I was almost finished. I looked up from my magazine, into the mirror, and saw almost a twin reflection of myself. I felt like I was seeing things. Slowly the picture came into focus; the woman sitting next to me, talking on the phone and making notations in her appointment book, had the same color hair, the same hairdo. *Exactly.* That's what had confused me.

Suddenly, everything clicked into place: she was the woman on the poster. The Wella Balsam Girl! She was talking about appointments, interviews, wardrobe fittings. I sneaked a peek; her book was completely covered with entries. "Excuse me," I said, when she hung up the phone. "Are you Farrah Fawcett?"

"Uh, yes," she said. Then she looked at me in the mirror, noticed the similarity in hair styles, gasped, and laughed. "Omigosh. We're twins! And you're . . ."

"Cynthia Garvey," I said.

"Good to meet you. Hey! I've heard of you and your husband," she said.

It was nice of her to say that. She asked me when I was due; we talked about babies and cribs and families. I told her, jokingly, that all the ballplayers had pictures of her in their lockers. She chuckled. Half-kiddingly, I told her about my own abortive modeling career.

"Yes, that's where I heard of you," she said.

"Oh, come on," I said. No, she insisted, she'd heard that I'd been taking my portfolio around.

"You should keep at it. After the baby comes," she said. Then, apologizing that she couldn't stay longer, she left. All the women in the salon stared at her, some whispering her name, as she went out.

I looked in the mirror again. Was that "the look" the photographer had talked about? Did we really have anything in common? For a second, the idea of having a life like hers excited me. But then I realized: I had no drive for it; no urge to become a public person.

Still, it would have filled up the time when Steve was away. For the first time in a while, I thought about my old plans for medical school. Then I thought about my baby, and about making a life with Steve. In a few moments, the feeling went away. I went back to my magazine. When my hair was finished, I got up and drove home.

* * *

"Hey! Are you the great Steve Garvey?" A man, well dressed, in his early thirties, was grinning mischievously at us from across the room. We were in the Stadium Club, at a Dodger fan club dinner. "C'mon over," said the man, walking us over to his table. "What's the matter? A big strong ballplayer like you afraid to lose his place? Drag him in over here, honey!"

This was certainly a different approach than we usually got. It was refreshing, a relief. We sat down next to him. The man whipped a card out of his pocket. "Sam Romano, at your service," he said.

Sam Romano was a sketch. He seemed less interested in selling furniture than in making Steve laugh. He kidded him about his height, his fielding, his "All-American" look. He talked to me, too, which was unusual. He asked me where I'd grown up, gone to school. He told us where he lived, which, he joked, was only five Freeway exits from our neighborhood. Another connection: he liked to play tennis, like Steve. "I'll swing by next week. We'll pick you up, and we'll play," said Sam, taking down our phone number.

"This guy's hilarious," said Steve. "A real character," I agreed. Eventually, I came to realize that Steve, who was not witty, liked to be surrounded by admiring friends —usually older men—who were.

The tennis date was a big success, Steve smiling and laughing at Sam's jokes. The Romanos became the kind of friends I'd felt we'd been lacking. I liked Virginia, Sam's wife, very much. She was a brunette about my height, with chiseled features and dark, intelligent eyes. She'd never had a career, but she had two bright children, a daughter and a son. She pulled me aside a few weeks after we'd met. "We feel we know you so well, Cynthia. Steve's a hard guy to figure out. But we feel we know *you.*" Steve got the Romanos tickets and parking passes, and from then on they drove me to the ballgames. Before I got too pregnant, we all went dancing at some of the local Valley discos. I liked to dance; Steve, who thought he looked clumsy dancing, hated it. The Romanos, to my surprise, managed to get him onto the dance floor anyway. "C'mon, Dad! Time to get out there, Jack Armstrong! Get out there and show 'em how it's done," said Sam. And Steve gave it a try. A miracle! A few of the dancers, recognizing him, nudged each other and pointed to Steve; the Romanos beamed at us from the table.

"Thanks," I whispered to Virginia when we sat down.

They could sense, I felt, that I was often lonely. When Steve was on the road they invited me over to dinner, sometimes two or three times a week.

"No, you don't need me over there again," I said, when I felt they were taking pity on me. "Oh for God's sakes!" said Virginia, over the phone. "We've got too much food. We'll see you at six-thirty."

I sat at their kitchen table and watched a happy family in operation: as she chopped vegetables, with short breaks for shouting instructions and good-natured threats to her kids, I'd ask her for advice about baby care. And about keeping a husband happy.

"You just have to be patient. And let them think they have more rein than they really do," said Virginia.

One afternoon, when the house was quieter than usual, Virginia told me that Sam had left her, a couple of years ago, for a younger woman. Then, after a few months away, he'd begged her to let him come back.

"My God!" I said. What if that ever happened to me? "How could you take him back after he embarrassed you publicly like that?"

"Well, what could I do?" said Virginia. "I had two small children. And I still loved him.

"You've just got to be patient."

"You know, Steve, I'm really looking forward to having the baby. And you being there—it's really important that you be there." Steve shuddered. I laughed. I knew that he couldn't stand the sight of blood; he was even a bit squeamish when he cut himself shaving.

His schedule didn't allow us to go to natural childbirth class together, so I hired a teacher to come to our house on Steve's free mornings.

The woman, an expert on the Bradley Method, gave us private lessons. Just for the two of us. It was Steve's job to support my back and guide me through the breathing exercises. I could sense he was uncomfortable about learning those things. Well, weren't all husbands? "Don't worry, Steve," I joked. "You don't have to have the baby for me. You don't even have to watch all the disgusting stuff.

"All you have to do is hold my hand."

"We're gonna get our boy on the All-Star team," said Sam Romano.

"That's great," I said. In order to do that, though, we had to work hard. And bend the rules a little. Well, maybe more than a little: although Steve was having a great year, the All–Star ballots—which were distributed to fans at the ballpark—had been printed up before Steve really caught fire. He wasn't one of the official candidates for the National League team. To elect a nominated first baseman like Tony Perez of Cincinnati or Billy Williams of Chicago, all the fans had to do was punch out a hole on the card. To elect Steve, the fans would have to punch out a hole marked "write-in," get out their pens, and actually write in his name.

Not even Sam believed that enough fans would bother doing that. "So we'll do it for 'em," he winked. During his visits to Dodger Stadium, he became friendly with the people who worked in the team office. He convinced somebody there to give him whole cartons of ballots. He took them back to our house, and we set up an assembly line. For the next month or so, we filled out All–Star ballots. Thousands and thousands of them. For hours and hours. Almost every day, Sam picked up a new carton or two and dropped off the completed cards. I went with him a few times. "But we won't have any ballots left for the fans," said a man in the office, once. "Thanks a lot!" said Sam, cheerfully, on his way out. Once or twice, Steve and I made the pickup. He was careful to park his car out of sight of the fans when he went inside.

Steve punched. Sam punched. In the beginning, I punched. We made sure that his name was written different ways, with different pens. We experimented: how many cards, stacked exactly on top of each other, could be punched out at once? After a while, I got tired of punching, and only came around once in a while—to vacuum up the thousands of little punched-out squares that were flying into every corner of the house. When the operation got into full swing, my brother Chris, who was going to dental school nearby, pitched in and helped us. Also, a young man named John Boggs, a family friend of the Lasordas, who'd become a sort of assistant to Steve.

Apparently, our card-punching primed the pump. Steve's name appeared in the early returns. Other fans got the idea. One day, Steve called me from the clubhouse:

"I made the All–Star team, Cyn!" he said. He was ecstatic.

"Yeah, well. You certainly worked hard enough for it," I kidded him. "Uh, yeah," he said, and hung up.

Dozens of letters and telegrams congratulating him came to the house. There were more articles, all about "the people's choice," than I could clip and paste. In mid-July I was six months pregnant. The weather was hot, sometimes over a hundred degrees outside. My ankles were swollen. I felt ugly.

About a week before the All–Star game, Steve came home with a swollen neck and a high temperature. The next morning, both sides of his neck were swollen. He was a straight line from his ears to his shoulders. He couldn't move his neck at all. He was shivering.

"Have you ever had the mumps?" I asked him. He

shrugged his shoulders. I called his mother in Florida. No, said Mildred, he had never had the mumps. I bundled Steve in a blanket, laid him down in the back of the car, and drove him over to Dr. Woods, the Dodger team physician, in Santa Monica.

"He's got the mumps, all right," he said to me, emerging from the examining room.

"Is he infectious right now?"

"Oh yes," he said.

That was wonderful. How would all the other teams react if they learned that their best players had been infected by Steve Garvey? Not to mention the fact that I was looking forward to having more children with my husband. Mumps made adult men sterile, didn't it?

I took Steve's hand and told him that he might have to miss the All–Star game. He sat up straight, panicked.

"But they wrote me in! They wrote me in!" he said.

Was he hallucinating? " 'They' all sat in our living-room," I told him.

"No. I've got to play. The fans wrote me in!" he insisted.

"Okay. All right, Steve," I said, soothing him. Dr. Woods and I worked out a plan: I took him home and put him right to bed. He missed the next few games with the Dodgers, and that brought a dozen calls from reporters.

"What's wrong with Steve?" they asked. Steve, I'm sure they would have loved to know, was in the bedroom with the lights out, sleeping eighteen hours a day. "Oh, he's just got a badly infected tooth," I lied. "Will he be ready for the All–Star game?" "Oh sure," I said. And that was what they printed.

On the morning of the game, John Boggs, Steve, and I took the last possible flight to Pittsburgh. His neck was still swollen rigid. The doctor had pumped him full of antibiotics, but his fever was high and he was sweating through his clothing. He looked terrible. The stewardess stared at my husband, slumped down in his seat with a blanket around him, and blanched. "He'll be all right.

Just get us some wet towels," I said. He slept most of the flight, and by the time we were in the cab to Three Rivers Stadium, he seemed a little better. Not good, but better.

"Don't be a hero," I told him. He walked groggily into the players' entrance. I waddled to the ticket window and asked for my reserved seats.

"I don't have them any more," said the ticket man.

"You don't? Why not?"

"The other Dodger wives said you weren't coming."

"What?" Several other Dodgers—their wives accompanying them—were in the game. But why . . . ?

"They were here a little while ago, and they said you weren't coming. So we turned them back in for sale."

"I'm not coming?" I said. I pulled out my driver's license and pushed it through the window bars. Looking worried now, he called over his supervisor. He was very sorry, said the manager, wringing his hands, but what could he do now? The section where I was supposed to sit was completely sold out. Would I like some tickets somewhere else?

John helped me huff and puff my way up the ramps. From the third deck, Steve and the other players were tiny. But even up there I could see that he could only look straight ahead. He stood at first base, hands on his knees, staring down the line toward home plate. "What if they hit a ball to one side of him? How will he see it?" I asked John. I didn't mention how scared I was of them hitting a ball right at him. The ball was very hard. And he couldn't move his head.

But Steve played fantastically! He hit a single and a double, driving in one run and scoring another. No errors at first base. The National League fans, meaning almost everyone in the stadium, cheered his every move. Steve was showing everybody what he could do. And the people up here in the cheap seats—the real people—all loved him. Maybe, if they knew who I was, they would have cheered me, too.

After the game, which the National League won, Steve

was named the most valuable player. "Let's go down to the field," said John. By the time we got there, Steve was holding up his MVP plaque for the photographers. Next to him, smiling proudly, were his parents, Mildred and Joe. Where had they come from? I hadn't even known they were in town.

I tried to talk to him. "Steve, how do you feel? Are you weak? You were . . ."

For just a second, Steve relaxed his pose, turned, and stared at me. Get back! said his expression. With his hand, he motioned me to move away, out of the picture. He wants me to go away?

All right, I thought. I watched from the side as the photographers shot Steve and his parents. He looked fabulously happy. I had seen this picture before. In his childhood bedroom in Tampa. With Mom and Dad and little Steve, holding a trophy in front of them.

"Good for you," I told him, grabbing his hands.

"Thanks, sweetie," he said. Sweetie? He gave me a peck on the cheek. A kiss for a female fan. Suddenly I felt timid, my feelings dampened. I followed him off the field.

We were only able to arrange four or five natural-child-birth lessons together. And Steve was still having trouble: when it came time to rub me, to let me lean on him, to touch me, he was awkward. Tentative. Poor Steve, I thought. So shy, so reserved. The teacher was incredulous. I could read her thoughts. This was the confident athlete, the famous, fearless Dodger?

"Come on, Steve, get in there!" she said to him. "You've got to support her better than that!" Steve reluctantly tried again.

"Your husband," said Jerry Kapstein, "is the quintessential all-American boy. He's everybody's sweetheart. And I can show you how to capitalize on that."

Kapstein was a professional sports agent, whatever that was. He'd met Steve at the All–Star Game, and invited us to dinner at a fancy Los Angeles restaurant. About twenty-nine, he looked—well, he looked like Steve. Same height, slightly smaller build, same dark hair, same face. He was a law-school graduate, although he hadn't taken the California bar exam. "Why not?" I asked. "It isn't necessary," he said smoothly, and proceeded to lay out Steve's future.

"You're very hot right now. And your contract year is coming up. I'll negotiate for you with Campanis. I'll work out some tax shelters. Handle your investments. Line up endorsements." He talked about getting Steve more and better press coverage, setting him up for commercials and television work, arranging speaking engagements and high-profile charity work. "Keep your sideburns short," he said. "That's the image we want." There was also, he said, a part in this for me. As Steve's all-American wife.

I laughed nervously. By the end of the evening, Steve had agreed to be represented by him. In a matter of weeks, sporting goods companies like Rawlings, Spalding, and Wilson were bidding for his signature on one of their fielder's gloves. Even more free merchandise flooded into the garage.

The Dodgers made it to the World Series that year. For the rest of the season, Steve was rarely at home. On game days he was so eager to get to the park that he left an hour or two earlier than usual. On most free nights he was doing the things that Jerry Kapstein was advising him to do: giving speeches to boys' clubs, meeting corporate executives, even, if I remember rightly, opening a supermarket or two. Reporters and businessmen called at all hours. For some reason, my name began turning up in the papers as "Cyndy." The autograph name. But why were they using it?

I was too tired to keep up with it all, much less get Steve's attention for more than a few minutes at a time. I knew I had to help him get through the season. And when the time came, he would be here to help me.

Towards the end of my pregnancy, I asked my mother and father to move in with us and help us out. Steve's parents were visiting, too. On October 16, at three-thirty in the morning, my labor pains started. Steve was in Oakland for the World Series. As soon as the second or third contraction ended, I felt an intense longing for him. This was my time. Our time. I called him at his hotel and woke him up.

"Hello?" said Steve, groggily.

"Steve. I'm in labor. Can you catch the next flight?" Silence.

"Come on, Steve. It's happening. I need you."

No response. Nothing. No, Cynthia, I thought. This can't be happening. This isn't happening. Steve *is* coming.

"Steve! Listen to me. It's only a forty-five-minute flight. It's three-thirty in the morning now. Your game doesn't start until eight o'clock tonight."

On the other end of the line, all I could hear was a man —my husband—breathing softly. In and out, in and out. For a second, panic. I fought it down.

He wasn't coming. I put down the phone. "Let's go," I said to my father. He drove me to the hospital.

It was a hard labor. Krisha, beautiful Krisha, came out shoulder-first instead of head-first. Without a partner, I didn't have the heart to do the Bradley techniques.

After eleven hours of contractions alone in my room, an intern came along, put his hand inside me, and turned her around. Finally, at 2 P.M. they gave me a general anesthetic. At 3 P.M. Krisha was born. At 8 P.M. I woke up, and they put my baby in my arms. The doctors and nurses gathered around. "Oh, she's so beautiful," said a nurse.

"Your husband must be so proud," said somebody else.

"He seems like a great guy. Is he coming up here to visit you?"

"We're all rooting for him tonight."

"Hey! The game's starting. Turn it on and let Cyndy watch!"

A wave of sadness swept over me. "Turn it off, please," I said. The nurse clucked sympathetically. Obviously, I was too tired and depressed to think straight. She took Krisha away. I turned my head to the pillow and began to cry.

CHAPTER 13

At midnight they woke me up for Krisha's feeding. The nurse looked unhappy. She broke the bad news to me.

"The Dodgers lost," she said with a frown.

Then she pulled her face into a big smile. "But your husband got three hits! He dedicated the game to his new daughter! And he sent you these beautiful flowers!"

"That's nice," I said.

The next day, the photographers and reporters from the newspapers arrived. They flooded into the room without warning.

"Hold her up, Cyndy!"

"What's her name, Cyndy?"

"This way!"

"Just one more this way!"

"How do you think the Dodgers'll do tonight, Cyndy?"

"What does Steve think about all this?"

I couldn't think of what I was supposed to say. "I don't know," I said. "And my name is Cynthia. C-y-n-t-h-i-a." But by then they were packing up and leaving.

They wired a picture of Krisha and me up to Oakland, and took pictures of Steve, in his uniform at the ballpark, smiling at it.

Surely he would fly down now and see his baby, I thought. Or at least call me. But Steve didn't come. I heard his voice only on the television. The nurse told me that Steve phoned the hospital once, while I was asleep.

On the third day after Krisha was born, after the World Series was over, Steve arrived, but not alone. He came into my room with his parents, Joe and Mildred. Right behind them was a wire service photographer Steve had brought. The man started to pose us for pictures.

Finally, the Garveys and the cameraman left. For a few moments, alone with my husband and new daughter, I watched Steve hold Krisha and gaze at her. We were all together now, I thought. A new family.

"Why didn't you come?" I asked him, finally. Steve just shook his head. He had no answers for me.

After he left, I rocked my beautiful Krisha in my arms and nuzzled my face in her neck. I drank her in. Suddenly, a feeling of love, of protectiveness, swept over me. It almost erased my disappointment with Steve. "It's going to be okay," I said to Krisha. "It's going to be okay."

I loved Steve. I knew that. Yet, I was disappointed in him —in a way I hadn't felt before. He had left me alone, abandoned me, at an important time. For the first time, I think, I began to look at Steve in two ways: as the man I thought I'd married, and as the person I knew he really was. Sometimes the two images fought in my head for dominance. Sometimes, when I was angry or tired, the second Steve won.

That frightened me. I was twenty-four, with a new baby I loved very much, but I loved Steve, too. Where was the man who'd written me those love letters? Who'd spoken about our future together?

After a while, tired of asking myself for answers, I came up with a sort of explanation: Steve *couldn't* come home during the World Series, I told myself. He felt he couldn't let his fans, his twenty-four teammates down. That seemed reasonable, until I remembered how little

Steve and his teammates thought of each other. Then it didn't make much sense. So there must be another reason. But now, I realized, wasn't the time to figure it out.

And didn't we have a family to raise? Krisha was a miracle baby, healthy and happy. She very rarely cried. Together, Krisha and I had a wonderful time. I bought every sort of stroller, carrier, and baby chest-pack on the market. We went everywhere together; she got excited when she heard the car keys jingle. I sang to her as I did the housework. I put on my old Motown records, pulled her out of her crib, and danced with her in the middle of the living room. I talked to Krisha all day long. I told her what our schedule was for the day, and asked if it was all right with her. I read her articles from the newspaper. When she made a face, I labeled her expressions.

"Krisha's angry!" I said. "Krisha's surprised!" "Krisha's worried!" "Krisha's *so* happy!" Eventually, I could call out her "faces" and she'd make them for me.

"Watch this, Steve," I said on one of the few occasions he was home. Krisha made her faces, and Steve looked so proud I froze the moment in my memory. Maybe, I thought, everything would work out. Krisha smiled at him; her look was one of unconditional love.

The first few months of Krisha's life, Steve was gone most of the time. Jerry Kapstein's big plan was getting under way: Steve gave speeches to corporate executives, played in charity tournaments—in short, talked to whoever wanted to talk to him, showed up wherever he was requested.

For company I bought a dog, a cocker spaniel I named Duffy, to keep us company. One day, a skinny thirteen-year-old girl from the neighborhood knocked on my door and asked if she could help with the baby. Her name was Laureen Lang, and she became my baby-sitter and helper —a younger sister, really—for the next five years. That was our family.

* * *

Later that year, one day when we were watching television together, Steve's face came on the screen. He was being interviewed somewhere, about something.

"Dad-dee!" said Krisha, and wiggled out of my lap. She crawled up to the screen and stared at her father. After a few seconds, she crawled around to the back of the set, looking for him.

"Dad-dee?" she said, looking at me in confusion. I gathered her up and gave her a hug. "Daddy's on television, honey," I said. "He's not here. Not right now. Soon."

In February, 1975, I made my own first appearance on television. The Dodgers and their wives were flown to Hawaii for something called the Superteams Competition: the baseball division champions competed against the National Football League's Super Bowl teams. Each team was scored in events like running, swimming, biking, and weightlifting. The whole thing ended with a huge tug-of-war.

It was being taped for ABC. The contest wasn't very serious, but Honolulu was beautiful, and—when Steve wasn't off running or jumping—we actually spent some time together.

I was still slightly puffy from Krisha's birth. Most of the other women, as usual, had nothing to do with me— but even so, I could tell they were intimidated by all the camera crews and cables and famous television commentators. Why? I wondered. All the commotion was interesting. I wandered around, watching the cameramen and the producers. I went over to the control booth to watch the director work.

The next morning, one of the producers gathered the wives together on the beach. "We need just one of you to say how much you like Hawaii," he said. "As a filler, you know?"

The other women shrank back nervously. Some of

Steve and Cynthia at their engagement dinner.

The wedding ceremony.
October 27, 1971.

The reception.

With newborn Krisha Lee in 1974.

In the dugout with Krisha, 1975.

Pregnant with Whitney, 1976.

Front door, 1976.

With Krisha, spring training,
Vero Beach, Florida, 1976.

Tom Lasorda, Steve, and Krisha Lee, spring training, 1976.

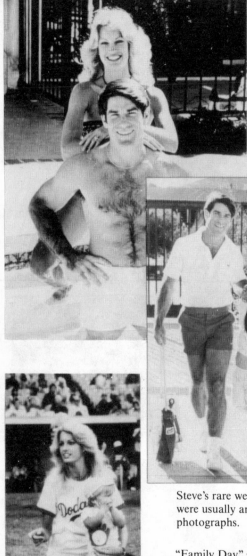

The Calabasas ho●
backyard, 1977.

Steve's rare weekends home
were usually an occasion for
photographs.

"Family Day" at Dodger
Stadium, 1977.

"The Image," *People* magazine, 1978.

The girls in 1980.

Krisha and
Whitney in 1983.

With Regis Philbin, "A.M. Los Angeles," 1981.

"A.M. Los Angeles."

Cynthia Truhan, 1988. (© Harry Langdon)

them began to giggle. Others looked absolutely petrified. To me, it seemed a perfectly simple thing to do. But I didn't want to volunteer. That would set me apart even more.

"Who'd like to do the interview?" asked the producer, a little impatiently now.

The announcer, Keith Jackson, trailing a microphone, stepped up. "Come on, ladies, I need somebody to talk to. Right now!"

I looked around. No one was coming forward. This was ridiculous.

"I'll do it," I said.

"Great!" said the producer. "Which one are you? Okay, let's go."

I introduced myself to Jackson. They brought up a camera, clipped on a microphone, and began.

"How do you like Hawaii, Cyndy?"

What do people say when they're on television? Something like this, I guessed:

"Oh, it's great here, Keith. You know, I haven't been to Hawaii in a long time. I'd forgotten how beautiful it smells. All the flowers. I even got Steve to go swimming with me. And he's not the best swimmer in the world," I said, archly. "You'll see *that* later."

I'd told a joke! Jackson seemed as surprised as I was. But, after a startled half-second, pleasantly so. He shifted gears.

"Well, we'll have a life preserver ready," he said, eyes twinkling.

"Keith," I said, matching his mock-serious tone, "I'm not kidding. You'd better. Steve's swimming is pretty bad. But entertaining."

We talked this way for a few more minutes. Then the producer said "Cut," and came over to take off my microphone. "That was great! You're good!" he said to me. What was? All I was doing was talking. I walked back over to where the wives were standing, and most were looking daggers. Several turned their backs and walked away. But why? I had stepped forward; they had chosen to hang back. What was the problem with that?

The problem was that for the next few days, it seemed, neither Steve or I could go anywhere without a camera crew around. Somebody asked me for a comment every few minutes. A crew did an interview with Steve and me in our cottage; they showed us where to go and filmed us walking, hand in hand, on the beach.

This made a few of the other wives even angrier. One morning, toward the end, one of them came over to me in the lobby, smiling.

"Did you have a good time at the team dinner last night? I know I did."

"What team dinner?" I said. "We weren't invited."

"Oh?" she said. Then she walked away.

By the time the 1975 season started, Steve was a bigger star than ever. Reporters from all over the country had called him for interviews all winter.

Steve loved to talk to the press. There was an article about him, or a television interview with him, nearly every day. And all the articles were similar; Steve had learned to steer his interviews into a few well-covered directions. The same anecdotes and quotes would appear, word for word, in different stories: there was the story of his riding the team bus as a boy in Vero Beach. This led into another story: Steve's dream of always becoming a Dodger. His patience paying off when he was just a pinch hitter. The miraculous move to first base. His squeaky-clean image.

All the stories were admiring, almost worshipful. I worried that the reporters would get bored; that they'd get tired of hearing the same stories. But I was very wrong about that. They never did.

Steve shrugged off my suggestions. He was getting deeper and deeper into his public image. One evening I discovered him in front of the bedroom mirror practicing facial expressions. Sincere. Attentive. Happy. Modest. Bold.

I watched him for a few seconds from the bedroom door. In a way, it was charming. It was nice; I'd caught my husband, for once, in a vulnerable moment. I sneaked up behind him and ruffled his hair.

"Practicing being an all-American, Steve?" I asked him, jokingly.

"Huh? What?" He turned around with a sickly grin. I'd caught him, hadn't I? He forced a little laugh, smoothed down his hair, and walked away. I suppose he was more careful in the future. I never caught him doing it again.

Steve spent very little time with Krisha and me. How could he? On off days, he was usually at a promotion or a speaking engagement. When the team was playing in Los Angeles, his daughter was already asleep when he came home.

I grabbed whatever opportunities I could to bring them together. On Sundays, when the team was home, the Dodgers usually played a day game. It started at one o'clock in the afternoon. It fitted into Krisha's sleeping schedule; three hours before game time, I started getting her ready to go to the game. I washed and dressed her, put her into the cute little dresses I knew Steve liked, and gathered up everything we needed. I filled up my big carrying bag with extra Pampers, sun bonnet, bottle, formula, toys, car seat, Kleenex, blanket. It was an hour's drive to Dodger Stadium; usually, Krisha needed changing in the parking lot before I could bring her in.

Krisha wasn't afraid of the crowds. I was so proud of her! In the big stadium, with the fans milling around and the organ music playing, she'd clap her hands, point and laugh, as if the whole stadium was a big, colorful mobile. A big toy for her.

The Dodgers would be on the field, warming up. I carried Krisha down to the field level, behind home plate,

and waved to Steve. He'd stop throwing to the other
players, come over to the rail near the photographers'
enclosure, put down his glove, and hold out his arms. I
passed her to him. It was wonderful; they looked almost
exactly alike.

It was a heartwarming scene. While the fans smiled
and cooed, Steve—looking handsome and manly in his
clean white uniform—held his daughter for a few minutes. He waved her little arms and showed her off to
Tommy Lasorda and the coaches. Inevitably, the photographers stopped what they were doing and gathered
around, taking picture after picture of Steve holding
Krisha.

Then he handed Krisha back to me. We went up into
the Family Section, where Krisha was more interested in
watching the people in the stands than the little men
running around down on the field. Usually, she lasted
four or five innings before she got cranky. I couldn't wait
for Steve in the Waiting Room; I had to take her home.
That meant that we wouldn't see Steve again; Sunday
was usually "getaway day," when the team packed up
and left on a road trip after the game.

By the time I'd gotten home and put Krisha to bed,
Steve would be on his way. The next morning, in the
sports pages, the pictures of Steve and Krisha would appear.

Surprisingly, with all the demands on Steve's time, our
social life picked up—but in a strange way. We didn't
socialize with couples our own age; instead, Steve became
friendly with a number of big businessmen in their fifties
and sixties. After the games, they came down from their
season boxes and talked to him. They invited us out to
dinner at fancy restaurants like Chasen's and Perino's.
We were always the youngest, by far, at the dinner table.

Steve seemed to enjoy these evenings very much. Inevitably, each evening began with the men grilling Steve
about baseball. This lasted about ten minutes, until the

topic changed to business or politics. Steve had no opinions on these subjects. He sat silently. To cover the silence, I sometimes joined in. The businessmen were pleased, if a little surprised, to hear my views.

Mostly, though, the executives seemed glad to have Steve around. I could sense that he made these older men feel younger. Almost always, they suggested he get together with their advertising men to talk about endorsements. (Sometimes that even included me; my "modeling" career finally began when Steve, Krisha, and I posed with soapsuds on our heads for a shampoo advertisement.) Or to give motivational speeches to their executives. More than once, an executive smiled, shook his head, and said he wished he'd had a son like Steve.

One evening, in the middle of a political discussion, our dinner host turned to Steve. Steve was looking silently absorbed, as usual.

"Our future senator," said the man, pointing his cigar at Steve. That was a joke, wasn't it? But nobody laughed. Not even me.

I tried to fit myself into Steve's schedule. I went with him to his speeches and public appearances as often as I could.

One evening, I left Krisha with Laureen and went to watch Steve give a speech to a local service club. The Romanos were with us, too. Steve was the featured speaker, the main attraction. He was happy, animated, smiling at anyone and everyone who came up to shake his hand.

He was in his element. The master of ceremonies gave him a long introduction: "Most valuable player . . . a true-blue Dodger . . . a fine young man . . . a real role model . . . something to say to both children and their parents . . ."

Steve sat listening, leaning forward, waiting for his cue. When the emcee finished, the applause started and Steve began to stand up.

I reached over to ruffle his hair.

"Do good, hon—"

My hand never reached his head. Quick as a flash—a reflex action—he reached up and stopped my wrist. I saw a flash of anger in his eyes. So sudden was his movement that a bracelet I was wearing flew off onto the floor. Luckily, only a few people sitting near us saw what had happened.

I was too shocked to say anything. Steve was gripping my wrist, hard.

Sam Romano half stood up, alarmed. "Whoa, Steve!" he said. Instantly, Steve realized what he had done. He regained his composure, smiled, let go of my wrist, and walked up to the podium. I barely heard his speech; I stared at the tabletop and tried to make sense of what had happened.

I felt, more than heard, Steve's speech ending. I became aware that strangers were looking at me again. I felt their stares on the back of my neck. What should I say to Steve when he came back to the table? I forced myself to smile.

"Steve must have had his Grade A Vitalis on tonight," I announced, as he sat down. Steve, the Romanos, and the people at the next table laughed nervously. Yet, deep down—no, not so deep down—I knew that something serious had happened.

It frightened me a little. It seemed to me that "real" Steve was being taken over by a made-up image. He wanted to be perfect all the time. As if he was always being watched.

In 1975, the Dodgers as a team were doing badly. In contrast, Steve was doing almost ridiculously well. His batting totals were the highest of his career. At first base he rarely made an error.

He started to act out his self-confidence on the field. From my seat, I noticed that Steve was becoming flamboyant. He didn't just catch the throws to first base: he

began making wide, theatrical sweeps with his glove hand
when he caught the ball. Then, he'd hold the ball over his
head for the fans to see. Sometimes, he'd race in front of
another infielder and made a difficult catch of a pop fly a
teammate could have caught easily.

It was too much for the other Dodgers; even in the
stands, I could hear them cursing him. He was a "show-
boat." A showoff. In the dugout, he sat alone. When he
struck out, some of the other players clapped derisively.
Walt Alston and his coaches stood on the front steps of
the dugout. They pretended not to hear.

In the on-deck circle, while Steve was waiting to hit, he
waved to me, in the stands, with his bat. Sometimes,
caught up in the excitement, I stood up and waved back.
The fans loved it; it became a sort of trademark for Steve.
Night after night, he was chosen as the "player of the
game" and interviewed on television. With each interview came fifty dollars' worth of gasoline and a hundred
dollars in merchandise from Sears. It was an embarrassment of riches. The free gas tickets piled up faster than
we could use them or even give them away to Laureen or
the Romanos. I went to Sears and "bought" their top-of-
the line appliances until there was simply no place in the
house to put another one. Then I started giving them
away, too.

In the middle of the season, the word was passed to me
that the team wives were getting together for a meeting to
decide "how to help morale."

Naively, I looked forward to it. They wanted my help?
I'd be glad to do what I could. Maybe, in the process, we
could clear up some misunderstandings. Maybe, just
maybe, I could build some bridges to the other wives.

The meeting was at Fran Cey's house; I made sure I
got there on time. I dressed Krisha, packed her diaper
bag, and drove across the Valley to her home. Almost all
the other wives were there; they were separated into the

usual cliques. I put Krisha down in the bedroom to sleep, and sat down on an ottoman, by myself.

Patti Sutton called the meeting to order. "We want to talk about," she said, "how we can support the team."

Fine, I thought. But then she looked straight at me. Or rather, six inches to the right of me. "We think Steve and Cyndy Garvey are getting too much attention in the press," she said.

"Too many interviews," said one of her close friends.

"Too many articles," said another one.

Wait a minute! "Is this meeting about *me*?" I whispered to Fran. She just stared at me.

"Well, that's it, then," I said, keeping my anger just barely under control. "I'm going." I stood up, marched into the bedroom, picked up Krisha, her bag, and my purse, and walked right through them to the front door. When I reached to turn the knob, Krisha's bonnet fell off. Nobody made a move to help me. I hooked the little hat with my toe, stood on one foot while I grabbed it with my left hand, stuffed it into my pocket, and left.

As I walked down the driveway, I could feel the sweat on the back of my neck. I unlocked the big Oldsmobile, strapped Krisha in her baby seat, and drove away. My eyes began to fill with tears. I drove home, put my daughter to bed, and cried the rest of that afternoon. When I told Steve what had happened he raised his eyebrows and cocked his head to one side.

"Don't waste your emotions," he said. Don't waste your emotions? Was that the answer? "It's not worth it, Cyn."

"Maybe you're right," I said.

For a minute, just a minute, late one afternoon, I saw the Steve I dreamt about. He was home after a day game, and he had been playing with Krisha in the nursery. I looked in. Steve was sitting there, asleep in Krisha's little rocking chair. His face was relaxed, peaceful. He'd obviously been holding Krisha in his arms when he'd dozed off.

Krisha had climbed down and was playing quietly with Duffy the dog at his feet. Her little wind-up swing, empty, was still playing its little baby tune. I was touched. I think I loved Steve as deeply, that moment, as I ever had. I kept that picture in my memory over the years, and brought it out whenever I needed it. Often, at bad moments, I turned the image over in my mind. It was rare and precious. My family. And I hoped, pushing back the doubts, that it was real.

I had to keep the feeling alive. I started leaving Krisha with Laureen—and a nice older couple I knew—more. I went on a couple of road trips with Steve, following the team to San Francisco, Seattle, the Midwest. He seemed to enjoy my company.

By that time, the rift between Steve and his teammates was apparent to everybody. When the Dodgers visited another city they traveled in two buses; the coaches and reporters in one bus, the players in another. Except for Steve. He rode with the coaches and the press: I sat with him, in the same seat every time, behind Walt Alston and Tommy Lasorda.

By the end of the year I knew I was pregnant again. That was wonderful, but it meant an end to my road trips. Steve, though, kept going around the circuit. Alone, I solved another problem: our address was so well known by then that whole caravans of cars drove slowly by, honking their horns and calling out Steve's name.

"Hey, Steve! Come out!"

"Yay, Dodgers!"

"We're Number One!"

"Come on out!" "Come on out!" "Cyndy, send him out!"

Steve, of course, usually couldn't come out. He wasn't home.

"Can't you get them to stop?" asked a neighbor.

"How?" I replied. We lived on a wide, long street, and

the drivers could just roll by, loop around, and come back for another pass.

One clear winter morning, I saw the answer. On top of a hill in the distance, bulldozers were scraping the ground flat. Surely, the fans couldn't follow us up there? I got in the car and drove over. The salesmen, in a trailer on the site, were glad to see me. I picked out a lot on a cul-de-sac. That would give us some privacy, I thought. Steve left the whole thing in my hands.

"It looks fine, Cyn," said Steve. By early spring they had begun to build our new home.

"Listen, Cyndy," said Fred Claire, the public-relations man for the Dodgers, "could you do me a favor?"

It was the beginning of the 1976 season, and a local show called "A.M. Los Angeles" wanted some baseball wives to interview. Fred had called me and asked me to be one of them.

"Not with those other women, Fred," I said. "They don't like me. You know that."

Silence at the other end. "I, uh, it would be great if you could help me out here. Regis Philbin has asked for you personally. The Garvey name is a big draw. *Please,* Cyndy."

"Oh, okay. As a favor to you, Fred. You'd better watch, though," I kidded him.

I was six months pregnant. I arranged for Laureen to sleep over and take care of Krisha, left the house at 6:30 A.M., and drove to the KABC studios at Prospect Avenue in Hollywood. Lyn Lopes, Patti Sutton, Terri Monday, and Fran Cey were already in the makeup room. They pointedly ignored me.

"What's with them?" asked the makeup woman. I shrugged, and waited outside until they were finished.

We were scheduled to go on near the start of the show. Regis Philbin, the host, was set to interview us. He was a short, bouncy man in an expensive gray suit. His co-host, Sarah Purcell, was nowhere to be seen. We were all led to a semicircular couch. I sat on the very end. I decided to keep my mouth shut, let the other women have the spotlight. Show them I wasn't a publicity hog. Not make them any madder at me than they already were.

I folded my hands on my big stomach. A commercial ended, and Regis began talking to the other wives. I thought, This will be over soon, Cynthia. Just sit back and relax.

"So! What's it like, this glamorous life of a baseball wife?" asked Regis Philbin. His voice was—sarcastic? No, just on the edge of sarcasm. As if this was a big joke we were all in on.

He looked around for an answer. I looked at the other wives. They were sitting rigidly on the couch, obviously terrified. I wasn't nervous at all.

"Oh, it's not that glamorous." Then nothing.

One of the women giggled.

"What's it like to have your husband go away for spring training?" asked the host.

"Oh, it's not too bad."

"You mean," asked Philbin, eyebrows arching, "it's okay for your husband to be gone (pause) *on the road* so much of the time?"

A couple of murmured answers. Philbin tried again. "What do you feed your Big Guy before the game?" A few words about steak and mashed potatoes and gravy. The women looked even more nervous, if that was possible.

From my spot on the end, I saw that Philbin was getting impatient. He leaned forward, cocked his head to one side, and began to rock back and forth. That made me uncomfortable for him. And it wasn't easy to sit still with a beachball in my lap. I leaned back, draped my arms over the backrest, and crossed my legs.

Regis whirled and faced me. "WHAT?" he yelled, mock angrily. "What are you DOING over there?"

Now I *had* to say something. So I did. And for some reason, without even thinking, I began to play his game.

"I'm all right, Regis," I said, in a exaggeratedly relaxed voice. "I'm just sitting here. Having a good time."

"Oh, that's nice. Isn't it, folks?" He looked at the camera in make-believe exasperation. "Well, what've you got over there? A little first baseman?"

"I don't know, Regis, what do *you* think?"

He smiled. I could see the wheels going around, read his mind. This was *working,* he thought.

"Well, what about you, Cyndy? Do you go to every game? Do you live and die with every pitch? Does he go nuts if he doesn't get a hit?"

"Oh no. I just double his dose of chocolate cake."

Regis looked "shocked." Out of the corner of my eye, I could see the other women glaring at me. But it was too late to stop talking now.

"Well, if you don't live and die with every pitch, what do you do for your Big Guy?"

I pointed to my stomach. "Hey, Regis. Isn't this enough?"

I looked past him, to the monitor. With a shock, I looked into my own eyes on the screen. The other women were completely out of the picture. I forced myself to look at Regis. We bantered back and forth about baseball, babies, changing diapers. When the segment ended, the other women glared at me again and stalked off.

"Hey, stick around awhile. We'll have a coffee after the show," said Philbin.

For the rest of the hour I stood outside the set. Just watching. First, Regis interviewed an actor. Then a man named Joe the Greengrocer talked about vegetables. From behind the scenes, the live television show was fascinating. The cameras rolled around without hitting each other, the director gestured wildly from his booth, the assistant producers, most of them young women, got everything set up in time. The pace was hurried, and it looked chaotic, but I could see that everyone knew exactly what to do.

When the final segment was over, Regis took me out to

the commissary. He asked me about Steve, the Dodgers. We talked about our kids.

"You know," he said, suddenly, "if Sarah's ever gone, do you want to sit in?"

"Oh sure," I laughed. That was a joke. Wasn't it? From the smile on his face, it was hard to tell.

The season began. A few weeks later, I took a short road trip with Steve to San Diego. Something strange and uncomfortable happened: one afternoon in the hotel, I got into an elevator. So did one of Steve's teammates, a man who disliked Steve intensely. We were alone in the elevator. He stood right next to me, almost touching. And leered. "Too bad you're pregnant now," he said. The elevator door opened and he walked out.

I was too astonished to say anything. What did he mean by that? He hated Steve, didn't he? His wife hated me. I was as big as an elephant. And he had—well, wasn't he coming on to me? Or had I gotten it wrong, somehow?

After that night's game, I told Steve what had happened. He raised his eyebrow. "Let it go," he said. Then we went back to our room.

A male voice on the telephone. "Hello. Cyndy?"

"Yes?"

"Is Steve home?"

"No, Steve's not home. Who is this?"

"This is so-and-so. I met Steve in Pittsburgh, and he said to give you a call if we were in town. Can you get us any tickets for tonight's game? Good ones, if you can."

This was my daily routine. Steve gave out our home phone number freely: before each game, dozens of acquaintances, business contacts, and absolute strangers would call for tickets.

In the mornings, I wrote down everybody's name, with the number of tickets each one wanted, on a piece of yellow paper. "Here, Steve. Here's the list for the comp sheet tonight," I said, handing it to him as he went out the door. It was Steve's job to write the names down on the sheet posted in the clubhouse. About half the time, he'd lose the list or forget what to do with it. Then the people he promised tickets would start calling at 6 P.M., just as I was leaving for the ballpark.

"We're at 'Will Call.' There are no tickets here!" they'd say angrily. They were furious at me! Then I had to call Billy, the Dodger ticket manager, a nice little old man who loved the players.

"Billy? Did Steve leave his comps on the list tonight?"

"No, Cyndy," he sighed. "Do you remember them?" I did the best I could, and sometimes the people even called back the next day, very occasionally, to thank us. Most of the time, that part slipped their minds.

I had to hand it to them, though, they weren't shy. "Did you have a good time at the game?" I'd ask.

"Yeah, well," they said. "We would've had a better time if we'd had better seats." Then Steve's good friends would ask for four more—or eight?—behind the Dodger dugout, if possible.

"Look," I said to my obstetrician, "I was alone last time. I don't want that again."

"No problem," said Dr. Myers. It was July, the Dodgers were on a home stand, and I was, as he put it, "ready to pop." He performed a procedure that induced labor.

The contractions started the next morning. And Steve was there. He drove me to the hospital. His—our?—arrival caused quite a stir.

"Steve Garvey!"

"Look!"

Doctors and nurses peered curiously at us as we went through the hall. "Hi, Steve!" They wheeled me into the birthing room, laid me down on the table, and gave me an epidural injection. There'd been no natural childbirth lessons this time.

After a minute or two, a smiling face leaned over me.

The nurse. "Does Steve want to be in the room?" Good question.

"There he is. Ask him." She nodded reassuringly and went away.

This time, my labor was surprisingly easy. Only a half-hour later, I was ready. And there was Steve! He was wearing hospital greens and a surgical mask. He stood off to the side, out of my line of sight, watching. Detached. Calm. I was so focused on what was happening that I didn't reach out to touch him. Nor, I realized later, did he come over and hold my hand.

It all happened quickly this time. The doctor held up Whitney. "Look, Steve," he said, "you've got a b—no, a girl. Here you go." Steve held his new daughter for a second, then handed her to the nurse. He went back over to the side of the room. Somebody cut the cord, washed my little baby, and put her into my arms.

Another girl. Just what he had wanted. Steve leaned over, hands behind his back, and gave me a kiss. He took the doctor, a baseball fan, across the street for breakfast at McDonald's.

CHAPTER 14

Virginia Romano was the only person I felt safe to confide in. With her, I felt, I could be Cynthia, not "Cyndy."

When Whitney was an infant, I would feed her while Virginia and I talked on the phone. "I don't think I can keep this up, Virginia," I said. "I don't like posing with Steve. I hate it when he shows the same emotions to strangers in public that he shows me in private. I'm losing who I am. I try to tell him, but he doesn't hear me.

"It hurts, Virginia. It just hurts."

"Try not to worry, Cyndy. Steve is still growing up. He's like most men. This is an exciting time for him. He doesn't have the time, the need, to think about complicated things. Like the things you and I think about.

"When his life slows down, he'll grow into himself."

"I don't know any more, Virginia. I just don't know any more."

In the middle of the next season, something inside me snapped. Steve was off on a long road trip; he hadn't called home at all. Only his fans called. One especially hectic morning, a man who'd been given our number asked for good tickets for an entire two-week home stand. I wrote down his request, hung up politely, and decided I had to leave. To get out. I called the travel agent. I called my brother and left a note for Steve. I packed up the girls' things, got them dressed in their good clothes, locked the door carefully, and left for the airport.

I chose a city that had no major league sports teams. Nobody recognized us. We checked into an oceanfront hotel; I took the girls to the beach in the daytime; we ate most of our meals in our room.

On the beach, I wore my bathing suit and a big floppy hat. I sat on the sand, Krisha and Whitney at each hip. I saw couples, men and women, all around me. Many of the men, on vacation with their wives or girlfriends, were being openly affectionate. They weren't as good-looking or as well built as Steve, but they were holding hands with their sweethearts. They were stroking their hair. Walking arm in arm.

In the late afternoon, we'd pack up and go back to the hotel. There were no calls for me. No messages.

I came back to the same spot every day, just thinking. About my marriage. About Steve. About myself.

After a week, I checked out of the hotel, bought a ticket to Los Angeles, and flew back. Steve had still not come back from his road trip. He arrived a few days later; he was a little less distant than usual. He'd tried calling me at home, he said, and gotten no answer. Then he'd called Chris to find out where I'd gone.

"I had to get out, Steve," I said. "I had to get out."

"So you're back now," he said, evenly.

"Yes. I've been doing some thinking about us. We have to keep some privacy, Steve. We have to keep the people out of the house. And I've decided there have to be some changes made. We have to keep your business calls from coming here. We have to keep the fans away from the house. And you have to be home with us at least one afternoon a week."

Steve thought it over for a second. Would he care enough to try to help us?

"Sounds good," he said. It was, I thought, a start.

* * *

"Hey, Cyndy. C'mon over here and look at this." Steve waved me into the living room. He was sitting on the couch, holding a big piece of cardboard. "The people at Jockey want us to do this for them," he said.

He had recently signed to endorse Jockey underwear. "Do what for them?" I said. I walked over and took a closer look. There were five or six drawings of the same magazine ad: the artwork was rough—but, if you looked closely at the man and woman in the illustration, it was unmistakably Steve and me.

In all of the drawings, the man was standing in his underwear. A T-shirt and briefs. The woman was wearing a white full-length slip—and nothing else. Her hair flowed down to her shoulders. She had her arms around the man.

The funny thing was that the woman in the picture, although she had my face, had a different body. She had bigger breasts, a tighter bottom, better legs. I laughed.

"Steve, I can't do this. I don't look as good as that woman," I said.

He shook his head. "Just think about it, Cyn," he said. Leaving the drawings on the coffee table, he left the room. Could he really be serious?

The next day, after Steve left on a road trip, I propped the pictures in front of the hallway mirror. While feeding Whitney her bottle, I walked over and stared at them.

Steve *was* serious. Should I do this? It would make my husband happy.

But I'd be undressed—in front of millions of people. Inside my head, I heard my father's voice shouting, "What are you doing, Cynthia?" I shuddered. He was telling me I was the bad girl he'd always suspected me of being; I'd become a tramp, shameless.

When Steve came back, I screwed up my courage. "Steve, I can't do this," I said. "I have hardly any clothes on. It's just too much."

He gave me a disgusted, quizzical expression, and

walked away. It was the right thing to do, I thought—but had I missed a chance to please Steve? To get closer to him? After all, we rarely embraced like the people in the ad. Maybe I had driven him farther away.

The man from the New York ad agency had flown out, rented a car, and driven to our house just to meet us. His company was, he said, shooting an ad for Geritol. It was "repositioning the product" to appeal to "younger consumers." The high iron content, he said, was especially good for women. He wanted Steve and me to do a commercial.

"We think you two will be perfect," he said, beaming at us. Steve smiled back. His delight was contagious. Well, why not? I'd turned down the last one, right? I thought. The stuff couldn't possibly be harmful. It was full of vitamins, wasn't it? And I got to keep my clothes on. This time, I signed the contract.

There was no script. I was to read my lines, just one or two of them, off a teleprompter. The day of the shooting, we drove to an old, dark studio in Hollywood. The director, a genial, casually dressed man in his thirties, introduced himself.

"Just be yourself, Cyndy," he said. "That's all we want."

"Well, fine," I said. The camera didn't scare me. They led Steve and me to the "set," which was just an armchair in front of a solid-colored backdrop. "You sit here, Steve," said an assistant. They plopped him into the armchair. "You sit here, Cyndy." They perched me on the arm of the chair next to him. "Just grab him around the neck and look at us," they said. I felt uncomfortable sitting like that. But if that was what they wanted, that was what they wanted.

"Let's do a run-through," said the director.

"Let me see my lines first, okay?"

"Sure, Cyndy," he said. In a few seconds, my words crawled onto the teleprompter:

I MAKE SURE
THAT MY HUNK,
STEVE GARVEY,
EATS RIGHT
AND GETS ALL HIS
VITAMINS AND MINERALS.
TO MAKE SURE OF THAT,
I GIVE HIM
GERITOL
EVERY DAY.

My hunk?

"Okay! Everybody ready! Camera! Sound!"

"We have speed."

"Action!"

The director pointed at me. Smile! "I make sure that my, uh, hunk, Steve Garvey . . ." I trailed off. I just couldn't do it.

The director stared at me. Worried. He came over and took my hand. "What's the matter, Cyndy?"

"Well, everything's okay except that word. 'Hunk.' I don't feel comfortable saying it. Can't I just say 'husband,' instead?"

Now he looked more worried. "Aw, gee, Cyndy. That's the line. It brings out that kittenish quality we like in you."

The "kittenish quality"? I looked at Steve, sitting there. The expression on his face was blank. Neutral.

"Just a second," I said. I grabbed Steve's arm and pulled him into a corner of the soundstage.

"Steve, I can't do this. I can't say that line."

"Do it, Cyn."

"But—"

"Just do it!" he said, in a furious whisper. It was frightening. In only a second, he'd gone from completely calm to the angriest I'd ever seen him in public.

I stepped back, astonished and a little frightened. The moment was hard to deny: Steve was more concerned with what these strangers thought of us than with what I was feeling. That was the bottom line.

"Cyndy!" The director, smiling again, was walking over to us. "Tell you what. We'll do the line both ways. With 'husband' *and* 'hunk.' Then we'll see which one works better. What do you say?"

I looked at Steve. Most of the anger was gone from his face, but his eyes still scared me. He nodded. "All right," I said.

Making my mind as blank as possible, I did both versions. The director was ecstatic. "That was wonderful. You two are great together," he said. He gave me a kiss and shook Steve's hand.

Steve drove us home calmly, as if nothing had happened. Naturally, they used the "hunk" version. The commercial ran for months; it seemed to pop up and embarrass me every time I turned on the television.

"Pretty good, huh?" said Steve, when he saw it for the first time. I didn't say anything at all.

After the Geritol ad, many ad agencies wanted us. They wanted the same thing every time. We did a spot for Swanson's TV Dinners, shot at Dodger Stadium: Steve stood out on the on-deck circle, supposedly waiting for his time at bat. I ran out of the dugout holding his Hungry Man dinner.

"Steve, is this all right for tonight?" I said.

The ad people loved it. We were just what they wanted: Ken and Barbie. The Golden Couple. Steve loved it, too. He seemed to come alive when asked to show affection for me—in public. We kissed and hugged and held hands for the camera.

In "real life," though, things were different. In real life I didn't seem to be getting any closer to Steve. I was still home alone most of the time. Whitney slept next to me in her cradle, Krisha slept in her crib fifteen feet away. I breast-fed Whitney and spoon-fed Krisha. Steve left the building of the new house to me; every few days, I put the girls in the stroller and saw how the workmen were doing at the site.

On game nights, Laureen came in after school to take care of the girls. Virginia and Sam drove me to the stadium. It was nice to sit with Virginia. It meant I wasn't alone among the wives any more, and she would talk about topics other than baseball. After the game, they stood with me in the Waiting Room.

I'd get a meal prepared for Steve when he came home; he'd mark his hits on the calendar and unwind by watching Johnny Carson or a late movie. I'd sit down beside him and grab his arm. After a while he'd yawn, and we'd go to bed. Most nights he rolled over and went right to sleep.

There were more embarrassing encounters with Steve's teammate. At the ballpark, on road trips, this man winked and leered at me. If he found himself alone with me in a lobby or a hotel corridor, he'd reach out and try to stroke my hair. I leaned away from him when he did that; I tried to avoid him whenever I could.

Even more grotesque—and inexplicable—was a run-in with this player's wife.

I had gone on a short road trip to San Diego. I was sitting by the motel pool. She came over toward me with a mean-looking grin on her face. "Oh, Cyndy," she exclaimed. "My husband thinks your blond hair is *so* beautiful." Then she walked away.

I was speechless. This was the first time this woman had spoken to me in months. She hated me. And her husband had told her—what? It was weird. It gave me chills.

"I don't like this. What's going on?" I asked Steve that night. "Just ignore it," he said. Ignore it?

The only place our marriage seemed to really work was on television. That year, all the Los Angeles-based talk shows had us appear. It started with Merv Griffin; his show had invited Steve to be a guest. I went with him to the studio and watched in the wings as he was interviewed. For a few minutes, they talked baseball. The usual questions, Steve's usual answers. Griffin's smile seemed a little forced. He looked bored.

Then, craning his neck, he looked past Steve and right at me. "Say, Steve! Isn't that your pretty wife standing over there?"

What? "Sure is," said Steve, a bit startled by the sudden change in direction.

Griffin pointed at me and crooked his finger. "C'mon out. Cyndy! Let's take a look at you."

Me? No, no. This was Steve's interview. I was just standing there. Nobody ever walks in on a television show from the audience. At least, I'd never seen it happen.

"C'mon. C'mon out!" said Griffin. Now he was waving me in. One of the cameras had turned around and was pointing at me. The audience started to applaud. I looked at Steve. He was leaning back in his seat, a happy smile on his face. I walked in, squinted into the glare of the lights for a second, and sat down next to my husband.

"Wow!" said Griffin, and winked at Steve. "He's a lucky man, isn't he, folks?"

More applause. Now Steve looked really pleased. He took my hand! Now this famous man, Merv Griffin, was asking me the questions.

"Tell me, Cyndy. Does Steve ever help out around the house?"

"Well—yes," I said. Steve had a funny nervous habit. "Before he leaves for the ballpark, he vacuums the living room rug. He says he likes the neat grooves it makes. It's some kind of good luck fetish, Merv."

Merv's eyes lit up. "Ha-ha-ha-ha-ha!" roared the audience. It was good-natured laughter; I realized that, for some reason, these people really liked the idea of a big strong baseball hero vacuuming the carpets. Steve realized it too, and smiling broadly, shrugged his shoulders at them.

"Well, now, Cyndy. Does Steve believe that"—Griffin leaned forward and winked at me—". . . that athletes should abstain from sex before a big game?"

More laughs from the audience. Oh boy, Cynthia, I thought. The truth about our sex life is not what is wanted here.

So I scoured my brain for a TV-type joke. "Definitely not before away games, Merv—I hope," I said.

Oh God. "HA-HA-HA-HA-HA-HA!" went the audience. I'd messed up. I looked at Steve. No! He was laughing, too. He wasn't embarrassed at all by my answer. In fact, he seemed excited by the audience's response.

During the commercial break, Merv patted my hand. "Hey, you know something?" he said. "You can talk."

"She can talk," he said to Steve. Steve beamed. For the first time in a long time, I realized, he was looking at me with affection. But why now?

After that, the talk shows invited us on together. We did our act several times that season. On Merv Griffin again. Mike Douglas. Dinah Shore. Steve even got us booked on game shows like "Hollywood Squares" and "Tattletales."

"Tattletales" was the strangest. Teams of "celebrity" couples were separated from one another and asked ridiculous, slightly racy questions. The object of the "game" was to give the same answer. The problem was: who were we here? Should I answer for Steve and Cynthia Garvey, or the make-believe couple the public thought we ought to be? No, that was too dishonest. I'd tell the truth.

"Would your wife mind if someone painted a nude picture of her?"

Yes, of course I would, I thought.

"No. She's very artistic," said Steve, smirking. Gales of laughter filled the studio.

"Where did you two neck for the first time?"

Neck? I couldn't remember much necking. His apartment, maybe.

"We had a little romantic weekend in a country inn," said Steve.

More laughter. In the green room between shows, though, Steve sat as stolidly as ever. The real Steve was back. Or was he?

"Why did you say that?" I asked him. "Come on, Steve. Why?"

"It's only a game," he said.

That night I was too keyed up by being on television to fall asleep. After I put the girls down, after Steve dozed off, I put on my bathrobe and went out into the living room. The house was quiet. Duffy sat at my feet.

What was going on here? I wondered. It seemed, at least to me, that the only times Steve and I made any connection was when we were in public. A public couple —that was us. Yet, that was make-believe. This was real.

What was real, Cynthia? This marriage? Steve was rarely home—and even when he was home, I couldn't connect with him. Maybe, by making love to me in public, he was telling me he wasn't in love with my private self. Maybe he wanted me to become, in real life, more like "Cyndy."

But that wasn't really me. I *wasn't* the perfect baseball wife, the smiling blonde on the television screen. I didn't even like that person. I was a woman with ordinary needs and desires. I wanted my own life to share with my husband. I had my own thoughts. I had my own plans. Or did I, really?

For the first time in a long while, I thought of the medical school application still lying in my drawer. It seemed such a long time since I'd actually considered sending it in. Before the girls. Before Steve's fame. For a moment, I was filled with the old excitement, the old ambitions. Then I realized who I actually was. Who are you fooling, Cynthia? Too much time had passed. Too much had happened.

I turned on the television and tuned it to a late movie. In an hour or two, my brain numbed, I turned it off. I climbed into the bed beside my husband, and waited for Whitney's morning feeding.

CHAPTER 15

"Hey, Cyndy. Seems you've got a new nickname," said Sam Romano. The four of us had gone out to dinner; as usual, Sam was entertaining the rest of us with his jokes and barbed comments.

"What is it this time, Sam?" I said.

"You're 'The Lovely,' " he said. Virginia and I glared at him. We knew exactly what he meant. "The Lovely" was short for "Cyndy Garvey, the lovely wife of Dodger first baseman Steve Garvey." That was what the sportswriters, when they put me in their stories, almost always called me.

"Shut up, Sam," said Virginia. "That's not very funny."

No, I thought. But he's right. I *was* The Lovely. Cyndy. There was no big moment, no one decision, but by the middle of 1977, I'd thrown myself almost totally into becoming her. It was obvious: Steve preferred Cyndy, the person people saw, that he saw in public, to Cynthia, the woman I was in private. And what good was Cynthia, the "real" me, to anyone? I *was* blond. I *was* a famous baseball star's wife. As far as I could see, I'd done nothing to prove that I was anything more than that, anyway.

My job now, I decided, was to be the best Cyndy I

could be. The more I was like her, the more Steve would pay attention to me. I went with Steve to more of his public appearances, smiling and waving when my name was called out.

The talk shows began to ask me to appear. Not Steve, just Cyndy. My college degree, they said at "A.M. Los Angeles," qualified me to demonstrate exercises for pregnant women and new mothers. I also talked about nutrition and pregnancy. Regis Philbin seemed glad to see me at KABC; I did the pregnancy exercises wearing a jumpsuit over my leotards, with a pillow stuffed over my stomach.

"Are you finished?" asked Regis, on the air. He reached down and yanked out the pillow. "Wheeel!" he said. "You're now a New Mom!" Even the cameramen laughed. One of the talent bookers on "A.M." moved to Dinah Shore's show; before long, I was doing exercises over there, too.

I moved us into our new house on the hill. I wanted the kind of house I thought Steve would enjoy coming home to; I decorated it in blue and rust, Steve's favorite colors. I bought some Leroy Neiman paintings he'd admired. He hadn't told me he wanted the trophy room, the pool room, the office. But of course he did. I was just trying to stay a step or two ahead of him.

I began to pay more attention to my appearance. What should Cyndy look like, I wondered? I had my nails done professionally. I had my hair lightened. I wore more makeup, to look more like I did on television—the "look" Steve seemed to like. When I went to the ballpark, I planned my outfit—Did the blouse set off the pants? Did the purse match the shoes?—in the morning. I started to wear sexy lingerie and perfume, especially on nights he came home late from the Stadium or the road.

We needed, I felt, more interests in common. When he was on the road, I took lessons in golf, tennis, racquetball —every ball sport I could think of. For his birthday, I bought Steve a Jaguar sedan with the vanity license plate

GARV 6. He bought me a huge blue Cadillac, and a personalized license plate that read MY MVP. I stopped reading at the ballpark and, worse yet, in private. It was as if I had turned off a large portion of my brain.

I could see it: Cyndy was a big hit with the public. And, especially when we were *in* public, with Steve.

At the ballpark, fans' heads turned—dozens of them, all at once—when I walked down the grandstand steps to my seat.

We were in even greater demand for commercials and endorsements. I helped organize, and "co-hosted," Steve's celebrity tennis tournament for Multiple Sclerosis. It was a big success. I threw big parties at our new home for Steve's business associates, usually inviting the few Dodgers who were still talking to Steve. In the off-season, and on off-nights during the season, we were always dressing up, leaving the girls with the baby-sitter, and going to one big dinner party or another.

Political fundraisers, charity dinners, "man-of-the-year" awards, corporate conferences. They all seemed to flow into one another. At some, Steve spoke. At others, they just seemed pleased to have Steve and Cyndy Garvey present. Steve accepted almost every invitation, and we always created quite a stir.

Most of the approval, most of the affection I got from Steve was at these affairs. Steve looked wonderful in black tie or a suit. I wore shimmering gowns with plunging necklines, and lots of makeup. As always, the other guests were older men—businessmen—and their wives. We attracted attention from the moment we walked into the room.

"Oh, Cyndy, you're so stunning!" they said.

"Steve! She's just gorgeous."

"Young lady, you're really lucky to be married to Steve Garvey. You know that, don't you?"

"Tell me, Cyndy—what's it like to be married to a superstar?"

To Cyndy, to me, the answers came easily, automatically. "Oh, it's great. Steve works really hard at it, you know. And I really *love* going to the ballpark and watching him play. How many wives can go and watch their husbands at work?"

The other guests beamed. And Steve, I could see, was pleased too. I'd look at him. He'd smile and nod, take my hand. Sometimes, he even hugged me. "Good work," his expression seemed to say. I loved it when he did that. I was pleasing him. I was getting through to him!

At the dinner table, Steve sat silent, smiling and holding my hand, while I kept the conversation going. "What do you do?" I'd ask the strangers at our table. "Where are you from?" "Really?" "Where are you from?" To the women: "How many children do you have?"

Round and round it went. I rarely talked about myself. At the end of the evening, whoever was in charge would thank Steve for coming and invite him to his next event.

"And make sure to bring your lovely wife," they said.

Steve promised. Then we'd go outside, get in our car, and drive home in silence.

Steve was at the very top of the baseball world. Before the 1978 season began, he signed a six-year contract for two million dollars. The money was coming in faster than we could spend or invest it. He made the All–Star team for the fourth year in a row. The Dodgers were also having a good year. Walt Alston had retired at the end of the 1976 season. Tommy Lasorda was now the manager. By the middle of the season, the team was in first place by a wide margin.

It was that year that the fans started to follow us. Before, there'd been a few autograph seekers—a dozen at most—waiting at the players' entrance. Now there were hundreds of them. Mobs of them. They followed us to the car. Every few steps, Steve stopped and gave out autographs.

He loved it. "Hold your programs down, get your pens

ready, don't stick them in my face!" he said cheerfully. He signed slips of paper, pennants, shirts, everything. It would take a half-hour, sometimes forty-five minutes, just to get to our car. When we got in, Steve rolled down his window and kept signing. On my side, people scratched on the window. They seemed to be poor people, mostly, some shabbily dressed. They were in a frenzy—but over what?

"Cyndy, Cyndy! Get Steve to sign this!"

"Please, Cyndy!"

"For my son!"

"¡Señora Garvey!"

"For my kid in the hospital!"

"Cyndy, can you sign underneath?"

"Please! Please!"

"¡Por favor! ¡Por favor!"

Steve was in seventh heaven. Tireless. Usually, I rolled down my window and handed things across to him. But sometimes we sat there for fifteen, thirty minutes. It was hard, almost impossible, to get him to leave.

Finally I went to the Dodgers and asked for help. They assigned us two huge off-duty police officers to keep the crowds in line. When the crush got too bad, I turned to one of them.

"Tony, I'm tired," I said.

"Okay, that's it!" said Tony, pushing the crowd back so we could drive off. Steve handed out the last autograph, smiled, and shrugged. What could he do? It was out of his hands.

On the way home, he played rock music on the radio, the volume turned all the way up. Rarely did he talk to me.

"Do you remember Joan? She passed away," said my mother, over the phone line from Detroit. Her friends were dying. Every month, it seemed, another of the women she'd grown up with was gone. The winters were cold up there. "I want you to move down here with us," I said to my father.

"Can't. The company won't transfer me," he said.

With a burst of assertiveness that surprised me, I looked up the home office of the insurance company he worked for, dialed their number, and asked for the head of personnel.

"Hello?" said the head of personnel.

"This is Cyndy Garvey. Stephen Truhan's daughter."

"Cyndy Garvey? Steve Garvey's wife? The baseball player?"

"Yes, that's right. Listen, my father works for you in Detroit. Is there any way we can work out a deal to transfer him here to Southern California?"

"Southern California?"

"Yes. We live here, and we'd like to buy a house for my parents. Is there any way you can help?"

Pause. "Steve Garvey. Of the Los Angeles Dodgers?"

"Yes."

A longer pause. "Well, uh, Cyndy," he said, "we'll see what we can do."

A few weeks later my father called me, astonished, to say that he'd been moved to the Los Angeles office. In a few months, with Steve's tacit approval, they were living in a house just a few blocks from ours. On Sunday nights Steve, my brother Chris, the girls, and I went over to their house for dinner. My mother served, my father talked. When Anne ventured an opinion, Stephen shouted her down. It was just like old times. Except for Steve.

"How's the team doing? How do you feel?" my father asked him, respectfully. My mother dished him out helping after helping. They all loved him.

The Dodgers made the World Series that year; they played against the American League champions, the New York Yankees. My job was to travel with Steve, keep him company, and keep up the image we'd worked so hard to build. The newspapers helped; they had photographers at our hotel around the clock, shooting pictures of the happy Dodger wives, including the lovely Cyndy Garvey, out on the town and pulling for their husbands. And that's what went in the papers: except that when the photographers went away, so did the other wives. The team planned shopping trips and theater nights for them. As usual, I was simply not invited.

At Yankee Stadium, though, it was different. Worse. I was assigned a seat right in the middle of the wives, between Patti Sutton and Ginger Hooten. It was awkward and awful: they stiffened and recoiled every time our shoulders accidentally touched.

The Series was a disaster for the Dodgers: Reggie Jackson of the Yankees hit almost everything they threw to him and the Yankees beat the Dodgers in six games.

The plane ride home to Los Angeles was torture. Steve and I sat up front, with the coaches. In the back, I could hear the players loosening up, having a few drinks and celebrating how far they'd gotten. They were singing and laughing. Even though they'd lost, even though they'd been unlucky, they knew they were young and healthy and damned good ballplayers.

Where we were sitting, the cabin was dark. The coaches sat slumped in their seats. Tommy Lasorda poured drinks out of his briefcase—it had a hidden spout on its bottom edge.

"Ya want a drink, Garv?" he said, turning in the seat ahead of us and holding up his glass.

"No," said Steve. He didn't say much more on the five-hour flight. Every now and then a sportswriter would kneel respectfully beside us to get a quote. Steve obliged every one of them. "Tough game," he said. "That Reggie was amazing." "Don't worry, we'll be back next year." Then the writers went back to join the party.

When we got back to Los Angeles, a small crowd of fans was there to greet us. All the passengers on the plane pulled themselves together and got off. As Steve gave out autographs, the other players and their wives paired off.

"You want a ride?"

"Need a ride?"

"Yeah, sure."

"No thanks."

Nobody talked to us. I held on to Steve's arm and we went home alone.

Late that year, Regis Philbin called me at home. "Can you sit in for Sarah for a couple of days?" That meant co-hosting. Not guesting.

"Uh, I think so," I said, anxiously. "It'll be fun," said Regis, as if this was the most natural, most obvious arrangement in the world. I shared the big news with Krisha. "Your mommy's going to work on television," I said as I pushed her into her playsuit. She waved her arms and laughed.

Before the big day, I arranged for baby-sitters to show up at six in the morning. The night before, I had received a packet of information on the guests who were scheduled. Each guest had a segment. Each segment had its assigned length. I left the house at 6:45 A.M. and got to the ABC studio an hour later. "Hiya, Cyndy!" said the guard at the gate. As if I really worked there.

And I wasn't nervous. No, not at all! The producer, a nice woman named Ann Reddy, walked me through Studio 52. "This is 'home base,'" she said, pointing to the couch. "This is the kitchen set. This is the open area for exercises." I nodded, and kept nodding. Yes, I knew about the red light on the camera. I knew most of the floor manager's signals for "cut" and "stretch" and "wrap it up." And that was it? "You'll be fine," said Ann, and pushed me into the makeup room.

And I made it through. At 9 A.M., Regis introduced me. We started bantering about baseball and children. I can't remember a word of it. Then the guests: lots of guests. Soap opera stars. A man from the school district.

Authors. Chip Carter, the President's son. Albert Brooks, the comedian. Home base. Kitchen. Commercial. Home base. Exercises. And back again.

Chip Carter, I remember, was pushing some kind of antipollution program. The man from the school district talked about busing. Albert Brooks was our "guest chef." He made . . . cereal. "This is a real gourmet dish, Cyndy. You've got to get the mixture exactly right." He made an elaborate show of pouring Rice Krispies, then corn flakes, then Frosted Flakes, into a big bowl. *"Voilà!"* he said, triumphantly. The man was hilarious; I collapsed in laughter on the kitchen counter. But that was okay! One of the cameramen made a circle with his thumb and forefinger.

Regis teased me all the way through. "Take us out, Cyndy," he said, pointing to my line—WE'LL BE RIGHT BACK AFTER THIS MESSAGE—scrolling past on the teleprompter. I breathed in, opened my mouth to say it—

"Oops! Too late! She missed it! It's gone now," said Regis. He turned to the camera, shook his head with mock anger.

"Folks, that's the difference between working with a seasoned professional and a well-meaning amateur," he said. Another time he got on me for talking too fast. "Wait! Stop!" Another turn to the camera. "Does anyone out there understand what she's saying? You're talking faster than a Don Sutton fastball. *Please* slow down!"

But when the commercial came on, he patted my shoulder before he got up to leave. "We're working," he said.

I remember that. Also, Regis walking over to scream at the associate producer when a segment didn't go right. Then, a few minutes later, hugging and kissing her and making an elaborate show of forgiveness.

But mostly I remember a wonderful surprise: that when I asked the guests a question, they answered me. They talked. They were happy to! Words and words, sentences and sentences, paragraphs and paragraphs. No silences, no blank spaces. How long had it been, I realized with a shock, since anyone had talked to me like that?

I listened carefully, gratefully. Then I asked them another question. And miraculously, they kept talking.

At the end of my second day a tall, very Italian-looking man came down to the set. Unlike all the casually dressed crew members, he was wearing an expensive-looking gray suit. "Oh my god!" said Regis, rolling his eyes and throwing up his hands. "The Big Man. He never comes down here!"

It was John Severino, the KABC station manager. "Well, it looks like this is going to work out," Severino said to me.

"Thank you," I said. I wondered what, exactly, he meant by that. But I didn't have the courage to ask him.

CHAPTER 16

I didn't work on television again for a year and a half. That seemed perfectly normal: after all, despite the excitement I'd felt, despite the nice things they'd said to me at KABC, I wasn't a television performer. I was Cyndy Garvey, wife of Dodger first baseman Steve Garvey.

It was 1978. Steve was twenty-nine. He made over two hundred hits that year; he was named to the All–Star team for the fifth straight season. For the third year in a row—and this would become more significant later—he played in every game, all one hundred sixty-two on the schedule.

He was a guest star on "Fantasy Island."

The Dodgers won the National League pennant again, beating the Phillies; but they lost to the Yankees in the World Series again. The public appearances and the endorsements and the magazine stories and the fans and the interviews and the charity tournaments and the road trips were more frequent, more important than ever. In print, some of the reporters were calling us "Mr. and Mrs. America." In private, I saw Steve even less than before: the pretty pictures in the magazines of the Garvey family in its dream house were as big a fantasy as anything on television.

My plan wasn't working. Being Cyndy wasn't enough

to break through to him. His calls from the road were getting less and less frequent. Even when he was in town, weeks went by between lovemaking. Between *conversations*. Mostly, I talked to the girls.

I had them both in preschool exercise classes. I was so proud of them! In ballet school, Krisha was the resident nonconformist: I watched her, smiling, through the window; when the teacher lined up all the little girls at the barre, she danced to the rock-and-roll music she heard in her head.

At home in Calabasas, we all danced. At least once a day, Krisha looked at me solemnly and said, "Time to boogie!"

"Yes! Right now!" I said, and tuned the radio to the loudest rock station I could find. All three of us joined hands and danced in circles in the living room, until we dropped, giggling, to the floor. Wonderful moments with my family. Except, I realized when the music stopped, that something was missing.

Even when he was home, Steve stuck to his strict routine of silence. I found myself . . . *touching* him, reaching over nervously to grab his arm or his leg when he was eating or watching television. He didn't seem to mind that, but he didn't reciprocate. We slept back-to-back, not touching. With his beautiful body just inches away, the longing for him—for someone—was intense. And stronger all the time. I began to have trouble sleeping; over-the-counter sleeping pills didn't help. Many nights, with Steve sleeping beside me, I lay awake for hours. At two or three in the morning, I'd go out into the living room and sit with Duffy the Dog. I read, or watched a movie, or played the piano softly. I let Cynthia come back until the sun came up. Then I went back to work, becoming Cyndy.

One afternoon, gripped by some weird burst of energy, I turned the radio up full-blast and waded into Steve's closet. It was filled with clothing, most of which he got from the manufacturers for free. First, I dumped everything onto the floor. Then I rearranged all his clothes: first the tennis clothing, all the white shorts with the other white shorts, all the pink shorts with the pink shorts, all the navy shorts with the navy shorts. Then, next to them, the white tennis shirts, the pink tennis shirts, the navy tennis shirts. Then, all the right dress shirts and ties with the right sports jackets and slacks and shoes and socks. Complete outfits! All ready for him.

The next day, I went to Robinson's and bought every men's cologne they had, so when he came home, he'd be able to choose the ones he wanted. I arranged them on his bathroom shelf.

When Steve came home, I showed him what I'd done. "That's nice, Cyn," he said. Then I fed him the chocolate cake I knew he liked; then I brought out the girls to say goodnight to their father, and put them to bed.

This was also the time of Polly Berger. Polly Berger was a Dodger fan, a woman around twenty-eight or thirty—it was hard to tell exactly. She was short and very overweight, with thick eyeglasses and dirty, unkempt blond hair. She shuffled along the ramps and aisles of Dodger Stadium wearing a blue Dodger warmup jacket and holding a beat-up old radio to her ear. She was a Dodger season-ticket holder. She was at every game; in the front of every autograph line. Everybody knew her. She was a "character": she "loved" Steve and hated me.

She was mentally disturbed. I was terrified of her. The year before, she'd begun writing love notes to my husband. They were scrawled in black and red ink. "I love you, Steve." "If you were with me, you'd be the greatest ballplayer in the world." "If you could just get rid of Cyndy, you and I could be together."

Now, when I walked out of the stadium with Steve, Polly looked at me with an expression of pure hatred. Then she yelled, "Steve, Steve, Steve, Steve, Steve! I love you! Steve!", holding out the millionth piece of paper to sign. What scared me the most was that she always held a fistful of sharpened pencils. Would she poke Steve's eye out? Mine? At that time, Steve had the habit, in public, of kissing women fans on the cheek. One time, he kissed Polly.

That night, she blocked our way into the car. As Steve stood and signed autographs, she blocked the driver's-side door-handle with her body, trying to get his attention. That didn't work. The next day she blocked my side. The guards didn't see her; they were busy pushing the crowds back.

"Steve, I can't get into the car," I said. Frighteningly, Polly was waving her pencils in my face. There was nowhere to go. The crowd blocked any escape. Steve didn't hear me.

I started to panic. "Steve, I can't get into the car!"

He looked up. "Polly, we've got to go now," he said, in a matter-of-fact tone.

"Okay, Steve," she said, sweetly. Steve looked at me, smiling slightly.

One afternoon, when my mother was watching the children at our house, Polly showed up on Park Vicente—From where? How?—and walked in circles around our cul-de-sac, calling for Steve and yelling curses at me. My mother, terrified, kept the girls inside and locked all the doors and windows. I called the police when I heard the story.

"Did she physically menace your mother or the children, Mrs. Garvey?"

"No."

"Well, there's nothing we can do."

There was nothing anyone could do. This was just one of the things that happened, people told me, when you become "a public figure."

The letters kept coming. I looked for them in the piles of fan mail that Steve brought home. "Let's do away with

Cyndy," scrawled Polly. I began to scan the crowds at the Stadium for her. I could spot her a mile away. She was always there. After one Sunday day game, she attacked me and my children.

We were headed down the escalator from the Family Section to the Waiting Room. I had Whitney in my arms and was holding Krisha by the hand.

Out of the corner of my eye, I spotted a streak of blue coming down the escalator. Something hit me, and I lost my balance. Suddenly, we were falling down the last eight or ten steps to the bottom. I held onto Whitney, but Krisha slipped out of my grasp. We were sprawled at the bottom of the stairway—Krisha lying ten feet away from me. I looked up, and saw Polly running down the ramp ahead of us.

Krisha started crying. I got off the floor and went over to her. She hadn't hit her head, thank God; only her elbows and knees had been hurt. They were cut and bleeding. So were mine. Whitney was all right. It could have been worse.

It could have been worse! Now, as the pain started to hit me, I was furious. I began crying, more out of frustration and anger than injury. I stopped an usher. "Please help me! That woman has hurt my children!"

"I didn't see it, Miss," he said.

I grabbed my children, and pulled the usher down with me to the players' entrance. There was Polly, leaning against the wall and staring straight at me. I turned around. The usher was gone. There was nobody else to help us. For fifteen, thirty minutes, we stood there, waiting for Steve to come out.

He came through the door, and, as usual, began to sign autographs.

"Steve! We've got to do something about *her* over there!" He finally looked at me. I was a mess.

"Look!" I rolled up my sleeve. My arm was bruised from forearm to shoulder. "Look at my shins. Look at Krisha!" Then, finally, it sank in. Without looking at

Polly, Steve stopped what he was doing and pushed us out the door. Instantly we were outside, going to the car, and I was explaining to Tony and Bob what had happened. They hustled us to the car, Steve signing autographs as he walked.

We drove away. Leaning over into the back seat, I dabbed my daughter's wounds with a piece of Kleenex.

"Steve, you've got to do something about that woman."

"Yeah. I will, Cyn," he said grimly. But, when I asked him the next day and the day after, he confessed that he'd done nothing.

For several weeks, I stayed away from Dodger Stadium. Then I went to Peter O'Malley, the Dodgers' president. "Peter, there's a fan who is terrorizing Steve and me. Steve might be able to handle it, but I can't." Peter told me that they would tell the ushers and security guards to keep an eye out for Polly and instruct them to keep her away from me.

Afterward, when I walked down into the family section, Polly glared at me from behind a screen of blue-coated ushers. I tried not to look up. She was there, eyes full of hate, holding onto her sharpened pencils. For autographs.

Something terrible was happening to me.

Inside, in private, the lovely Cyndy Garvey was beginning to unravel. I could feel it, see it. I was sleeping less and less; I lost my appetite and began to lose weight.

As if that weren't bad enough, Steve's relationship with his teammates got out of control again. Late that season—even as his team was heading back to the World Series—he went through the worst experience of his career. It was a shock to me: even though most of Steve's teammates hadn't been friendly with him for years—on the Dodger bench, he sat at least ten feet away from any other player—I thought he had arranged his life so he could ignore them. I was wrong. And, in a way I still don't fully understand, I was involved in what happened to him.

I was with him that day, August 20. The Dodgers were in New York to play the Mets; I'd gone along with him on the road trip. After the game, I went down to the Shea Stadium locker-room exit. As usual, I waited for him. No Steve. Not after thirty minutes, forty-five minutes, an hour. "Where's Steve?" I asked the players as they came out. For some reason, none of them would look me in the eye. They shook their heads, shrugged their shoulders, and walked away. Something was wrong.

Very wrong. Could he have been injured? But I'd seen the whole game. Steve was fine. He'd waved at me and signaled to meet him downstairs, as usual. At five-thirty, Steve came out. He was wearing a big, wide-brimmed hat that he owned pulled low over his eyes. He had the collar of his sports jacket turned up. *He* wouldn't look at me, either!

"Hey, what's going . . ."

He grabbed my arm and yanked me through the door. The two team buses—one for the coaches and reporters, the other for the players—stood outside. He headed for the coaches' bus, paused, and then yanked me in the other direction. The players' bus? Steve didn't ride with the players.

"But . . ."

"Just get on!" he said. He pushed me up the stairs and through the door.

It was the first time I'd ever been in the players' bus. The players were startled to see us: as I stood at the head of the aisle, they stopped talking and, every one of them, gaped in astonishment. The moment is frozen in my memory: all the players—the black ones grouped together in the rear, the white ones up front—just staring. Silent. The only sounds came from their radios. A strange mixture of country music next to me and soul music farther back. Stereo.

Then Steve was beside me. He pushed me into a window seat and slumped down next to me, hiding his face in his hand.

"What's going on?" I asked, loudly. In the relative silence, my voice carried through the bus.

"Ssh, ssh. Be quiet. Ssh." he said. I pulled his hand away and looked at his face straight on.

Horrible! It looked like someone had attacked his left eye with a paring knife. I couldn't make out the iris or the pupil or the white of his eye. All the blood vessels had burst, and all I could see was blood, bright red. There was a huge bruise around the eye, too.

"What happened?" I gasped, starting to panic.

"Nothing."

"Nothing? Nothing?" I stood up in the seat and yelled down at him. "We're flying to Montreal. You might have a detached retina. You can't fly like that!"

Steve yanked me down. I bounced back up. I was trembling, out of control.

"WHAT HAPPENED?"

That did it. Steve winced, and looked at me with disgust. But there was only one way to stop me.

"Don Sutton and I got into a fight," he said, nearly whispering.

A fight? He hurt his eye like that in—a fight?

"That's it!" I said, loud enough for everybody to hear me. "We're getting off the bus. I've had it with this team! They don't care about you!" I grabbed his sweater and tried to step over him, to pull him off the bus with me.

He pulled me down. "It'll be fine, Cyn," he said, trying to quiet me. Now I realized I was shaking. And crying. I couldn't stop. And the radios had gone silent.

"Don Sutton? Don Sutton did this to you? Why, Steve? Why?"

"We had a fight in the locker room over the article in the Sunday paper," said Steve. I vaguely remembered it; Sutton had called Steve "a total Madison Avenue hype." Or something like that. "I confronted him over it," he said. "It got out of hand and then he brought up your name."

"My name? What did he say?"

"Never mind," said Steve.

"No! What did he say?"

"Never mind," he said, and just turned away.

Suddenly, the rush of anger and adrenaline ended and I was very, very tired. I slumped into my seat and watched the scenery go by. In Montreal, as soon as we arrived, I took Steve to an eye specialist. They taped his eye shut and gave him medication. "You're lucky it wasn't worse," the doctor told me.

The fight was big news in the papers for weeks; but Steve was just as popular on the banquet circuit as ever. That winter, I got a call from John Severino at KABC. I took it on the kitchen phone. "Sarah Purcell's going to be away for a while. Can you come in and do a week with Regis?"

"Sure," I said. I was no more a television star than before, but it was a good change, a lark. The people there were glad to see me, and Regis and I worked as well together as before.

The authors and soap-opera actors came through as smoothly as ever. I had fun with Regis; he was a Notre Dame graduate, and on the morning his team played Southern California in basketball, I wore a USC cheerleader outfit under my dress. In the middle of our opening segment, while Regis talked, I took off my outer layer. While the soundman played a tape of "The Trojan Fight Song," I led a cheer for USC.

Regis' eyes widened with pleasure. A few days later, Regis surprised me by sneaking Steve onto the set. Steve rushed onstage, brandishing a baseball bat, in the middle of our opening segment.

"Okay, Regis! I'm tired of you fooling around with my wife all week," he said.

Regis wasn't fazed a bit. "Oh, *he's* here," he said sarcastically, straight into the camera.

Steve was in fine form himself. He sat down on the couch next to me and presented Regis with his bat.

"I thought you might need this," he said, "for defense against killer tomatoes and blond co-hosts."

Steve and Regis bantered for a few minutes. ("Didn't you meet Cyndy at Michigan State, where you were a football star and she was a cheerleader?" "No, Regis, *she* was a football star and *I* was a cheerleader.")

Finally, he got up to leave. "I've gotta go now. Gotta go vacuum!" said Steve, rushing offstage as abruptly as he'd arrived.

"I thought he'd never leave," said Regis, in mock exasperation.

I giggled.

On another show, a makeup artist demonstrated his beauty ideas by putting light "daytime" makeup on one side of my face and heavy "evening" makeup on the other. "Which side do you want off?" he asked me during the commercial. "Leave 'em both on," I said, grinning.

"Okay," he laughed.

Regis loved it. All through the rest of the show, he raced from one side of me on the couch to the other. He talked to "Daytime Cyndy" in a normal voice. For "Evening Cyndy," with her shiny red lipstick and thick black eyeliner, he lowered his voice and whispered sweet nothings to me.

"Baby, baby, baby!" he said. Even the cameramen laughed at that.

And everybody involved with the show, I was thrilled to see, would still answer my questions. They listened to me! They talked to me so much it made me giddy with pleasure.

Except there was one question nobody would answer. "Where's Sarah?" I asked. "When's she coming back?"

The crew members, obviously uncomfortable, would mumble something incomprehensible and walk away. Something was wrong with Sarah Purcell. But what it was I couldn't figure out. After a while, I stopped asking.

"Where will you be next week?" asked Frank Kelly, the show's producer-director, on the last day of my stint.

"Why?" I asked.

He wouldn't tell me. About a week later, Regis called me at home and asked me to have coffee with him. The next morning, I drove in and met him after the show. Sarah Purcell was still not back. Another female guest host was working with him.

We went to the commissary, carried our trays to our seats. Regis leaned over the table, looked sideways at me with that bad-boy grin, and sighed impatiently.

"Well, Cyndy," he said. "Do you want this job or what?"

CHAPTER 17

D id I want the job? Yes and no. On some level, just below the surface, I knew that my brain—Cynthia's brain—was turning to mush. And that I would have to find someway to use it, or go mad.

But if I did take the job, I realized, I'd be away from the house for many hours each day. Who would take care of Krisha and Whitney? Who would give them their total attention?

And who would watch out for Steve, make sure his needs were met? I still half-believed—I still made myself believe—that I could finally reach the gentle, loving part of Steve. So I wanted everything perfect, everything correct. Any mistakes I made, any damage I caused, would reflect on my fitness as a mother. As a wife. And would justify Steve's going away, pulling back, retreating into his career even further.

The thought scared me. It was dangerous even to consider it. I called Regis at KABC and told him thanks, but no.

"Aw, c'mon!" said Regis, cheerfully. "Come on and *do* the show. We'll have fun. Come on, come on! What are you hedging about?"

By then, I knew that Sarah Purcell had left the show permanently. The next day, John Severino called to talk me into signing.

"I don't think I can do this, John. I've got two toddlers at home, and one is just starting to walk. And I live so far away. To get up that early—"

Casually, airily, he cut me off. "Come into the office tomorrow," he said. "I want to show you something." Then he hung up.

John Severino's office was huge and wood-paneled. As I walked in, he pushed a button on his desk. The big wooden door closed behind me.

"Look at this," he said. On separate television sets behind him, he was playing two tapes simultaneously. One showed me, pregnant with Whitney, as a guest on "A.M." The other, of me co-hosting, was recent.

"Look, Cyndy!" he said. He turned to face the monitors. "I've kept the first tape ever since you came on. You're thinner now, and you're more comfortable on camera, but you're the same person. You're you. We like that." He turned to me.

"Cyndy, I could see it from the start. You are a natural. We want you."

"I don't know, John," I said. I told him again of my misgivings. He brushed them aside.

Steve's theatrical agent, a nice, middle-aged man named Norman Brokaw, called me. "You should do this job, Cyndy," he said. "You've got a brain—and you can use it."

A brain. They wanted me for my brain. The words excited me; for the first time since I'd given up the thought of medical school, I could feel myself—the non-Cyndy part of myself—being challenged.

I was wavering. One morning, just as an experiment, I hired a baby-sitter and made the drive into the station. It took an hour. I'd have to leave the house very early in the morning.

All right. Fighting my guilt feelings, I made serious inquiries about a full-time housekeeper. I decided to ask

Steve; let him come right out and say whether he wanted me home for him. If he did, I'd turn down the job.

It was hard to find the right time. The truth was, with his schedule, it was hard to find any time. Finally an opportunity presented itself: on the way home in the car from a preseason Dodger publicity function, I tried to put the question to him just right. Except that there was a sports call-in show on the radio, and Steve was engrossed in it all the way back from Dodger Stadium. They were talking about him.

I waited. After the show moved on to other subjects, I snapped off the radio. Then I put my hand, nervously, on the gearshift lever.

"What do you think about this job for me?" I said, hesitantly. "Do you think I can . . . do you think I should . . . do you think it would be all right if I did the show?"

Steve took his hand off the wheel and patted mine. He turned to me and smiled.

"Do what you want to do," he said. Then he turned the radio back on.

I decided to try to do the best I could.

Norman Brokaw negotiated my contract; it was for sixty-five thousand dollars a year. There was a clause in it— "We thought you'd want this," they said—that let KABC drop me if Steve was traded to another city.

I got very lucky and found Priscilla, a single mother, small and dark-haired, with three children of her own. She lived only two miles away. I was still nervous, but I felt relatively confident that I could trust my girls with her. She knew the neighborhood and who belonged there and who didn't. I told her about Polly. I told her not to identify the children to strangers. She understood.

When the children were taken care of, I went to work at the station full time. After a few weeks, my routine was set: every weekday morning my alarm rang at five-thirty; I got up, being careful not to wake Steve. Usually, he'd have come in late from a game the night before.

I'd go to the kitchen, the part of the house farthest away from the bedroom, and get ready for the day. I scanned the *Los Angeles Times* and the *Herald-Examiner*, started the girls' breakfasts, and packed their lunches. At six forty-five, on the dot, always, Priscilla arrived. At seven I woke up the girls. They were wonderful; totally unfazed by Mommy's new job. They'd rub their eyes sleepily, toddle downstairs, and we'd talk while I got dressed in my skirt and blouse and stockings. My "TV clothes," the girls called them.

I'd leave at seven-thirty. The show aired from nine to ten in the morning. Depending on whether we were doing any extra taping that day, I'd be home as early as noon or as late as two-thirty.

The girls would be home from preschool by then. I'd say goodbye to Priscilla, change into jeans and a T-shirt —my "Mommy clothes"—and do the grocery shopping and the dry cleaning and the banking and whatever chores needed to be done. Sometimes, but not as often as before, I'd feel energetic enough to call the babysitter and drive into Dodger Stadium for a game. I'd take the manila envelope, filled by the producers with books and magazine articles and research material for the next day's show, and read it during the game.

Steve and I were driving home in separate cars by now. When the game ended, I'd leave the Stadium immediately. Before I went to sleep, I'd sit up in bed, a yellow legal pad propped up in front of me, writing down questions to ask the guests the next morning. Sometimes, but not usually, I'd hear Steve coming home in the middle of the night. He'd leave the house for the ballpark at ten-thirty the next morning.

The feelings of guilt, the idea that our family would fall apart if my concentration wavered, were always in the back of my mind. Most days, I called Priscilla from the station to check up on the girls. I kept track of Steve's whereabouts as best I could.

But between the worries, a wonderful thing was happening: I was beginning to fall in love with my job. My work! It was the same work as when I was guest-hosting, except now it was . . . *mine*. The guests, the books, the interesting people came at me in an unending stream. Five days a week, four weeks a month: politicians, actors, writers, doctors, psychiatrists, lawyers—and again, overwhelmingly, *they all wanted to talk.*

It was like water to someone dying of thirst. Every day, I saw something new: cleverly double-talking senators and congressmen; writers pushing their books— some interesting, some silly; famous performers who were witty, entertaining. Like Burt Reynolds, for instance: after he mentioned in his interview that he'd like to get married, he agreed to entertain "proposals" from female callers. We sat in front of the camera. I punched up the phone lines.

"I could make you really happy, Burt," joked the woman on Line One.

"You look like you need someone to take care of you," said Line Two.

"I'm married, but my husband's at work, Burt."

"I want you to come over to my house right away."

"Hey! You sound nice," said Burt. "Where do you live?" His eyes narrowed with make-believe sexiness. He took a sip of his coffee.

"Um, how old are you, caller?" I said.

"Sixteen."

Burt Reynolds choked, his eyes bugged out, and he spit his coffee across the room. It was hilarious.

There was a famous person to talk to every day. Some were "real"—they acted out their image in front of the camera, but during the commercials, before and after the interview, they deflated, became themselves again. They talked calmly and normally to me about their lives, their background, their children.

Some celebrities, on a long tour to push a movie or television show, or dragged to the studio by their publicist, looked like they were in a coma when they arrived in the studio—but snapped to life when the red light went on.

"Do you regret never winning an Emmy?" I asked a well-known soap-opera star.

"Yes, I do," she said. And then she burst into tears!

She cried until the red light went off. Then, during the commercial, she turned to me, smiling. "Did I do that okay?" she asked, cheerfully.

And then there were the "ordinary" people. We called them civilians. They were social workers, men and women from Los Angeles-area charities who struggled to get their heartbreaking stories out—and get some help with the problems they were fighting—in the five minutes they were on camera.

Many were painfully camera-shy. Some were so nervous that I could see their hands trembling. When the camera cut away from them I patted their hands to reassure them. "You did great," I'd say, as the production assistant unhooked their microphones and led them away.

I was learning, learning. And most importantly, most excitingly, there were people, friends around, to help me. I was part of something worthwhile. A team.

I soaked it all up like a sponge. "Hiya, Cyndy!" Jimmy, the guard at the ABC gate, would shout as he checked my name off on his clipboard.

"Hey, you made it!" my makeup woman, Sunday, would say as I came in at eight-thirty. She'd kid me good-naturedly about my ridiculously long commute. We'd sit and have a quick cup of coffee; I started my makeup and, while she finished me off, Ann Reddy would come over to talk to me.

Ann Reddy was my producer; she was also, I realized

after the first few weeks, a wonderful new friend. She was unmarried. A career woman. She was my height, had a wonderful smile, and long blond hair that—to her eternal, good-natured despair—had a mind of its own. In the time before the show started, we'd go over my questions, talk about any last-minute changes, and discuss what we'd read in the newspapers that morning. She'd tell me about her boyfriends. I'd babble on about the kids, about the house. She was encouraging, upbeat.

Many of the people who made the show happen, I realized, were smart, hardworking women just like Ann. Women like Barbara Chacon, Claudia Ortiz, Vicki Testa; talent bookers, producers, writers, researchers. For the first time since I'd left college, I was part of a group of women I could talk to, who were interested in the same things as I was. It was exhilarating—and a little sad, because now I knew what I'd been missing all those years.

But things were moving too fast to dwell on that. I needed to pick their brains, to get better on the air. "Tell me what you see," I told them. "Criticize me. I need it." And they did. They told me to slow down my speaking voice; to let it lower in pitch. They warned me not to talk with my hands, and to keep them away from my face. They gave me clues on how to work with Regis. "When he's talking, let him lean forward in front of you. Don't break in by saying, 'Excuse me.' Lean back, give him a little intake of breath, so he can sense you're going to say something.'

"It's all done with body English."

Regis appeared to like what I was doing. On the air, my presence seemed to inspire his sense of humor. "She does it all, folks! She just does it all. Tell us how you cleaned your closets out again, Cyndy. And then you got all dressed up and went out with Mr. G. the same night. What are you? Cinderella?" When he ran out of topics, he could always bring up Steve. "How's Mr. America? Jack Armstrong? Mr. Tree Trunks?"

I knew that the Steve Garvey he joked about—a happy, modern nice-guy superstar who sat back, grinned, and enjoyed his marriage to a fast-talking, slightly domineering, slightly feminist, slightly famous wife—didn't really exist. But thanks to Regis, thanks to our "Golden Couple" image, this make-believe person was there between us. Like a prop to be used. It made me uncomfortable. But I convinced myself it was just part of the game. Part of Regis' routine. Part of show business.

Sometimes, not always, I managed to tease Regis back. But I sensed my main job was to counterbalance him, to smile and ask a serious question when he got too carried away with his wisecracks. "My top second banana," he called me.

A woman named Beth Forcellito took me under her wing. Beth was KABC's head of daytime programming: a powerful position, just under John Severino in the station hierarchy. She was, I was astonished to learn, a former nun. She was short, heavyset, and wore stylish, well-fitted clothes with wide shoulders. She had red-blond hair and a strong, open face. My first week on the job, she came down to the set to introduce herself.

"Hi, how are you doing?" she said, briskly. No nonsense. "Don't be nervous. You're good. We're going to work together. And I'm going to help you. This is what I know how to do."

She certainly did. After I got through the first few weeks, we began to look at tapes together after the show. If I did a good interview or asked a particularly good question, she said, "That's it!" If I giggled or acted coy, she frowned, pushed the stop button, and rewound the tape to show me my mistake. No harsh criticism, no unearned praise.

The advice and the no-nonsense confidence she had in me were beyond price. After a few months, Regis took a short vacation. The station brought in a substitute host. I sat down in my usual place on the couch, to the left of center.

Beth must have seen me on the monitor in her office. She came down to the stage.

"Whoa! Wait a minute! *You* sit in the middle and *he* sits on the left. *You're* the host. Get it right!"

She was talking to Cynthia, I realize now. And I was listening.

My mother was thrilled about my job on television. To her, I suppose, it was the culmination of all those etiquette lessons and beauty pageants. She watched me every morning, without fail, and for every one of our guests —especially the actors and actresses—she had a compliment and a question. "Is she really that good-looking in person?" "Oh, I wish I could tell him how much I liked him in his last movie." "How old are their children now, Cynthia?"

What I knew about these people wasn't particularly interesting, but it gave her such pleasure to hear any bit of innocent gossip that I happily obliged her. She still, I realized, had to live twenty-four hours a day with my father's violent temper. I heard it often, whenever I visited her.

The Voice. It was the same voice. Around the dinner table, in the den, lashing across, like a whip, from room to room. Criticizing. Belittling. Killing her.

Sometimes she would escape to my house, to play with the girls alone while I was at work. One afternoon, when I got home, I found her sitting at my desk. She seemed fascinated by the papers—my notes, my reading material, my appointment calendar—scattered on it.

My appearance flustered her. She quickly straightened up the books and papers she'd been looking at.

"Busy, busy, busy!" she said, pointing to the calendar.

"Yes, but it's all scheduled, Mother," I said wearily. "My busyness is all up there on the bulletin board. In black and white."

"But what's all this red writing, dear?"

"That's Steve's life. That's his schedule."

"But look, Cynthia. There's so *much* of it. It fills every evening. It fills all the weekends. Why," she said, amazed, "he's gone all the time!"

An unhappy moment. An awkward pause.

She grimaced, blushed, tried to recover. "Well! You know, Cynthia," she said quickly, smiling a sad smile I'd seen a thousand times, "your father was gone a lot, too."

"Yes, Mother. I guess I do."

Between my father and me there was a sort of grudging truce. We didn't talk much, hardly at all, although the girls spent a lot of time with their grandparents now. At first, when I went to work, I worried whether he would treat his grandchildren as he had treated me. I watched for signs, ready to get my girls away from him instantly if he did.

But, to my surprise, he was a normal, if a bit distant and crotchety, grandfather. He was at his best with them in public, proudly showing off his grandchildren to neighbors and strangers alike. He grumbled sometimes about the noise and left them to my mother, but he seemed to have no problem spending time with the girls, taking them for walks in their stroller, even hugging and holding them.

"Does Grandpa ever get mad at you, honey?" I asked Krisha one day, bringing her and her sister home in the car.

"Grandpa mad? Not at me, Mommy. No! He says I'm his favorite," she said, proudly.

A wave of bittersweet relief passed through me. I took my precious girls upstairs for their nap.

Before I knew it, I'd been on the show six months. The same actors began to come around again; the same books —this time with different titles, different authors—came back around, too. I felt more confident on the air. I didn't giggle as much. More and more, instead of hanging back, just laughing at Regis' wisecracks, I jumped in with questions and jokes of my own.

In public, too, things began to change a little. Some of the women in the supermarket, after their questions about Steve, talked to me about the show, about an interview they'd seen me do. At some of the gatherings Steve took me to, the people we met asked me about my job as well as his ballplaying.

"Do you watch her on TV?" they usually asked him.

He shrugged; his schedule, he said, didn't allow him to get up that early. Actually, he'd begun to leave for the ballpark earlier and earlier.

I rarely saw Steve at all during the day. How could I? I was a whirlwind; a full-time working woman and mother. My adrenaline was flowing all the time. I started skipping meals, forgetting to eat. That was not a problem, I thought: slightly underweight people, I knew, looked very good on television.

In fact, nobody noticed my weight loss at all. One evening, a business associate of Steve's, a Hollywood agent we'd known for several years, came up to me at a party.

"I watch you every morning, Cyndy," he said. "You look very good. It looks like you've loosened up. It looks like you've taken off about twelve coats."

"How many coats do I still have on?" I asked. One day, in the fall of 1979, I began the long process of finding out.

CHAPTER 18

I t started as a show like any other: opening spot with Regis. Interview. Interview. Exercise segment. Then, in the second half, an expert on child-abuse prevention and counseling. A woman. Her first time on the show.

I'd expected that we'd talk about rapists and child molesters. Criminals. In the first part of the interview, which was very heart-wrenching, we did. But then the segment took an unexpected turn. "It must be terrible to have your child kidnapped, at the mercy of a sadistic person," I said.

"Yes," said the expert. "But what is worse is to have a child suffer within his own home."

"Oh yes. I—" *What?*

I snapped to attention. Riveted. It happened too fast to be a rational response. For some reason that I didn't have time to figure out, this change of subject startled, and maybe even frightened me. I began to stare at the guest, just a few feet away, across the couch.

"It's true," said the woman, until that moment just a nice, slightly nervous, ordinary-looking person, about forty. "Millions of children suffer in silence. They're physically abused, or more insidiously, verbally abused— yelled at, belittled, humiliated—by one or both of their parents. And it happens in the 'best' of families.

"From the outside, everything looks fine. But that's the saddest part. Because these children have no one to go to. They're told subconsciously to keep the abuse secret. That it's their fault. They caused the problem. Sometimes they believe this terrible lie all their lives."

She kept talking, but her words turned into a roaring in my ears. I could feel myself breaking into a cold sweat. This had never happened to me before. I leaned forward, toward her, in front of Regis.

Her voice faded in and out, blurred, then formed meaningful words again.

". . . who were abused as children can go either way. They can either continue the pattern, and abuse their own children, or overcompensate in the other direction. Become the opposite, and not repeat the cycle."

Now I was sweating even more. A kind of electric current was running through my body. I was leaning so far forward that, oblivious to everything, I was letting my body come between Regis and the camera.

And then the segment was over, and before I could say anything at all to them, the guests were off the set. "Hey, what's with you?" said Regis to me, irritated, during the break.

Frank Kelly, the producer, came over.

"Are you all right?" he asked.

"Why?" I countered. I was coming somewhat back to normal.

"You didn't look so good during that segment, Cyndy."

"I'm fine," I said, unconvincingly. He went away. I tried to focus on the next segment. What had just happened, Cynthia? The question echoed in my brain. I shook my head, forced myself to concentrate on the show. I stared down at my notes and went back to work.

Something had happened to me, I knew. Some connection had been made during that interview—although I wasn't sure what it was. In truth, I did know. But I wasn't ready to acknowledge it.

I did some quick rationalizing. I told myself—talked myself into believing—that I was simply "interested" in the problem of child abuse. After the show, I contacted the woman I'd interviewed; she was glad to hear from me and excited about my offer to "help." She sent me some pamphlets in the mail; one weekday evening, after everybody had gone to sleep, I sat down in the living room, Duffy at my feet, and began to read.

One of them was about "adult survivors of childhood trauma"—a phrase I'd never heard before. There were descriptions of physical, and, to my surprise, something called "verbal" abuse. There were some statistics about the percentage of children who were constantly belittled and/or beaten by their emotionally disturbed parent or parents. There were terms like "sense of isolation"; "deep-seated anger/hostility"; "fear of intimacy"; "learned helplessness."

It went on and on. It was terrifying. Could these awful words mean . . . ? Have any connection to . . . ?

I felt that electrical current again. A voice, Cynthia's voice, made itself heard. These things have happened to me, I thought. No!

Panic. Frantically, I read through the material, looking for problems, for terrors I hadn't experienced. There were a few.

"No, no. I'm fine," said Cyndy. Then I put the pamphlets in a drawer, went back to bed, and waited for morning.

During the day, I could push most of the fears and doubts away from me. The job, my children, filled up almost all of my time. I was still learning, still absorbing information, still getting better.

I felt Regis and I were beginning to work well together. "Married on the air," was the way the producers put it. Sometimes, when we were doing our opening segment,

I'd even find myself reaching out to straighten his tie, or adjust his collar, or brush some lint off his jacket. "Will you stop fussing?" he complained, with fake anger. "This woman can't keep her hands off me!"

He liked that. I enjoyed the interviews we did together. Sometimes, when Regis had trouble formulating a question, I'd jump in to help him.

That, it seemed, was a problem. He never complained directly to me, but during one of our early morning talks, Ann Reddy explained how to stay on Regis' good side. "Try not to finish his sentences for him, Cyndy," she said. "Also, try to compliment him on his appearance. *Never* make fun of it. If he comes in looking a little tired, don't mention it.

"And when he's doing an interview by himself, he wants you to stand offstage and watch him, so he can play off your reactions."

"Oh sure. Okay," I said. That all sounded very reasonable. After all, he was my partner. He knew what he was doing.

"We really appreciate your coming down here," said the woman sitting next to me. I was on a bus; we were going to a home for abused children out in the desert. It was near Riverside, east of Los Angeles.

Try as I might, I'd been unable to get those pamphlets completely out of my mind. Once again, I was "interested." I'd called up an organization called Childhelp, U.S.A., and asked what I could do to "help." As, of course, a "celebrity spokesperson." They'd quickly enlisted me as an emcee for a benefit dinner. That had gone well. Now here I was, to learn more about the problem.

The children in the shelter—from tiny babies to adolescents—had been beaten, tortured, abused so badly that the courts had taken them away from their parents. Some had almost died at their parents' hands. It was obvious that many, along with their physical injuries, had been psychologically scarred for life. All the dedicated staff members could do was to get the poor children to express their fears—and to give them as much pure love as they could.

It was awful. But along with the sadness, I felt a tired anger. Not just, I finally realized on the long ride back to town, at the parents of these children.

It was time, I knew, to face my own past.

My seatmate turned to me, interrupting my thoughts. She was smiling politely. Just making conversation.

"What got you interested in helping us?" she said.

I began to stammer.

"I was, uh . . . my father . . . I grew up . . ." The woman's expression changed to surprise. Alarm. Concern.

Then it all came out. All at once. It was as if someone else, someone cool and rational and objective, were talking.

I told her about the beatings, the yelling. The fear. "I think I grew up in an abusive household," I said.

The woman nodded gravely. We understood each other. Then I looked straight ahead. We rode back to Los Angeles in silence.

The main guest for the day was a well-known movie actress. Regis and I were to interview her together. She came to the studio just a few minutes before air time. She was accompanied by a huge, fierce-looking German shepherd on a short leash.

"He's my bodyguard. He goes on the air with me," she said.

The producers were aghast. A dog on the air? They tried to convince her to leave it off-camera.

"No. I need his protection," she said. She looked pale, tense. Very small. She said there had been threats on her life. There were people out there who wanted to kill her. Either both of them went on, or she went home.

"Well, that's it for me," said Regis, clearly terrified by

the dog. He went to his dressing room. I did the interview myself.

It went fairly well. Before we started, the actress explained that the dog was trained to attack if she said a certain word. "It's better I don't tell you, so you won't say it accidentally," she said.

On the air, the actress made a magic transformation. She was happy, vivacious. Not a care in the world. The dog sat quietly at her feet; she explained that he was her dear pet, that he went wherever she did. I gave it a friendly, but tentative pat.

When the commercial came on, though, the actress seemed to turn off. She looked smaller, grayer, shrunken back into her fear.

I reached over and took her hand. "Are you really so afraid for your safety?" I said.

"Yes," she whispered. Until the segment began again, I could see the terror in her eyes.

"Mom, I want to ask you something important. Remember when Chris and Mark and I were small?"

I was visiting my parents' house. My mother looked up from her ironing and smiled. "Oh yes," she said. "You were beautiful children. I was very proud of all of you."

I screwed up my courage. "Mom? Dad was pretty violent toward us back then. He beat us up a lot, didn't he?"

Her smile disappeared. My mother turned her head away from me, back toward her work.

"Well, yes. I suppose there was violence," she said. Her voice was barely audible. "But you have to forgive your father. He was under a lot of pressure."

She turned to face me, her face crumbling with embarrassment and pain. I instantly regretted bringing up the subject. "There were things happening back then, Cynthia, that you didn't know about. Many, many things that you didn't know about."

She thought for a second, turning inward, then shook her head. "Hmmph. Yes," she said, shaking the memories away. The iron thumped down on the shirt again, hard.

"You have to help me deal with this. You have to tell me why I'm so sad inside," I said.

I was sitting across from a woman psychologist I'd been referred to. I knew I needed help. But I was also terrified that, being a public figure—Cyndy Garvey, part of a golden couple—the press, the public would somehow find out. How could I get well if my problems became public knowledge?

The psychologist assured me, with a patient smile, that everything I said would remain in this room. For a few weekly sessions, haltingly, I told her about my fears, my doubts. Why I said what I'd said to the woman on the bus. A cleaned-up, toned-down version of my childhood. I didn't mention Steve much at all.

She wasn't fooled by my evasions. One afternoon, about halfway into the session, she held up her hand and smiled at me.

"I strongly believe, Cynthia," she said, "that you were a verbally abused child." She started writing something on a piece of paper. "I think it would help you to talk to other people with similar problems," she said. "This is the name of a woman psychologist. She runs a therapy group for adult children of abusive parents."

"But I can't do that," I said. "I'm scared. I'm Cyndy Garvey. I'm a public figure . . ."

She smiled again, a little sadly, and held out the paper. "Don't be afraid," she said. "Don't worry about that. Go."

The group met two evenings a month, in the basement of a community center in the Valley. Nothing special; just metal folding chairs and concrete walls. There were eight or nine group members—patients, I suppose—plus Jo-anne, the psychologist. All of the group members were parents. It was about equally divided between men and women; between professionals and blue-collar workers. It had been going on for several sessions. Only first names were used. But that, I knew, wouldn't work for me. Many people knew my face. I was absolutely certain that my problems would get in the paper—my name was in them nearly every day, anyway.

I sat down quietly in a chair at the end of the semicircle. "Cyndy," said Joanne, "stand up and introduce yourself to the group."

"My name is Cyndy. I . . ."

"Oh!" said several of the members, their eyes opening wide. This is no use, I thought. There's no way I can be completely open here. It's not safe. I stopped talking and stared at my feet.

"Why are you here, Cyndy?" prompted Joanne.

I was trapped. "I . . . I think that when I was a child, I had some incidents that made my life very afraid." Thoughts, memories, boiled through my brain. This was too much. I was forcing myself to talk and censoring myself at the same time. It was impossible.

"My father was a pilot, and . . . uh, we moved all around . . . and, um, he was angry a lot of the time. I'm, uh, afraid a lot these days—and I want to get in touch with what happened to me."

I sat down quickly. Had I escaped?

"No, no, no," said a man in his mid-thirties, sitting across from me. "You can't get away with that. You have to be more specific."

Joanne rescued me. "That's fine for now. We'll get back to you later, Cyndy."

I stared at the ground again. "I'd just like to listen awhile, if that's all right," I said softly.

"That's fine for a little while," said Joanne, and thankfully, blessedly, moved on.

Steve knew about my therapy, but we rarely if ever talked about it. We rarely talked about anything.

At the time, Steve was in the next-to-last year of his famous "streak." For seven years, he played in every single Dodger game. It was the longest streak in the history of the National League; it was the record he most valued.

By the 1979 season, he was counting down the number of games to the record on the kitchen calendar. The streak lived at our house; it was a physical presence between us.

The streak was physically and mentally grueling. By now Steve was thirty; most players his age took an occasional day off to rest or to let an injury heal. But, because of the streak, Steve couldn't. He was being literally ground down by playing baseball; he was about twenty pounds lighter than when I'd met him. His body was covered with bruises and calluses; cuts and sprains never had time to heal.

Another problem was that the streak wasn't entirely under his control: Steve, like any other baseball player, could fall into a slump or get injured at any time—or, if Tommy Lasorda, for any reason, got mad at him, all he had to do was bench Steve for one day and the streak would be broken. It made me sad to think about it. In fact, the whole streak made little sense. A line in a record book didn't seem worth what he was going through.

"Steve, this is killing you," I said one evening. "Why don't you stop the streak? Take some time off? Let up on the pressure a bit? Spend some more time with us?" He frowned and shook his head, as if what I'd said, too, made no sense at all.

Maybe it didn't, I thought. Maybe the streak really did mean more to him than anything else. More than his health. More than his wife. More than his children.

The streak lasted far beyond the time we were together. I never asked him to stop again.

I simply saw him less and less now. Steve left for the ballpark earlier and earlier; he liked, he said, to stay close to Tommy before the game. On weekday mornings, Priscilla told me, he took to leaving the house at eight-thirty or nine. Dressed in his tennis clothes, he'd get into his car and drive off.

"Where do you go so early?" I asked him.

"Oh, uh, I play tennis with Sam. It lets me get rid of some of the tension."

It seemed strange that he would spend his energy that way. But who was I to question him? By that time I was on my own round-the-clock schedule.

At night, tired myself, I lay next to Steve's exhausted, battered body. I felt a longing for physical contact—not sex, necessarily, just comfort. Contact. Affection. Sometimes, as Steve's body relaxed into sleep, his exhausted muscles went into spasms. He slept right through them. I watched with horror as he moaned, convulsed, and gradually fell into a deeper sleep.

"You had death throes again last night," I told Steve—if I saw him—the next day. He'd smile grimly and cross another square off his calendar.

I began noticing other men. Watching them. Studying them. Comparing them to Steve. It was wrong, I knew.

In my new life, they were all around me. Television executives, ABC colleagues, guests: none of them heroes —or as handsome or as "perfect" as Steve—but all of them interesting. They wore adult clothing; they said adult things about life, politics, books. They laughed, told jokes. They talked to *me*.

A man named Marvin Hamlisch, a famous New York composer in town to promote a musical he'd written, hung around the set and played funny tunes on the piano, wisecracking behind me while I did an exercise segment. I nearly fell off the set laughing; despite his antics, or maybe because of them, the segment "worked." After his segment was over, he lingered in the studio, watching; afterward, we talked some more. Nothing too serious. Just polite chitchat about what we were doing with our careers.

It was a pleasure just chatting with him—or people like him.

"I don't know who I am. *I don't know who I am.* Tell me. Tell me! Who am I supposed to be?"

Beth, a member of the group who sat near me, had her head in her hands and was crying uncontrollably. Nobody moved to comfort her. That wasn't the way the group worked.

It was agonizing. Like most of the other group members, Beth was braver than I was. They all told their stories; I sat and listened and said as little as I could possibly get away with. Except that it was impossible to just listen. How could I? This wasn't a talk show. Not a "moving" article in *People* magazine. More often than not, their life histories veered dangerously close to mine. It was obvious, too painfully obvious to ignore. Even in my silence, I felt exposed. They were chipping away at my excuses, my rationalizations.

Like almost all the adults in the group, Beth had had a cold, violent father and a mother who rarely interfered. Most of the men had been beaten severely by their fathers; most of the women had been hit less severely, but all of them had been verbally abused and belittled by their parents—and several, like me, had served as protectors of younger male siblings. But that was in the past. Now, a generation later, their childhoods were being repeated. Several of the men in the group had either beaten their own children or were constantly afraid of giving in to violent feelings. The women, most of whom had married men much like their fathers, all had trouble forming relationships. Some could not even relate to their own children.

"Who am I supposed to be?" sobbed Beth. "I've gone through three marriages. I have a fourteen-year-old daughter. If I don't know who I am, how am I going to tell a teenager what to do? I can't handle it.

"I—I want her to go away!"

Then, only the sound of Beth's crying. Nobody had any answers for her. I thought about my own daughters. If I didn't get my own identity straightened out, what would I pass on to them? And then I thought about my own father. Suddenly, with a startling clarity I pictured him standing, smiling, next to Steve.

In the silence, I tried to get the picture out of my head. But Joey, a burly truck driver who sat opposite me, must have read my mind.

"What about you, Cyndy?" he said. "What about your marriage? The great Steve Garvey can't be such a bad guy, can he? You've got a good life. You look good. What are you here for?"

That's what I'd been afraid of. There was so much to say. But if anything about Steve got out . . . *disaster*. I'd been so frightened of that that I'd talked it over with Joanne privately before the group met.

Joanne stood up. "Cyndy is here for herself. Her problems don't have to do with Steve Garvey. We don't have to talk about him here."

"Thank you," I whispered to Joanne. She had protected me. But I couldn't stop thinking about Steve and my father. About Beth. About me. About my loneliness.

That spring, the program traveled to Las Vegas for a few days. I missed the girls terribly; I felt guilty about leaving them with Laureen and Priscilla. About leaving them at all. I called back home every night.

One evening, Krisha answered the phone. The receiver clattered and rattled as she wrestled it to her ear.

"Hi, Mommy!" she said.

"Hi, honey!" I said. "What have—"

"We went to Sea World, Mommy!"

"You *did?* Oh, my! With who?"

"With Whitney and Daddy and Judy!"

Judy? "Who's Judy?"

"Judy, Mommy," she said impatiently, cutely. "Daddy and Judy. Daddy *kissing* Judy."

"What?" I laughed. A new little friend of theirs that Steve had taken along? And whom Krisha was jealous of because Steve kissed her? "Now, Krisha. Who's—"

Then, immediately, I heard the phone being pulled away from Krisha.

"Hi!" said Steve.

"Who's Judy?" I laughed, teasing him.

"Judy was our guide," said Steve.

"And you kissed the guide?"

"Oh no, no," he said, exasperatedly. "The guide gave *Krisha* a kiss. She got all mixed up."

We talked for a few more minutes. A pleasant surprise; he was more animated, more affectionate, than usual.

About three weeks later, I went with the girls to pick up some snapshots at the drugstore. There was Steve with the girls, at Sea World, pushing them in little dolphin-shaped strollers. And there was Judy, the guide—a dark-haired young woman in shorts and tennis shirt—smiling alongside them.

"This'll be fun," said Steve, heading the Jaguar toward Los Angeles. I'd agreed to pose for a well-known fashion photographer named Harry Langdon for the cover of a new magazine called *Shape.* Because of my exercise segments on the show, they'd done a story about me. I, too, was losing weight; I was down to one hundred and eight pounds at the time, but on camera I looked the picture of health.

To my surprise, Steve had volunteered to drive me over and watch the entire session. It was the first time in a long time that he'd asked to accompany me anywhere.

"Good to meet you," said Harry Langdon, politely, to Steve. A lean, good-looking man, dressed all in white, he seemed only mildly interested in meeting him. He quickly steered Steve to a seat at the back of the studio; it was a stark, tastefully decorated loft. Soft music played in the background; young assistants, a makeup person, a hair stylist, moved efficiently around Harry.

I had my hair and makeup done. The first part of the session was for head shots only; then, after an hour or so, I changed into a bathing suit and posed in front of a neutral-colored backdrop.

It wasn't working. Although Harry asked me to loosen up, I couldn't seem to relax. I moved stiffly, kept my arms rigidly in front of my body. It took almost an hour before I realized the trouble: for some reason, I was uncomfortable posing in front of Steve. I kept glancing at him out of the corner of my eye. Why was he here? I wondered. He could see me, if he wanted to, any time. Did he want to be in the picture himself? He was sitting, as he'd done for hours, straight up in his chair with a small smile on his face. Not saying anything. Just watching.

We struggled on. It embarrassed me to tell the photographer that my own husband inhibited me. But Harry, with only a slight show of puzzlement, figured out the problem on his own.

He walked over to Steve. "I would really appreciate it if you would leave now," said Harry; Steve nodded and left the room.

"Okay. Let's begin again," said Harry.

By now it was dark outside. Harry turned on a small fan and aimed it at me. The background music changed, became softer, more sensual. Without Steve in the room I immediately loosened, became more responsive to Harry's suggestions.

"Okay, put your hand here."

Click.

"Lean forward."

Click. Click.

"Now, put your hand over *there* and put your hair up."

Click.

Suddenly, for the first time in a long time, I was totally

relaxed. And the mood that Harry had set took control of me. I felt all the pent-up longing, all the need for intimacy flow through me. I began thinking of the men I'd met in the past year. About my need for affection. About Steve.

"Fine! Fine!" said Harry, as we moved smoothly from shot to shot.

The feelings began to overwhelm me. I began swaying, posing more provocatively, making love to the camera. The longing was flowing up from inside and spilling over. I was in a trance. A kind of sexual trance.

I must have gone too far. My needs must have been too apparent. Harry stopped directing me and stood quietly next to his camera, a look of concern on his face. I went on by myself for a few seconds.

"Okay, Cyndy," he said soothingly. "We've got what we need. That's enough for now.

"Are you all right? Take all the time you need to get dressed," he said. It took me a while to pull myself together. I sat and talked with Harry, asking him about his work, until I felt ready to go. Then Harry called Steve back into the room, and, without talking about what had happened, my husband and I drove home.

It was the last session before Joanne's vacation. Somebody had asked Joey about his relationship with his daughter.

"Well," he said offhandedly, "my daughter doesn't talk to me."

His daughter doesn't talk to him, I thought. The neglect, the pain, the hypocrisy of that sentence rang in my ears. His daughter doesn't talk to him! I thought of my father, the man, *the men* I didn't dare disturb. Whom I so much wanted to talk to me.

I was so angry that I broke my silence.

"Why doesn't she talk to you, Joey?" I said. "Do you hit her?"

Infuriatingly, Joey grinned at me.

"Why do you say that, Cyndy?"

What? I pushed on. "Are you angry at her all the time?" I asked.

Then Joanne's voice, softly: "What issues does this bring up for you, Cynthia?"

There was no holding back. I stood up, burning, and stared at Joey. "I got beat up by my father until I was thirteen. I was verbally abused until I left home for college."

But there was more, much more, I realized at that moment. And I couldn't keep it all inside of me. The terrible thoughts, the realizations, were forming just ahead of my words. I was crying, sweating, shouting.

"It was horrible," I sobbed. I told them about the shame, the humiliation, the pain of keeping my secret all these years.

"And the most painful part, the most horrible part, was to watch people in my family masquerade as normal people. And *I* did it, too! That's led me to where I am, today."

"Where is that, Cynthia?" asked Joanne.

Oh God. "I'm in a marriage where *he* pays me no attention and I can't talk to him and . . . and . . . *this is not who I really am!* I have to leave you soon and become somebody else. I have to become somebody . . . *somebody named Cyndy.*

"I have to be Cyndy on television. I have to be Cyndy in my home. *My name isn't Cyndy!*"

I stopped. Suddenly, I was aware of everyone in the group staring at me. And that I was drained. Totally spent. I sat down, put my head in my hands, and cried.

I cried in the car all the way home. When I got home, about ten-thirty at night, Krisha toddled down the stairs to greet me.

My face was still wet. "Mommy, are you sad?" she asked.

"Oh no, honey," I said, picking her up for a hug. "I've

just been crying a little bit tonight. Sometimes, even grown-ups have to get some bad feelings out. But now I'm all better. It's okay."

"Oh. Okay, Mommy," she said. And we went upstairs to bed.

CHAPTER 19

Unfortunately, that was the last group therapy session I attended. I didn't go back to Joanne after the summer break. Part of the reason was that the KABC management, noticing the "A.M. Show" 's good ratings, had started "A.M. in the P.M.," a half-hour version of the program with Regis and me, starting at three every weekday afternoon.

The new job meant I couldn't get home until late afternoon. With even less time to spend with the girls—and hopefully, with Steve—I couldn't afford the time.

But there was another reason. That summer, I convinced myself that I didn't need the group. Not any more, anyway. Now that I'd talked about my problem, I told myself, I could deal with it myself. I'd confront my childhood, all the old habits and fears, and work them through alone.

That way, nobody would see me cry. Yes, that made perfect sense: I went to the library, checked out all the books on child abuse I could find, and read them from cover to cover. I found time to keep up my volunteer work. I visited the station's news department, convinced the news director I could work for him, and, with the help of a very good producer, reported a five-part mini-documentary on child abuse.

Everybody over there seemed to like what I did. That

meant, of course, that I was on top of the problem. Wasn't I?

My career, said my agent, was going fine. He began sending me out for other jobs. CBS, he told me one day, was looking for a woman to co-host their pregame football show.

"Let the people at the network take a look at you," he said; though I didn't know much about football, and didn't really want to work in sports, I took the girls over to my parents' for the weekend and flew to New York.

It all went smoothly. I sat in a mocked-up studio, reading make-believe copy with Frank Gifford and Irv Cross. They were very nice, though I wasn't offered the job.

On the flight home something interesting happened. I was in my seat, trying to read. But I couldn't help noticing a man in the row ahead of me. Earlier he had smiled and said hello.

He appeared to be in his early forties, short, thin, and intelligent-looking. But he was confusing me. The annoying part, the part that I couldn't figure out, was the way he talked to our flight attendant.

"Honey, can you get me a cup of coffee?" he said.

"Honey, can you get some water?"

"Honey, how about another pillow?"

"Thanks, honey."

"You're welcome," said the flight attendant. Honey? I thought. She probably resents being called that. But, of course, it was her job to be friendly no matter what.

But why was he calling her "honey" in the first place? He didn't seem the type. He was reading *The New Yorker*. He was conservatively dressed in a dress shirt and sports jacket; no chains or chest hair or big cigar. Then, a thought, a possible explanation, flew into my head. Could it be . . . ?

I had to find out. I tapped him on the shoulder. He turned around.

"Excuse me. Is the flight attendant your wife?"

A blank stare. Complete puzzlement. Then his eyes lit up in comprehension. He threw back his head and laughed.

"Come here, honey," he said to the flight attendant. He seized her arm, gently, and turned her so that I could see her name tag. HONEY it read.

He laughed again. "See?"

Oh God. I blushed. "I'm so embarrassed," I said.

"Why should you be?" he said, his eyes still twinkling. He stuck out his hand. "I'm . . . ," he said. I'll call him Seth Greenfield here.

"I'm Cyndy Garvey." His smile stayed the same. I realized, with a surprising feeling of relief, that he'd never heard of me.

"What do you do, Cyndy?" he asked. I told him that I was co-host of a show called "A.M. Los Angeles." He said, apologetically, that he didn't watch television in the mornings, but he'd heard the name.

"Well, I'm married to Steve Garvey, the Dodger base-ball player," I said.

A polite nod; he didn't seem too familiar with baseball, either. He told me that he was an independent producer. He named a few of the films he'd made. The titles sounded familiar. They were mostly "quality" movies: no car-chase thrillers.

We talked for several hours, all the way into Los Ange-les International. He told me that he was divorced and had two sons. We showed each other our pictures. He asked me about what it was like to be a talk-show host; who I thought made the most interesting guests.

The rest of the flight went quickly. It was easy to talk to Seth Greenfield. He listened with more than politeness. When we landed, he offered to give me a ride. I thanked him, but told him my car was in the parking lot. We shook hands and parted company at the terminal exit.

The next day, at the station, somebody handed me a phone message. It was from Seth Greenfield. He wanted to invite me to lunch. Have lunch with me? I'd told him I was married. "Not a good idea," I said, and threw the paper away.

Seth called me several more times. Not compulsively, just a message or so a week. I didn't return his calls.

I was very lonely. The Dodgers were doing well that year; Steve had, for all intents and purposes, left home. His streak was becoming more and more talked and written about; he was having, despite his aching body, another fine season. Despite, or maybe because of that, he kept up his nonstop schedule of speeches and personal appearances.

At least, I thought, things would slacken off after the season. But in late summer, I learned that some—but not all—of the Dodgers were going to make a playing tour of Japan in November. It was an optional trip. It seemed irrational to me that he'd want to make his season even longer.

That was a mistake. Toward the end of the season, I realized I hadn't even asked him about it. "You're not going, are you?" I asked him one evening.

He turned away from the television set and just stared at me. That meant yes.

"Come on, Steve," I coaxed. "Not everybody is going. You don't have to. Why don't you take some time off? Enjoy it with your family? You'd have a good time."

Nothing.

"Steve!" Now my voice was rising. "You know November is Sweeps month. I can't go with you. Why are you doing this?"

Just a blank, faintly curious stare.

A thought: was he enjoying watching me argue with him? I choked back my anger. "All right, Steve. Do what you want to do."

He turned back to the television set. The conversation was over.

* * *

My agent kept sending me out for other work. In addition to the usual guest talk-show appearances, I cohosted a one-shot network special, a sort of "Superstars" for television actors and actresses. The word filtered down that John Severino didn't like my doing this. One day that fall, after the show was over, he called me into his office.

As I came in to sit down, he pushed the button that closed the door behind me. He scowled at a piece of paper on his desk. "Your agent," he said disgustedly. "Your agent wants you to do other shows."

He looked up at me, still frowning. "Tell him you can't do anything without asking me."

A tingle of fear and shame. He was angry at me. I had done something wrong. But . . . wait a minute. Wait, Cynthia. Nobody at KABC, John included, had ever mentioned this subject before. As far as I'd been told, there was no rule against working on other shows. If there was, would my agent have deliberately broken it?

I screwed up my courage. "John. Is there anything in my contract against my doing this?"

He looked at me, a big man in a gray suit, as if he couldn't believe what he'd heard.

"Cyndy," he said angrily. He was talking slowly, deliberately. "If you want to do anything on your own," he said scornfully, pausing as if to consider the stupidity of that notion, "you've got to ask me. If you don't, we'll fire you."

Just like that. As if, I realized, he was talking to a child. Like my own father had talked to me. And now—surprisingly!—an anger began to well up inside.

That feeling scared me even more than the fear I already felt. But I didn't give in.

"All right," I said, trembling with fear and anger. I didn't cry in front of him. I stood up, pulled open the door, and went home. Later that day, my agent told me what I'd thought all along: there was a clause in my contract stating that outside appearances were expressly allowed.

Steve left for Japan. There were no more arguments, no big goodbyes; when the time came, he just flew away with the team. Another road trip. I didn't have the Dodgers' itinerary, and he didn't call or write at all. I was out of touch with him for three weeks.

One morning, a few minutes before air, the phone in the makeup room rang.

"Yes, she's here," said Sunday, my makeup person. She handed me the phone.

"Hello?"

"Hello! This is Seth Greenfield. Do you remember me?"

"Of course I do," I said. Damn. "Listen, I'm really embarrassed that I haven't returned your calls."

"What? Oh, that's perfectly all right," he said. We chatted for a minute or so. Then he asked me to have lunch with him. I realized, with a sting of loneliness, that I wanted to very much. Something clenched inside me relaxed, but just for a second.

"Oh, Seth, I don't know if I should do that. What if a reporter, or somebody who knows Steve, sees us?"

"So what?" he said. "What's the harm? We both work in the same business. And besides, this is perfectly innocent."

Perfectly innocent. Two days later, I met him at a small French restaurant. He was the same as before: intelligent, witty, kind. A gentle man. A gentleman. A good listener. He ordered our wine, our food, with interest but without pretension. We talked again about my work and his. He told me about his latest movie projects and his children. Somehow, after a little while, more serious subjects came up; I told him how much I disliked living my family's private life in public.

"That's terrible," he said. "It's impossible for a sane person to live like that. I keep my home and business lives completely separate. That's something I absolutely insist on."

He asked how I managed things with Steve away from home so much. I talked a little about the problems, about my loneliness.

I felt comfortable, open with him. Yes, and attracted, too. For the first time in a long time, I told someone—him—that I preferred to be called Cynthia. He nodded seriously when I told him that.

As we had coffee, as he paid the check, he told me that he lived nearby. In his own house, that he'd lived in for many years.

"You know, Cynthia," he said, "if you want to really understand me, you have to see my house." He invited me to dinner there. It was my turn to nod yes.

Two days later, at six o'clock, I drove down the tree-lined street on which Seth lived. It was in one of the oldest areas of the Valley; it sat several blocks from the main boulevard. There was no other traffic. Very little noise at all. Still, I was afraid someone would see me. I parked down the street from his address and walked over. Seth's house was completely surrounded by a six-foot-high wall. From the street it was totally invisible.

I rang the bell. After a few seconds, the door swung upon.

"Hello! Come in!" said Seth, wiping his hands on the apron around his waist. He hugged me. "I'm glad you came. I can't wait to show you everything," he said, closing the door behind me.

I was astonished. Behind the gate was a miniature mansion, a little Tara, complete with front porch and columns. It was painted a cool white. The path to the house was lined with flowerbeds. There were rosebushes. Pieces of sculpture were scattered on the lawn. Around back, where he led me next, there was a small swimming pool with a waterfall emptying into it.

Inside, the rooms were decorated sparsely—almost

minimally—with low, light-colored modern furniture. On the walls were pictures from Seth's art collection. He pointed several of them out to me: a Klee, a Miró, a Picasso. He showed me a space where another piece, which he had lent to a museum, usually hung.

"They're wonderful. But I don't know anything about art," I said.

"Don't worry. I'll teach you," he said.

Then he dashed into the kitchen to "rescue" the dinner. I noticed the huge poster-sized pictures of his children. We ate slowly, talking all the while. The food was delicious. And his house was quiet. No ringing phones. No television. And it was gloriously, deliciously private.

I thought, Other people live this way. Why had I missed it all? I felt more relaxed, more myself than I could remember.

Seth was as charming as always. He didn't try to kiss me; I was grateful for that. After dessert, after we'd talked some more, he walked me to the street.

"Come back whenever you can," he said. He hugged me again, and closed the gate. I got into my car—the one with the license plates that read MY MVP—and drove back to the real world.

Two or three times a week, after the morning show was over, I made the drive to Seth's house. I was much too afraid to go out in public with him again. But behind his big, white walls, we were safe.

He'd be home for lunch before me. We sat and ate together, talking or reading the newspaper. Sometimes he'd talk about art; explaining why he enjoyed his pieces, why he bought them, why he'd hung them where they were.

Frequently, wonderfully, he'd touch me: he'd touch my knee to make a point. Or absentmindedly stroke my arm or twine his fingers through mine.

The quiet, the security, was what I valued most. I loved being in Seth's world. My physical relationship with him was secondary. We didn't make love until a month had gone by—and, I discovered with some guilt and sadness—I didn't enjoy it as much as I should have. My guilt was controlling me. But Seth never pressed me. And I tried my best to give him pleasure.

After a few visits, I began taking along a change of casual clothing. For sunbathing, healing, in his backyard.

"Ah-hah, the transformation!" laughed Seth, after I'd go into his bedroom, take off my "Cyndy" clothes—the high heels, the dress, the hose—put on a pair of shorts and a T-shirt, and go back outside to relax with him.

After a couple of hours, our time was up. Time to change, time for a final embrace, and then back to work. And back to the guilty feeling that I was betraying my marriage. My girls, my family.

The show was doing well, and I felt I was improving every week, but my relationship with John Severino was deteriorating.

He wanted, I realized, to establish a kind of absolute power over me—over and above what his job entitled him to. But why? What was the point? How could that possibly help what we were doing together? I couldn't figure it out.

And I couldn't, for reasons that were only half-formed inside me, give in to him. Become the child he was treating me as. Become, I realized to my horror, the old Cyndy again—the person he had thought he had hired.

It was hard. Very hard. One morning, with Los Angeles wrapped in a huge rainstorm, there was a truck accident on the Ventura Freeway. Traffic was stalled: for the first time in my television career, I was late for a show.

I was frantic. I made it to the studio just at nine o'clock. Sunday slapped on my makeup. I ran toward the set. Regis was sitting alone, talking into the camera.

"Well, Cyndy must have gotten caught in traffic," he was saying. I waved at him, and I was fairly sure he had registered my presence out of the corner of his eye.

All right, no problem. I got ready to walk into camera range. This would work fine. I was late, the co-host was late to work, just like thousands of other people in the city this morning. In my mind, as I moved forward, I rehearsed my first line: "Regis, you won't believe what . . ."

Suddenly, I felt myself being stopped short. A hand was gripping my shoulder! I spun around, frightened. It was John Severino. He was very close, towering over me.

"You're not going on," he said, in a low, flat voice. "This is live television. Nobody comes in late for their own show."

"But, John," I whispered, "there was an accident. I couldn't get here."

He shook his head.

"John! This is the first time this has ever happened!"

"Cyndy, you might as well go home."

Go home. Go home? I looked up at the set. Regis, I could see, knew I was here. There was a hint of a smile on his face. But he was still improvising on his "Where is Cyndy?" monologue.

The members of the crew, embarrassed, were concentrating on their work, avoiding my eye. It wasn't their fault.

Don't cry yet, I thought, as I walked as slowly as I could back to the dressing room.

The next day, surprisingly, John was as friendly to me as he'd been in a long time.

"Well, did you learn your lesson?" he said jokingly. He was giving me a chance to become Cyndy again.

For a split second, I was tempted. But no. Too late. "John," I said, shaking my head, "I couldn't have gotten here on time yesterday, even if I could fly."

"Regis doesn't treat you very well, does he?" said Seth. We were sitting in his backyard, next to his pool. He'd been watching the shows in his office, he said, and he'd noticed that right away.

It had never really occurred to me, I told him.

"He's really threatened by you. As a man, I can see it —in the way he holds himself, in the way he talks down to you. He doesn't like the fact that you're growing, getting better. And so he's doing little things to upstage you.

"Stop cooperating! Don't sit facing him so often. Talk more to the camera, like he does. Establish your own territory."

I looked at him closely. In his face, I saw only a fierce, selfless concern for my future. Who else like him did I have on my side?

I told him I would try.

I tried very hard to love Seth. To satisfy him physically, to give back all that he had given me. But sadly—much more than sadly—it was impossible. It defied all logic, all sanity: I couldn't love this warm, gentle man as much as I loved my cold, distant husband. A terrible thought: was it Steve's very coldness that attracted me to him? Was I attracted to unattainable men, to men who challenged me to win them over? Men like Steve. Men like . . . my father?

The thought horrified me. It was a horrible, wrenching dilemma. Neither Cyndy nor Cynthia could see a way out.

"Why don't you leave Steve?" said Seth. "His world is not your world. It's bad for you to live in it. You know that, don't you?"

I shook my head. Seth, understandably, had been getting more and more intimate. He had begun talking about my going out in public with him; about meeting his friends, his children. About possibly moving, with the girls, away from Steve and into his house. With him.

It was impossible, I realized. A terrifying thought. And now, because of his gentle pressure, the guilt and anxiety were beginning to reach into his sanctuary. I had to do something.

The time came that winter. The show had relocated, for a week, to a hotel in South Lake Tahoe. The second morning there, sitting on the set during a commercial break, I looked up and saw Seth standing beyond camera range. He didn't wave or acknowledge me. Just a quiet, good-looking man. Waiting for me.

I fought down the panic. What if anyone saw us together? I forced myself to look away from him; when the show was over, he was gone.

He had, I found out, checked into the hotel. From my room, behind my closed door, I called his. I asked him to come over, making sure that no one saw him.

"Seth, we can't do this," I told him. "You know I can't risk anyone seeing you with me here."

A beat. "All right, then," he said, softly, "I'll leave."

I plunged ahead, every word hurting. "And I can't see you any more. It's impossible. I'm just not ready to make the commitment."

Seth, wonderful, gentle Seth, stared at me for a few seconds. I saw, I knew that I had hurt him badly. But he took my request with dignity. Understanding. Manliness.

"I wish you would reconsider," he said.

I was crying now. What was I throwing away? I shook my head. We talked for a half-hour, an hour, but nothing changed.

The phone rang: it was one of the producers. I had to change and go to a production meeting. Seth hugged me, one last time, and left.

Now I knew what I had to do: to rejoin my marriage, if Steve would have me.

It took all the courage I had, but when I got back to Los Angeles, I managed to get to Steve before he left the house in the morning.

"Steve. While you've been gone—while you've been away—I've been seeing another man."

For a horrible moment, I waited for his reaction.

Finally, he spoke. "I know," he said.

He knew?

His expression barely changed. His accountant, he told me, had spotted my car parked in front of Seth's. After seeing it there several times, he'd told Steve. This had all happened months ago.

I was reeling. Steve had known? He'd known all this time, and hadn't asked me about it, hadn't said a thing?

Finally Steve, for once, broke the silence. "Is it over?" he asked.

"Yes, it is," I told him, my head spinning.

"Okay then," he said. My answer seemed to satisfy him. Neither of us had anything more to say. He left for whatever appointment he was going to.

For a little while longer, my life with Steve—if you could call it that—went on. Neither Steve nor I ever brought up my affair. Nor, of course, did he tell me about his own. On the surface, at least, things were almost the same as they'd been before.

In truth, my relationship with Steve had only one more sick, destructive spasm left. Filled with guilt, I tried for one last time to get his attention. It was more out of fear —of the future, of the problems I knew I had yet to face —than from any real conviction it would work out. There were no real reasons, I realized in my less self-deluded moments, for Steve to make any changes at all.

He was who he was. He liked things the way they'd always been. But even that conscious, sad knowledge didn't stop the old fantasies. I pushed the logic away.

The magic formula was simple. We were living separate lives. But couldn't our two worlds come together? I could make it happen. I had the entire house repainted white. No more blue and rust.

My plan: Steve and I would buy some real art; learn about it together. We'd go out in public together with creative people, interesting people, people who led interesting lives. Not just sports fans and politicians. We'd start as soon as his schedule permitted it.

As for my part of the bargain, I'd cut down my working hours. I'd put the girls in Saturday dance and art classes. I could spend more time in his world; I'd follow baseball, stay up to greet him after his games, go to the stadium more often to watch him play. He'd be sure to notice.

And we could have another child.

Yes. That would bring us closer together: I loved Krisha and Whitney so much, they were getting old enough to handle a little brother or sister, and I'd always dreamed of a bigger family. That March, I took a week's vacation, flew to Florida, and joined him in training camp.

I took him out to dinner at a restaurant in Vero Beach. I waited for dessert, then brought up the subject.

"Let's have another child, Steve. Another child would be wonderful."

Steve leaned back in his chair and smiled. "Oh, I don't know, Cyn," he said.

"It'd be a great time for it," I insisted, leaning forward. "Krisha and Whitney came so close together, but now my body is rested. I'd love to do it now."

Steve shook his head.

"We could have a boy, Steve. Wouldn't you like a boy?"

"No, I don't think so," he said. "I like just having my girls around me."

My heart fell. Now he was leaning so far away from me that his chair was tipped back on two legs.

"I kind of like things," he said, "just the way they are."

The awful emptiness I felt was my final fantasy, dying. Now, only the fear was left.

CHAPTER 20

The man who would finish off our marriage was waiting patiently in the corridor. It was fifteen minutes before airtime, my second week back at work. Whitney had broken her arm a few days earlier; it was the time that Steve had deserted us in the hospital. I'd stayed home a little longer to take care of her. I had to leave right after work to take her to her doctor's appointment.

I was a little late, but everything was under control. I parked the car, grabbed my briefcase and suitbag. As I headed for the studio, I ran through the day's guests, the opening segment with Regis, in my mind. What was it that Vicki had told me about the second segment? I pushed open the heavy door to the sound stage; I was out of the bright sunlight into the cool, dark interior. My eyes needed a few more seconds to adjust, but that was all right. The makeup room was right over—

"Hello, Cyndy."

The deep voice was only a foot or two away. Startled, I looked up. My eyes were just starting to work again. Somebody was standing in front of me, blocking my path. A man. A big man, in jeans and a workshirt. A leather jacket. And a full brown beard. Standing behind him, off to one side, was a small, dark woman.

"I'm Pat Jordan," said the man.

"Yes?" I tried to focus my attention on him.

"I'm from *Newsweek,*" he said.

"Yes?"

He smiled. "We're doing an article on Steve and you. You don't know that I'm supposed to be here?"

"Uh, no."

"Well, I talked to your husband last night, and he said it would be fine to come to the studio and meet you."

Last night. Last night. I zipped back through my memory. Last night? Last night Steve had come home after a night game. I'd been asleep when he returned. We hadn't talked at all. And now there was another problem. The producer, Frank Kelly, was beckoning me angrily from across the studio. And it was getting really late.

"Just a second," I said to the tall man, and left him standing there.

"What's the matter, Frank?" I said.

"Cyndy. You cannot have reporters on this set. You cannot have this show written up without my permission."

"But, Frank, I don't know who this man is."

Frank shook his head impatiently. "He came to me, Cyndy," he said, "and told me he was going to watch a few shows this week and write about you."

What? "Frank, I really don't know anything about it."

No reaction. "Please ask him to leave," he said.

Now I really had a problem. If I just told the writer to leave, it would almost certainly be in whatever story this man was writing. The publicity would be awful. On the other hand, if I took the time to explain my problem to him, I would be late. And that was worse.

One chance. "Frank," I cajoled, desperately, in my best Cyndy voice. "Would it be okay if—listen, I don't know this man, but—would it be okay if he stood just behind the camera?"

It worked! "Okay," he said grumpily, "but only if he stands behind camera range. And no tape recorder."

"Thanks, Frank," I sighed.

I rushed back to the writer. "Listen. You've really caught me off guard, but the producer here, Frank Kelly, said that if you stand right here, and don't turn on your recorder, you can stay."

"Okay," he smiled. "And can I see you afterward?"

"Okay, sure," I shouted over my shoulder, as I ran to the makeup room. Sunday pulled me over to her, hastily powdered off the shiny spots, penciled on some eyeliner, grabbed whatever lipstick she could reach, and drew my mouth in bright red. Ugh. I looked terrible. A clown.

Too bad, no time.

Run, Cynthia. I made it into my chair, past a still-scowling Frank Kelly, only seconds before the red light. Regis looked at me and smiled slyly. "So! Doing an article for *Newsweek!* A major magazine! Am I gonna be in it?"

Oh great. Regis, as usual, was doing his bad-boy act. Calling attention to the situation; making it more embarrassing. I turned to him and whispered, because I didn't want the reporter to hear, "Regis, it's just one of Steve's sports articles."

"Well, I can be in that!" said Regis, mock-angrily. His voice boomed through the studio. The writer, standing next to the camera, laughed appreciatively.

I jerked my mind back to the show. But I couldn't quite focus on it. All through the hour, whenever my camera light was off, I stole a glance at . . . what was his name? Pat Jordan.

I noticed now that he was listening intently. The woman was still standing by his side. And the little red light on his tape recorder was glowing.

"Give me a minute," I said to Pat Jordan, when the director released me from the set. With Jordan walking right behind me, I went to the makeup room to call the house. Had arrangements really been made? Maybe Steve could—

"You must hate Regis Philbin," said Jordan, into my ear. "You must hate men."

What? I stopped and faced him. "I don't hate men," I told him, puzzled. "I love men."

The writer nodded gravely. I called Steve. But Priscilla answered the phone. It was ten forty-five. Steve had just left to play tennis with Sam Romano, she said. He'd be going to the ballpark from there.

Damn. Now I had a choice: I could take the risk of alienating a real reporter, from a big national magazine, or I could answer some questions, spend some time with, a man who might be an imposter.

"Okay," I said. "I've got a little while. Let's talk right here."

"All right," smiled Pat Jordan. He seemed to be in no hurry; for a few minutes, with his tape recorder off, we made small talk. "This is Susan," he said, and I shook hands with his companion. (His wife? His girlfriend?) He asked me whether I'd always lived in Los Angeles; I shook my head and told him about being an Air Force brat and living all over the country. Curiously, I thought, he took no notes. Instead, he listened closely, nodding, as if we were just having a friendly conversation. He even told me some things about himself. He told me that he lived in Fairfield, Connecticut. That he had five children. ("Five children!" I laughed, half amused, half envious. "You don't see that much in Los Angeles.") That he'd like to come back tomorrow for a longer interview.

Five children, I thought. "Well, let's see," I said. "Can you come back here tomorrow, after the show is over?" I walked him outside and pointed out the studio commissary. "I'll meet you there at ten forty-five," I said.

"Great," he said. I went back home to my children, and to ask Steve who this man was.

"Pat Jordan? Oh, he's all right," said Steve.

I'd phoned my husband from home at five-thirty that afternoon, when I knew batting practice was over, in the

Dodger clubhouse. The connection was bad; there was organ music, rock music, and players were shouting in the background.

"I'm just working with him on an article for *Newsweek*. It's not about you. It's about me."

"Yes, but, Steve, listen to me—why didn't you tell me about this man? You can't just send a reporter over to the set. I got in a lot of trouble at work this morning."

"Cyndy, Pat Jordan is standing right here next to me. He says hello. Gotta go now. Bye."

Pat Jordan was right on time. This time, alone. We sat down at a booth and ordered coffee.

"You're doing this piece for *Newsweek?*" I asked.

"Well," he grinned. "Not exactly. This is for *Inside Sports,* a sports magazine owned by *Newsweek.* "

Inside Sports? I'd never heard of it. I didn't want to tell Pat Jordan that, though; that was impolite.

"This article isn't just about Steve's career, or just baseball," said Pat Jordan.

"We want to do a piece," he said, leaning forward, "about the real side of baseball. Not the statistics, not the games, but how baseball families cope. You don't have to tell me the problems they face. I know about them. The traveling, the schedules, the life they have together."

That sounded interesting. No sportswriter had ever asked me about that before. I looked more closely at Jordan. He certainly didn't look like a typical sportswriter. More like a poet, or a college English professor. He seemed genuinely intelligent, genuinely interested. Not just looking for an easy angle to fill his notebook with quotes.

"Who else are you talking to?" I asked. Pete and Karolyn Rose, I thought. Tom and Nancy Seaver.

"Oh, we're still working on that," he said. "We won't take up too much of your time. But we want to get a different kind of look."

Hmm. Nobody had ever done this type of article, as far

as I could recall. It might be good for Steve and me, I thought. Break through some of the "Ken and Barbie" stereotypes. Curious about this different kind of sportswriter, I asked him his background. He had, he said, pitched briefly in the major leagues. "But I guess I just didn't have what it takes," he said, unapologetically. There was none of the usual head-shaking, exaggerated regret with which most men talked about their sports failures. He'd been writing, he said, for a while now, and had had one good-selling book.

"It's called *A False Spring*," he said. "But you've probably never heard of it. You don't read sports books," he said.

"Oh, that's not—wait a minute!" I said. I *had* heard of *A False Spring*. It was one of the books, I told him, that I'd put in Steve's suitcase for road trips.

"Oh?" he said, pleased.

"I loved living in New England as a girl," I told him.

He asked about my girls. We chatted about them for a while. He was easy to talk to, I realized. His dark eyes registered what I was saying. I barely noticed it when he turned on the tape recorder and the interview began.

His questions were different from any I'd ever been asked by a sportswriter. Interesting. We talked about my middle-European ancestry. My life in the Air Force, carefully skirting the troubles with my father, my parents. I told him what it was like always to be the new girl, to be considered a threat. Excluded. Then—a moment of caution. Was I whining? I thought. Complaining too much? Ready to pull back, I looked for any hint of skepticism in his eyes. But they were open. Sympathetic.

I told him about turning inward, toward my books and schoolwork. About Michigan State, my botched pre-med program, about meeting Steve.

I talked about my problems with the Dodger wives, with the invasion of our privacy. As an ex-ballplayer, I was sure that Pat Jordan understood the problems that families had in coping with "The Life."

I talked about the challenge of my new job.

"When I'm fulfilled and I'm busy," I said, "I'm happy. When I'm lonely, I'm not happy. And in baseball there's a lot of loneliness. To come home from a show like that— you're busy, and your mind is stimulated. You've had a good time.

"I love the show. I have a good time on the show. I hope it comes across that I do, because I'm not putting that on. It's truly me."

At that, the sadness welled up inside me. I'd never told the next part to a stranger before. But this man seemed to understand. To be worthy of the truth.

"And then I come home to an empty house at night. There's no male or adult person there. Repeatedly. It can make you nuts."

"Well," he said, encouraging me, "at least you know you've done something during the day."

We agreed to talk again on Friday. At one o'clock that afternoon, still coming down from the tension of that morning's show, I pulled up to the Beverly Hills Hotel. Pat Jordan, who was staying there, was waiting for me in the lobby.

"Just a minute," he said. "Let's go out and see Susan." We went around to the swimming pool, where she was lying in her bathing suit, sunbathing.

I sat down on the chaise longue next to her. "Hello. How are you?" I said.

She barely acknowledged me. "Hello," she said frostily.

I certainly wasn't expecting that. Before I could react, Pat Jordan jumped in. "She's not going to join us today."

"All right," I said. They must have had a fight, I thought. Too bad. Jordan took me back inside, into the Polo Lounge. It was filled with well-dressed people, laughing and clinking glasses and gesticulating. It was very noisy. At first, we were seated at a table next to the service bar. The rattling of plates and silverware was so loud that I wondered whether the tape recorder would be able to pick up our conversation. I called over the maître d', and he gladly moved us to another table, for four, in the middle of the room.

Pat Jordan sat down next to me. He put his tape recorder, not running yet, on the table.

He pulled his chair closer. "Did you and your wife have a fight?" I asked.

He smiled. "Susan isn't my wife," he said. He explained that Susan was his girlfriend. Though he still lived with his wife, who was back in Connecticut with the children, the two of them had grown apart over the years and that Susan, who was an ex-Broadway actress, was the woman he loved. His wife accepted the situation, he said.

"I see," I said, a little stunned at this news, but not wanting to appear unsophisticated or judgmental. After all, I thought, he hadn't tried to lie about or hide this arrangement.

And he didn't seem embarrassed or ashamed, either. This trip to Los Angeles, he said, was one of the few times they'd been able to get away together for any length of time. He told me what a good time he and Susan were having; what sights they'd seen; and what other sights should they see? I made a few suggestions.

They were, he told me, going to stay an extra few days in Los Angeles. "And the best part is, it's all on *Newsweek!*" he laughed. I smiled back.

We ordered lunch. Still no tape recorder. I asked him a few questions about his work; he started to talk fervently, eagerly, about his writing. He leaned closer, maybe a little too close, I half-realized. His eyes gleamed. What he wanted, he told me, was to write great novels—that was his real goal.

"With a realistic base to them," he added. I nodded. "That sounds wonderful," I said. An interesting man, I thought. An athlete and a writer. A person who's grown up, made unusual choices, and put his sports life behind him.

He told me that Susan, his girlfriend, had once been married to a professional basketball player. That she, too, knew what it was like to be married to the sports world.

Our salads arrived. Jordan reached across the table, and I saw that his shirt-sleeve—half rolled up—was about to fall into the salad dressing. "Hold it!" I said. He froze. I reached across, grabbed his arm, and rolled up his sleeve. When he realized what I was doing, he laughed sheepishly and rolled up his other sleeve.

I excused myself and went to the ladies' room. A few minutes after I came back, he turned on his tape recorder and we continued our talk.

We talked some more about my marriage and career. About the difficulties of meshing Steve's and my schedules. After a while, the conversation shifted; the tape recorder was still running, but Pat was doing most of the talking. Well, what was wrong with that? He obviously liked and trusted me. And listening to him was much more interesting than talking about myself.

His girlfriend, he said, had four children of her own.

"And she has good help?"

"No, she doesn't have good help," said Jordan. "She left her husband with the kids. She did 'Kramer vs. Kramer' a long time ago."

"That would be hard," I said, shocked by her decision.

"Yes," said Jordan, abruptly.

Was I being too judgmental? "Well, are there any ideal marriages any more? The old marriages of thirty, thirty-five years ago?"

He smiled grimly. I could see he was talking from his own experience. "Marriages are ideal in only two ways: either both people grow and develop simultaneously, or neither of them grows. They're both nineteen, and they stay nineteen until they're forty, and then they're happy. But if one is nineteen at forty, and the other is forty at forty, then they've got a problem. So if they both either grow together or if they don't grow at all, they're happy. But if one starts growing in one direction and the other doesn't—"

"You know," I said.

"It's nobody's fault. That's the sad part," said Pat Jordan. "It's nobody's fault."

"This is funny," said Pat. "When Susan was at the station, she took one look at you and said, 'She's exactly where I was ten years ago.' And now she's found which way to go."

Ten years ago, I thought. When she was married to the basketball star.

"I had one man tell me," I told Jordan, " 'If you divorce Steve Garvey, you might just as well get out of town.' "

"You're kidding."

"No, I wouldn't kid. I wouldn't make that up. 'Where would you be without Steve Garvey?' Do you know what it's like to be told that? That's a real kick. Especially when he doesn't beat me or anything. You know?"

"Oh! You mean because he's such a good guy that that automatically makes you the villain." Pat leaned back in his chair. "Where do you think a guy with five kids goes when he leaves his wife?"

"Better hide out," I laughed.

"I don't care. I can't think that way," he said.

Lunchtime at the Polo Lounge was almost over. The restaurant was emptying out, quieting down. We were sipping our coffee. "Did you ever have anyone interview you?" asked Pat. "Is this the first time anyone has ever done this?"

"No. I've been interviewed by women's magazines, stuff like that, but we talk about being a mommy and things like that." I laughed. "We talk nice. I feel like a kid. Nobody has ever asked me what it's like to be a baseball player's wife."

Pat thought for a moment. "I think," he said, "we'll change the title of the story. Originally, it was something like 'Superstar's Wife' or 'The Star's Wife.' The title now is just simply 'The Wife,' period, end of report. Because you are typical of what has happened to many women at this point in the beginning of the 80s and the late 70s. The old story."

An old story, he said. Could that be true? And yet, I realized, I'd never really told it to anyone. A fleeting thought: I'd only known this writer for a few days. Was he the right person to tell it to?

I worried about our unusual conversation, turning it over in my mind whenever I had a chance, for the next few days. Pat Jordan wasn't through yet, though; he'd arranged with Steve to visit our home for a joint interview that Sunday evening. On Saturday afternoon, I was home alone with the children while Steve was at the ballpark. I had just put the children down for their naps. The house was quiet.

The doorbell rang. I got up to answer it, a little annoyed. We had very few, if any, friends who just dropped in unannounced. This was probably an autograph seeker.

No. It was Pat Jordan and his wife. No, no. His girlfriend. They were both smiling broadly. "Steve told me to come out here and take a look at where you live," said the writer. "And we wanted to make sure we could find this place before it gets dark. We were in the neighborhood, and we thought we'd see if you were home."

"Well, come on in," I said. It was strange of them to drop in like this—but in truth, I realized, I could use some company. At least until the girls woke up. "Would you like something to drink?" I said.

"That would be great," smiled Jordan. I got them some sodas from the kitchen.

"What a beautiful house!" he said, standing in the hallway, peering into the living room. "This is real California, isn't it, Susan?"

We went into the TV room, sat down on the couch, and talked. Susan's attitude seemed to have turned completely around; she was friendly and open with me. Perhaps, I thought, that was because at the hotel I hadn't known about her and Pat's arrangement. Now that I knew, and hadn't disapproved of it, she could trust and be open with me.

Pat talked about Los Angeles, about the sights he'd seen, about his writing. He said that he would send me all of his books. "That would be very nice of you," I said.

Susan told me about her life with the professional basketball player; all the absences, all the disappointments, all the loneliness. I understood perfectly, I said. Without really thinking about it, I told Susan and Pat a bit more than I'd intended. About Whitney breaking her arm, for instance. About Steve deserting me. As the story came out, so did the anger. This is probably good for you, Cynthia, I thought. Get it out at last. Pat and Susan nodded sympathetically as I began to tell them my sad story.

"Wait a second," he said. "Let me get this." Pat reached into his coat pocket, took out his tape recorder, and turned it on. Was this part of the interview? Well, why not? I thought. I was among friends. I'd trusted Pat with my feelings already; what do I have to hide? And what does Steve, I thought, what does Steve have to hide?

I told them about Steve's passivity that day; about his disappearance from the hospital. I tried to explain Steve's side of the situation, but I was too emotional. Too angry. I failed.

"He felt," I said, "that I was secure with my father and knew that the doctor was going to be there—but I'll tell you what, I've had a baby without him being there. When he was playing in the World Series. When I had my first child and everyone was watching him on TV, and when I came back from the labor room they were still watching.

"That's okay. But to me, the man I married should come back—I mean, what if I had died in childbirth, or the child had come out wrong or something? Your mother and father are great, but they're not it. What if Whitney had gone into shock the other day?"

Pat agreed. "What if it had been major?"

"Or a decision had to be made?" I said. "It's on my shoulders all the time. You lived with it, Susan."

"It does happen all the time," Susan said.

I gave them a brief tour of the house. When we got back to the den, we talked some more about my problems with the other wives. About a couple of magazine articles that had tried to exploit my differences with them. About the wives of some other star ballplayers, like Nancy Seaver and Carolyn Rose—who was going through a divorce with her husband, Pete.

We talked about my problems at the ballpark; about the autograph seekers and the other wives. About my reluctance to be "The Lovely" at baseball functions Steve attended. About my dilemma: if I were to spend all my time with Steve, people would think I was hogging the spotlight; when I spend more time on my own, which I do out of necessity, it makes people think I'm not a dutiful wife.

Pat told me a sad story of his final year in baseball, when the team wives, knowing that Pat was on his way down, treated his wife with condescension.

"She'd come home crying all the time. She'd say, 'What horrible women.'" I felt for her.

Pat told me his hopes for his story. "You know," he said, "I could have gotten a different person. I was open for the possibility that I would come down here and find you just loved being Mrs. Steve Garvey—and there wasn't a thought in your head other than having your picture in every Sunday magazine section. And that would have been the scope of the story. Very easy, very safe. I tried to avoid a Pete Rose thing because there is so much bitterness going on there that it could be distorted."

"I don't have a lot of bitterness toward Steve," I said. "No. I love Steve. I want—I always tell him we're going to work this out. And he can't do it. I'm trying to put him back in the perspective that I met him. I want to love him for the man I met. He is so covered, just jumbled up in his career and other outside interests, I'm trying to see him clearly—and see if what I fell in love with is still strong enough. And the time factor in baseball deteriorates that a lot.

"You just don't have enough time."

Upstairs, the girls began to stir. Pat asked me if he could tour the house himself, making notes for his story. "Oh sure," I said. The next night, Steve brought Pat and Susan to our home again, for their "official" visit. This time Jordan concentrated on talking to Steve. After I offered them something to drink, I went upstairs to soak Whitney's arm and cast in warm water; I had to do that every three days. By the time the girls were asleep, Steve, Jordan, and Susan were sitting on the couch together, watching a funny sports show on television.

Steve and Pat Jordan were talking baseball, as if they were old friends. Or, as close to an old friend as Steve had. I sat at the other end of the couch for a while, then went back to my room to review material for the next day's show. Pat told me he had all he needed, and they left. The next day, Monday, Pat and Susan came to the station to say goodbye. It was nice of them, I thought.

That was in the early spring of 1980. A few weeks later, Pat Jordan sent me a set of the books he had written. I sent him back a handwritten note, thanking him. Steve handled the arrangements for the photo session without telling me. Steve, the photographer, and the photographer's assistant all drove up to the house together on July 4, while I was sitting with the girls by the pool. I went inside to change out of my bathing suit.

"Oh no! Don't do that," said the photographer. "You look great in that suit." I compromised by putting on a pair of shorts; in a few hours, they were gone. They weren't certain when the article was going to run.

I heard nothing more about the article, although I continued to think about what I'd said to Pat. I was looking forward to seeing what he had written. Maybe reading it would even help Steve and me understand each other.

Late one night, in the middle of August, I got a call at home from Vicki Testa, my associate producer. She was calling from her house.

"Cyndy, have you seen it?" she asked. She sounded upset—more upset than I'd ever heard her.

"What, Vicki?"

"Cyndy, you'd better call Steve. It's very bad."

"What is it, Vicki?" I sat up in bed. Could somebody we know, a staff member, have died? Could the show have been canceled?

"It's the article. The one written by the man who came on the set."

"Pat Jordan?"

"Yes, that's the byline," said Vicki. "It's awful, this article. Just awful."

"Oh, Vicki," I said, relieved that it wasn't something worse. "We've had bad articles about us before. All I did was talk to this man. How bad can one article be?"

CHAPTER 21

There was no way to get to a newsstand that night. Nor could I look at the article before we went on the air the next morning. Someone told me, though, that there was a piece about the article in the *Herald-Examiner* that morning.

When I sat down on the set, Regis was ostentatiously folding back a copy of the *Herald.* There was no time to talk to him before we were on the air.

"So!" said Regis. "Ya got something hot out today, huh? What happened?"

Automatically, Cyndy answered perkily, "I really can't talk about it, Regis, I don't know."

Regis held the newspaper off to one side and silently "read" the item. Then he turned to me. "So you want to cuddle, huh?" He reached over and wrapped his arm around my waist. "You could cuddle me!"

Cuddle him? Why was he asking me to cuddle him? And why was he leering at me? I vaguely remembered saying something like that to Pat Jordan, but I hadn't meant . . .

Somewhere inside my brain, an alarm bell went off. I recoiled in shock. I was so surprised, so confused, that I broke all the rules. I leaned over Regis' shoulder, on the air, and began to read the item.

It was by somebody named Jeff Silverman. I skimmed

through it as fast as I could. ". . . America's Fun Couple . . . August 31st issue . . . *Inside Sports* . . . writer Pat Jordan . . . couple in crisis . . . seams in their marriage . . . 'It looks like *everybody's* getting to first base these days' . . . 'My career doesn't fill the void of not having my husband home,' admits the candid Cyndy. 'Sometimes I wish I could cuddle with someone. When there's no man around, you can go nuts . . .' "

What was this? I'd never said those things. This item was awful. Untrue. For a moment, stunned, I forgot where I was, what I was doing, and looked away from Regis, straight into the camera. No answers there. Out of the corner of my eye I saw Vicki standing beside the camera. She had her hands over her face. She was crying.

This is just a misprint, I thought. It's all a mistake. Somehow, by concentrating on that thought, I managed to get through the hour. When we were released from the set, Vicki walked me into the ladies' lounge. I sat down on the couch and took her copy of *Inside Sports*. It was a thick, glossy magazine. Steve and I were on the cover. The article about us, placed strangely at the very end of the magazine, ran ten pages.

With a growing sense of dread, I began to read. The article was divided into sections, each under its own heading: THE HOUSE; THE WIFE; THE JOB; THE HOTEL; THE HUSBAND; THE PROBLEM; THE COUPLE.

Vicki sat next to me, her hand on my shoulder. Our house, wrote Jordan, "was decorated in a style common to people who have the resources for instant gratification, but who have yet to grow into a style of their own."

The young wife had neither the style nor the patience to coordinate every detail . . . There were photographs in the bedroom hallway. Photographs of the husband and wife and children. Photographs of the husband and wife. Photographs of the children, two young girls, ages 4 and 5, with windblown hair—one blonde, one dark. There were more photographs downstairs. The husband in a

Dodger uniform, holding two small American flags in each hand and smiling. The wife in profile, her blonde hair as unreal in its perfection as that of a Breck girl. The wife *posed* getting out of a car, the wife smiling as she points one leg out of the car, her silky dress hiked past her thigh . . .

There were mementos, too . . . all the mementos were the same. Unblemished. Disposable . . . It was as if, for this family, all these expensive-looking objects were needed to fill in the gaps in the unformed natures . . .

Posed. Unreal. Fake. *My children.* Is that how he saw me? I thought. Wait a minute. "This is wrong," I said to Vicki. She gave my shoulder a squeeze. I read on.

THE WIFE

Cyndy Garvey is 30 years old. She is tall and thin. She has long blonde hair. She is pretty in the manner of a Miss America contestant, a look she embellishes—bleached hair, heavy make-up—to give it distinction. It is a look thought glamorous in certain regions of this country, and despite her protestations ("I don't try to look this way. I just always was glamorous") it is not a look acquired without effort. She claims her looks are a burden, which is not uncommon among women who have been pretty all their lives.

"No!" I said to Vicki. "That's not the way it is. That's not what I said at all!"

"I know," said Vicki. She tried to gently take the magazine away from me. I shook my head, held onto it, and kept reading.

THE JOB

There is a call for quiet on the set. The stage manager, a slim black man with a gold earring in one pierced ear, begins counting down. "Nine . . . eight . . . seven . . ." He whirls around and snaps, "Quiet, LOVE!

If you please!" The battery of cameras moves forward, towards the talk show host, Regis Philbin, a dapper man in a pinstriped suit, who is sitting on a large sofa. Sitting beside him is Cyndy Garvey, the co-host. The stage manager points at Philbin, who begins his monologue. Cyndy smiles at the camera. She is sitting up very straight, legs crossed, hands folded in her lap, leaning slightly toward the host. Every so often she interjects a comment. Philbin responds without looking at her. She smiles at the camera. Philbin goes on. From the shadows, a New York actress, who is a guest, whispers to someone. "It's a regional look," she says of Cyndy. "It would never play in New York."

. . . Her blonde hair is pulled back into a ponytail, revealing a pair of oversized bulb earrings. Her hair is pulled back so tightly from the sides of her face, stretching the skin, that her face looks gaunt. She is too thin. Her arms appear as sticks protruding from her sleeveless blouse. On screen she appears only as slim, but in person she is emaciated. There are deep lines, parentheses, on either side of her wide mouth.

Philbin is telling a funny story. Cyndy adds a word here and there. She seems content to react to his lead. As Philbin is finishing his monologue, Cyndy interrupts him with a funny comment. The crew breaks into laughter. Philbin turns his head toward her. "What the hell do you know?" he says, half-kiddingly. "You've only been doing this show for a year. I've been doing it for five years." She smiles at him, as a dutiful wife would a husband who has chastised her in front of guests. While the camera is on their faces, she kicks him in the shins.

"Oh Jeez," says someone on the set. "No wonder she doesn't have much confidence. He won't give her a break. He's a real c——."

Later, someone asks how she puts up with Philbin. She smiles and says, "You mean Bozo? Oh, he's my big bad brother. He's always teasing me, but I can put up with it. Because I don't need it. The show, I mean. They told him the show would be a lot better if he'd do less. But he won't."

For a second, fighting for control, I pulled myself out of the article, and shook my head in pain and disbelief. There was some truth in what Jordan had said, but in his hands these were cruel truths, cruelly said. And Jordan had a right to his opinion—but wait. I couldn't remember myself saying one tenth of that—and what I did remember had been pulled out of context. Spliced together from different places. Made up. I started to panic. What was going to happen to me if Regis, if *anybody* believed I'd actually said those things? I forced myself to keep reading. Unbelievably, the worst was yet to come.

THE HOTEL

The maître d' sighs, scoops up the menus he had just deposited on the table near the service bar, and leads Cyndy Garvey and her gentleman companion to another table in the center of the nearly deserted restaurant.

"Will *this* do, Madame?" he says.

"Yes. Thank you very much," she says, smiling. They sit down. After the maître d' leaves, she says, "Well, I just don't care. I will not be seated near the service bar." Her companion nods. He is a tall man, in his 40s, with a salt-and-pepper beard. He unbuttons the cuffs of his silk shirt and is about to roll them back when she says, "Here, let me do it. I think it looks sooo sexy." She rolls back the cuffs twice, smiling at the man as she does so. It is the smile of a woman who thinks she is being sexy. It is merely a dessert filled with empty calories: she knows, and she assumes her companion knows, that her flirtation is meant to lead nowhere. She is used to flirting without having to deliver. It is safe. Most men are gratified by it, by her laying a hand on their arm, a small blessing, for which they are grateful.

Not true. "Not true!" I said to Vicki. I'd never said these things. These paragraphs were about Jordan, not me. They were the fantasies of a man with a dirty mind. Filth!

"Actually, this show is my kindergarten," she says. "I'm working, learning, and someday I'll graduate. I'll be all right. I'm not 22 anymore. I'm no little nymphet. But I'm no ballsy career woman either. I'm just trying to balance a career with being a wife and mother. I have all this energy and nowhere to channel it. Now I have a voice of my own. I'm going to do something with my life. Maybe I'll do news, or straight acting, or a talk show. Whatever, I won't go through life wondering what I might have been . . . Would I like a career in New York? You mean if my husband was traded to New York? Oh, you mean just me." She laughs, as if embarrassed. "I can't answer that right now. The way things are . . .

"When I married my husband, I never intended to be anything but a wife and mother until a few years ago. I was bored, so I took a job. I know my husband wants me to be happy and fulfilled, and if this job does it then that's what he wants for me. In the long run, my career might be even bigger than my husband's."

She laughs again, as if contemplating a fantasy. "You know, a woman in her 30s needs mobility to grow. When she gets into something she's hard-pressed to give it up . . . even for a man. I know, in my own case, if I was single now, I'd be a hard person to marry. But still my career doesn't fill the void of not having my husband home during the baseball season. He's gone 92 days out of the summer, and during the off-season, he's very active in business. He's got to take advantage of his peak earning years as a ballplayer. But God, sometimes, I wish I could cuddle with someone. I have to have someone to talk to at night. Baseball is a tough sport for a wife. A baseball wife can't work at a conventional job, like teaching, or else she'll never see her husband. Baseball doesn't leave much time to be together, unless the wife goes to the park and sits in the stands and cheers her husband on . . . Jeez, when there's no man in the house you can really go nuts.

"I have to be a constant support for my husband. If I'm angry at him when he leaves the house for the stadium, I feel guilty. Maybe he won't do well. Of course, he always does well," she says with sarcasm. "At first I channeled all my energy into him. Now he calls home and I'm not there. A lot of wives discover a need for an identity at 30. We think all we need to get rid of the frustration is a new man. We trade up, we think. It's a halfway measure. If the new man's an athlete, we'll outgrow him, too."

The wife is speaking in a brusque, nasally voice that sounds almost whiney except there is no self-pity. Her voice is flat, objective, punctuated by quick smiles and brittle laughter that rarely correspond to her words.

Pat Jordan had tricked me. He had used me. I recognized things I had actually said, but they were spliced cleverly between his fabrications and his fantasies. Reading his poisonous words sent sharp needles into my stomach: I felt myself becoming hysterical. Losing control. My house, I thought, pathetically. *I had let this man come into my house. To sit and talk to me. To meet my girls.*

"My god, Vicki! He makes me sound like a lonely, sex-starved maniac!" She shook her head.

"It's all a lie, Cyndy," she said. "I know that." I looked at her. I could see her fear—for me—in her eyes. After reading this, what would anyone who didn't know me think? Underneath the panic, I felt the first sting of guilt.

Eyes burning, I rushed through the rest of the article. In the section titled THE HUSBAND, there was the usual summary of Steve's career; some cheap shots at his "calculated" image. " 'This is not a concentrated effort. I am the same as I was 10 years ago. Everyone has their own space and they have to decide how they want to use it.' " Under THE PROBLEM, he quotes only me:

" '. . . I'm out here in the land of fantasy and I see relationships come and go and I don't know whether it's worth it to cash in on anything stable . . .

" '. . . I want electricity, a spark, some idiosyncrasy . . .

" 'I'm a girl who needs a regular sex life.' " *How dare he!*

" 'The suburbs drove me nuts. I had to get out . . .

" 'I haven't had any affairs yet, but I wonder what it would be like . . .

" 'If I divorced my husband, I'd have to get out of town.' "

Now, Jordan talking:

> She falls silent for a moment. She is still staring straight ahead. The tone in her voice has remained constant. Unemotional. How can she reveal such intimacies without emotion? She does not cry. In fact, she flashes her brittle smile precisely at that moment one expects her to cry. Now, at 30 when she is feeling unpleasant emotions, she knows of no other way to express them.

When Jordan's words came to an end, I dropped the magazine onto my lap. I sat silently, Vicki next to me, for a few minutes. I tried to figure this out: this man, whom I barely knew and whom I had let into my home—let near my children!—had told lies about me.

No. He'd done something worse than that. He had invaded me. Assaulted me. He had used my words, turned them into *his* words, to strip me of the little bit of privacy I had built up over the years. Somehow, in the little time we had spent together, this man had sensed my sadness and loneliness. Then he had gone away—to warp and twist these feelings: the sadness into the bitterness, the loneliness into bitchiness. Bitterness. Ugliness.

What a fool I was. I was gullible. Defenseless. Powerless. Stupid. A child!

Then, from somewhere, an awful thought: *What would my father think when he read this article? Would his worst suspicions be confirmed?*

In an awful moment, I was awash in shame. Maybe this was what my father had meant. Maybe this was why he was angry with me. Maybe you were a bad daughter, a bad person. Maybe everybody—Jordan included—had known it for a long time.

Yes, Cyndy. Now it all made sense. I could hear my father's voice, telling me all the things that Jordan had written. I was useless. I was sinful. I was a bad wife. A bad mother. Yes, it was true. I deserved any punishment I received.

And then, for some reason, I flashed back to another, even more terrible scene: my father beating me, for the last time, when I was thirteen. "No more!" I'd said to him, way back then. "No more," I heard myself saying now. "No more."

There was no time to figure it out. In a second, just like before, I felt my shame turn to anger. No! It was not fair! I thought. *That was not me. I was not a bad woman.*

Suddenly, I was furious. Focused. Concentrated in my thinking. It was time, I saw with awful clarity, to stand up for myself. *It was time to put a stop to this.*

My first thought was to call Steve. He was not home. I called our lawyer, Alan Rothenberg.

"I want you to stop this, Alan," I said.

He was sympathetic. "Yes, we're aware of the article, Cyndy. We haven't had a chance to study it, though. We'll do that today."

"It's all false. It's all lies about us, and I want it stopped. I want you to call up the newspaper, call up the station, and get them to stop writing about it or mentioning it. I don't want Regis talking about it."

"We'll see what we can do. Don't worry," he said. I hung up.

I don't remember driving home. I took care of the girls, and when they went upstairs for their naps, sat in the living room, alternately shaking with anger and crying with shame. Thinking about Jordan. The article. My marriage. Steve.

Later that night, alone in the house, I called Information for Fairfield, Connecticut, and got Pat Jordan's phone number. I dialed it. A woman answered.

"Hello?"

"Is Pat Jordan there?"

"No, he's not. Can I take a message?" The voice was timorous, hesitant. I hadn't heard it before. It was Jordan's wife, I realized. I was too angry to even feel sorry for her.

"This is Cyndy Garvey. Do you understand what your husband has done to me?"

"I don't . . . I don't know where he is."

"Well, when he comes in, you tell him to call me."

Later that evening, he called me back.

"You fooled me," I said to him. "How dare you!"

Silence.

"I let you into my home!"

More silence. Something clicked. For a second, a searing second, I saw the connection. My father. Steve. Pat Jordan. Three different men. All the same. "I'm going to sue you," I said, angrily.

Finally Jordan spoke. "I had to do the assignment they gave me," said Jordan. I hung up the phone, sat back down in my chair, and waited until morning for the fight to begin.

CHAPTER 22

The next morning, there was another gossip item about the article in the *Herald-Examiner*. I noticed, to my dismay, why the *Herald* was playing it up so much: the newspaper, beginning the following week, was planning to print the entire *Inside Sports* article in installments.

Regis was ready, newspaper in hand, to mention it on the air. But this time I was ready, too.

"So!" he said, eyebrow raised, during the opening segment. "What's happening? What's all this about?"

I was careful not to smile at him. "I can't discuss it, Regis," I said. "It's in the hands of our lawyers." Then silence. He was forced to change the subject. Toward the end of the show, I noticed that John Severino was in the studio. He stopped to talk to me as I was coming off the set.

"Well, Cyndy. Your lawyers called us," he said. "They asked that the article not be mentioned on the air, and I've told everybody not to."

"Thank you, John," I said.

"But think about this, Cyndy—you've come very close to violating the morals clause in your contract. We could let you go, if we wanted to, because of the things you said in that article."

Morals clause? Let me go? "John," I said, pleading.

"There's no morals clause involved. That's not fair. I didn't say those things. They were made up, twisted. That article, that man, injured *me.*"

Severino nodded. "I understand," he said, and walked away.

From that day on, neither the article or the lawsuit was mentioned on "A.M. Los Angeles." But it didn't matter. Jordan's article, so "frank" and "revealing," opened the door to torrents of press and public criticism of me. Not Steve. Just me.

"I'm taking calls on Cyndy Garvey," said the talk-show host on KABC Radio, the Dodgers' station. I gripped the wheel, shaking, as I drove home from work. A few minutes earlier, this man, whom I had never met, had read some of the worst passages from the article. As if the article were all the proof he needed, he'd stated the opinion that I was an ungrateful woman who did not appreciate that I would have gotten nowhere, been nothing whatsoever, without my husband's help.

"I absolutely agree with you, Michael," said the woman caller. She did not like me, either, she said.

"You said what I've been thinking," said another woman.

One after another, for an entire hour, the host drummed up dislike of me. Caller after caller, person after person, commented disparagingly on my looks. My career. My marriage. My sex life. I was a blond bitch. A flirt. A frustrated bimbo. An ingrate.

By the time I got home, I was in shock. Dazed, my anger almost a numbed reflex, I called the station to talk to the host. They would not put my call through. "He'll call you back after the show," said the receptionist. I left my number. He never returned my call.

It was as if, for some reason that had nothing to do with who I really was, thousands of columnists and broadcasters and the people who believed them had been storing up dislike for me. No, not for me. For the person they thought I was. For the image, the *idea* of Cyndy Garvey.

SHED A TEAR FOR CYNDY. LIFE CAN BE SO UNBEARABLE was the headline on this story by a local sports columnist:

> Today, you would call Steve [Garvey] a roaring success, a beneficiary of hard work and dedication. And a beneficiary of the many advantages his money and renown have brought his wife, Cyndy, who, through her husband's efforts, has been placed in a position contending enough to indulge the luxury of a big mouth.
>
> In the current issue of *Inside Sports*, dear Cyndy has bared her hardship living with this hero. It has been emotional hell. Her identity has been dwarfed, her feelings ignored.
>
> Her husband hasn't grown as she has, she contends. And even her sexual needs have been neglected . . .
>
> Long ago, Cyndy outgrew baseball and baseball wives. She describes herself in the interview as "glamorous," and says she often has trouble with men on airplanes. At times, in fact, she has left first class and fled to coach to get away from male seat companions.
>
> It hasn't occurred to her, though, that without Steve Garvey, she might be flying standby.

This was by a man who talked to my husband several times a week. I'd met him often, talked to him pleasantly. But that didn't count, I realized. I wasn't a sports hero. I was just a wife. And, apparently, no kind of insult—personal, sexual—was against the rules now.

> *Beautiful and intelligent but neglected wife and television personality looking for warm, dynamic All-American man to cuddle with during husband's busy sports season. Interests include Barbie dolls and working out at Jack La Lanne's.*
>
> Cyndy Garvey has given America's men hope.

I have always had this thing for Cyndy Garvey. So
have a lot of guys I know. But we've all felt she was out
of our league. How could the rest of us compete with her
husband, Dodger star Steve Garvey?

Ah, but then came last week's publication of Cyndy's
controversial interview with *Inside Sports* magazine.
Well, I don't care what anyone else says, that article has
breathed new life into every man in love with Cyndy
Garvey.

It was like one big personal ad crying out for love and
companionship in some lonely hearts club magazine . . .

This is how a writer named Tony Castro started his
column. And there was more of the same. Much more. In
my mind, the anger and shame fought for dominance. I
searched my memory, my conscience. What had I ever
done to provoke these men? I wondered.

And then, terrifyingly, their abuse spilled out of the
media into the real world.

On the freeway, on my way to work, the license plate on
the car marked me. I noticed leering male drivers following my car. They pulled alongside me, rolled down their
windows, and shouted obscene suggestions. When that
happened, I cut across the freeway to the nearest off-
ramp. I parked the car and waited, shaking, until I was
sure the men were gone.

"Hey, baby! Hey, Cyndy!" shouted the man across the
parking lot at the shopping mall. I froze. He was young,
skinny, decently dressed. Just an ordinary man. He
walked towards me, spewing filthy suggestions. As I frantically loaded the groceries in my car, people stood and
stared at both of us. I managed to get in the car, lock the
door, and drive away before he reached me. I called the
police. They came to the house, took a report, and left.

I forced myself to go outside, to live my normal life. I
was just a normal person, just like them. Surely, everybody could see that?

It was no use. At the supermarket one day, I stopped at the checkout counter to glance at a *National Enquirer.* The headlines leered at me. This is what I'm up against, I thought.

"More trash," I said to the cashier. I saw his expression change—then, before I could react, felt my head yanked back. I was looking into the face of a furious woman! She had grabbed me by my hair.

"No. You're trash!" she said. For a second, I looked into her wild, furious eyes. Then just as suddenly, she let me go. She walked away, out the door, as the other shoppers just stared at her. It wasn't until she was gone that the physical pain registered through my shock. The humiliation and fear, which started when the shock wore off, lasted much longer.

Steve was no help. I asked him, pleaded with him, to talk to the baseball writers and ask them, as a favor to him, to lay off me. His wife. But he never did. And he was gone just as much, if not more, than before the article. I had no one to turn to, no one I could trust.

I was alone with the pain. In the middle of the night, when it was hard to fight back, I sometimes gave into the guilt. Yes, I was bad. Yes, I must have done something wrong. I was a poor mother, an unfaithful wife. But if that was really so, what terrible things had I done? What horrible things had I said?

No!

No, Cynthia, I repeated, shaking, to myself. I *was* a good mother. I did love my children. I would give my life for them.

I'd done the best I could to get through to Steve. I had a job. I had a *real name.* But did that matter?

Maybe, when people looked at me, nobody saw Cynthia. Maybe nobody believed she really existed. Maybe Cynthia was a bitch, a witch, an ingrate. Maybe I should be satisfied with being Cyndy. Maybe Cyndy was all that I was. Maybe Cyndy was all that I would ever be.

No.

I was Cynthia. And Cynthia's big mistake was that she had trusted Pat Jordan. Trusted him enough to explain who I really was. He had nodded and smiled and used my own words, or what he falsely claimed were my words, to attack me. Now I had to fight back. To stop the attacks. Just like, I realized, I'd stopped my father from hitting me, all those years ago.

And the only way to do that, the only way to hold onto my sanity, was to fight back, as best I could, *as* Cynthia. To hold onto her. To hold onto the truth, to whatever self-respect, whatever identity I could.

That was my only option. My only way out.

The thought of what I would have to do, with what I would have to face, filled me with nothing but terror.

Our lawyers filed suit against *Inside Sports* and *Newsweek*. Immediately, they got a temporary injunction stopping the *Herald* from reprinting the article. After ten days, though, the newspaper got the order rescinded.

When the reprints began, in daily installments, things got worse. The parade of cars in front of our house, which had slackened somewhat, picked up. People stopped, peered into our window. Our mailbox was filled with obscene letters, addressed to me. I threw them out.

Neither my mother or father ever directly discussed the article with me. "If there are things you need to do now, we'll take care of the girls for you," said my mother one morning. That was the closest we came.

I had less contact with my neighbors than ever. At the dry cleaner, at the bank, at the post office, the people I dealt with every day seemed too embarrassed to look me in the eye. Strangers stared at me unashamedly—wondering, I assumed, how I could be bold enough to show my face in public.

The *Herald* advertised the reprints by putting my picture on the placard on the bottom of their newspaper machines. The pictures, the machines, the newspapers were everywhere; there were several of them on the route I walked with Krisha and Whitney. *They were out on the street for my children to see.*

One morning, after a sleepless night, I got out of bed at dawn, dressed, went outside, roamed the neighborhood, and ripped up every *Herald* placard I could find. Then I went home and made breakfast for the girls. In a couple of days, all the placards had been replaced.

I made it clear to Steve that I was going to sue Pat Jordan whether he helped me—whether he wanted the "distraction"—or not. Reluctantly, he agreed to join me in the suit. A few weeks after the article came out, I managed to find an empty space in his schedule, and Steve and I went to Alan Rothenberg's office to plan our long-term strategy. Alan introduced me to his associate Gary Bostwick, an ex-Peace Corps volunteer, a pleasant-looking, mustachioed man a few years older than me, who would be doing most of the actual work on the case.

We were suing *Newsweek* for $11 million, but that figure was being used mainly as a bludgeon. "I want an apology. I want a retraction," I said. Steve sat next to me, saying nothing, while I went through the story line by line.

"I didn't say this."

"He twisted this."

"You have to understand. This was taken out of context."

Alan Rothenberg was tough with me. "I have to warn you, Cyndy," said Alan. "Proving libel can be very difficult. It's going to take up a lot of your time. Maybe most of your time. This is going to be a very long, very painful, and very expensive procedure."

He named some dollar figures, a time frame—hundreds of thousands of dollars, years. The numbers didn't matter, I told him. Neither did the years.

"I don't care. It's worth it. We have to do this," I said.

Now Steve spoke up for the first time.

"Wait a minute," he said. "You know, I've got a streak of consecutive games going. I can't miss a ballgame. Will this interfere with my baseball schedule?"

Alan looked shocked.

"Oh no, no, no!" said Alan. "We can work around your schedule."

"Okay then," said Steve.

After the meeting, heading toward a restaurant for lunch, I lagged behind the rest of the men, with Gary. At lunch, the men talked about baseball. I couldn't eat.

Alan Rothenberg was right. The lawsuit took over my life. It kept the wound open. It kept my anger flaming, eating me up from the inside. But it had to be done. I had to show the world how Jordan had made up quotes, quoted me out of context, twisted my words in order to hold me up to ridicule. This was my turn, my chance to explain all of this. I was going to punish Jordan and put things right.

Weekday mornings, while I was actually doing the show, were the only times I could force the lawsuit out of my mind. In the afternoons, barricaded in my house, I talked to the lawyers. At night, the fear and rage and shame took control.

As their first step, our lawyers subpoenaed Jordan's interview tapes. By comparing the actual quotes with the published article, we could show how he had distorted my meaning. The other side's answer came back: the tapes were lost, erased, reused. Then they said that they would hand over a transcript, but only after some "irrelevant" material had been deleted. Their transcript arrived, full of deletions; huge holes. "They're stalling. They've got something to hide," said Gary Bostwick, smiling to keep up my spirits. He told me that their evasions were a sign of weakness; they obviously had something to hide. I wanted to believe that, but their lies and evasions just made me angrier.

At first, I spent my afternoons meeting with Alan and Gary, pointing out the lies and distortions. Then the depositions began: Steve and I had to go to the office of *Newsweek*'s attorney—a famous libel specialist named William Masterson—and answer hundreds of questions while a court reporter took down everything that Masterson and his assistants asked us.

There was a chance the Dodgers would make the playoffs that October, so the depositions were scheduled around possible games. They took our depositions in a big, wood-paneled conference room in downtown Los Angeles. Five lawyers on their side. Four lawyers on ours.

"Don't let them see you get angry or excited, Cyndy," said Gary. "Just give them yes or no answers. That's all. Don't give them anything more than you have to. They don't deserve it."

They took me through the article line by line. Between questions, they joked and smirked and whispered to each other. The deposition went on for hours, days, weeks. Steve, when he wasn't away playing baseball, sat behind me and to my right, impassive. Gary Bostwick, with whom I'd talked almost every day over the months, and felt was a friend, sat on my left. He watched me closely for signs that I was losing my temper. When he saw that, he reached under the table, secretly, and took my hand. He looked at me and smiled sympathetically. He knew it was awful, said his smile, but what could we do? Just treat the other side with inward contempt. That was our best weapon.

MR. MASTERSON: Were you angry with baseball at the time you had this session of interviews with Jordan?

MRS. GARVEY: You know, now that I think back to it, I speak so freely probably I interchanged the words "frustration" and "anger" as one. It would not seem impossible to me, but I was not angry at Steve per se, I was angry at the situation, the total situation.

Q: Is it probably then, Mrs. Garvey, given your speech pattern that you just said, that you probably said to Jordan, "I am now open because I am angry"?

A: No, I did not say, "I am open now because I am angry."

Q: Did you say, "I am angry now"?

A: I might have said, "I am a little angry, I am a little frustrated."

Q: In the next paragraph, Mrs. Garvey, did you say to Jordan, "The suburbs drove me nuts."

A: No. The suburbs drive me nuts, they drive me nuts now.

Q: Did you say to him, "I had to get out. That's why I went back to work"?

A: No.

Q: Did you say to Jordan, "Maybe my job will be a way out"?

A: No.

Q: Did you say to him, "I don't want to give up what I've got unless I can go to something else"?

A: No.

Q: I'm sorry, ma'am?

A: No.

Q: Did you say to Jordan, "I don't want to drag my kids around during my indecision"?

A: That I do not disagree with, because I don't want to drag my kids around through my indecisions.

Q: What decision or indecisions do you have reference to?

A: The suburbs drive me nuts, because since taking on a job that is in Hollywood I fight that freeway traffic for an hour and a half every morning five days a week, but I don't want to drag my kids around because they are in good schools and they like their neighborhood, so that decision will be taken care of sooner or later, but I am not going to drag my kids around through it.

Q: Is the indecision or indecisions the question as to whether you should live in a different place that would be closer to your place of work?

A: Among other things, or whether I should take a job that is closer to where I live. I don't know.

Q: Is it your testimony that the indecision to which you referred, indecision or indecisions, does not have anything to do with your questioning your marriage and your role in your marriage?

A: Where you live goes along with your marriage. It confines your marriage if you are not real happy where you live.

Q: Is the answer to my question "yes" or "no"?

A: I am sorry, what was your question?

"Mommy's tired. Mommy's sad," said Krisha, climbing up on my lap as I sat, after a deposition, in the living room.

I looked at her beautiful face. She was sad, I realized with a pang of guilt. She was concerned for me. My troubles were getting through to my children. I was stealing time from them for other purposes. That was wrong, my fault. I had to shield them from this terrible time.

"Oh no, no, no, sweetheart!" I smiled my biggest smile.

"Mommy's not sad. Mommy's happy to be with you! Come on! Mommy wants to play!" I put on the radio, turned up the music, and began to dance with her.

I tried hard to keep it up. Whenever I came home from work, I made sure to be the happy mommy. "Come on! Let's go for a walk! Let's go shopping! Let's buy some toys! Let's get something for Krisha and Witty!" I signed the girls up for more lessons, more activities. In the afternoons, in the time left over from the job and the lawyers, I drove them from place to place. At night, when Steve was out of town, I took them into bed with me. They needed the extra comfort, I thought.

The depositions, the motions, the conferences dragged on and on. I slept less and less. I lost more weight. There was a pain in my stomach that would not go away. I went to my doctor and discovered I had a bleeding ulcer. The doctor prescribed Tagamet, Valium, and sleeping pills. And told me not to worry so much.

Early one morning, on my way to buy a Christmas present, I parked my car in Beverly Hills and started to walk down the street. A wave of weariness swept over me, and I leaned up against a light post. I looked across the street, toward the Beverly Wilshire Hotel. A tall, vaguely familiar man, wearing glasses, dressed in a conservative dark suit, was standing there, staring at me. He was holding a rolled-up umbrella. In Beverly Hills. How silly, I thought.

The light changed. He started to walk across the street toward me. It was, I realized, Marvin Hamlisch.

He had a puzzled expression on his face. "Hello, Cyndy," said Marvin Hamlisch. "You look terrible. Just terrible."

I looked up at this strange man and began to cry.

CHAPTER 23

That Monday, there was a phone message for me at the studio. "Marvin Hamlisch called," it said. "I can't deal with this now," I said, and put the message aside.

By then, our lawyers had taken Pat Jordan's deposition in New York City. They had gotten him to describe how he had spliced quotes together and put his own words in my mouth. When I had nodded, or said "Yes" or "I understand" to an opinion Jordan had expressed, he had felt free to use it as my own quote. He had even "recorded" scenes and dialogue after they had happened—by talking into his tape recorder during times when Steve and I weren't actually present. Those were the parts of the tapes that he and his lawyers didn't want us to have.

The lawyers thought that Jordan's testimony had helped our case. But their enthusiasm didn't make me feel better. Far from it. Seeing how Jordan had trapped me, and how I had let him do it, made me even angrier at him. And myself.

The anger burned into my stomach. It fed on itself and spread through my body. But my anger wasn't all bad, I thought: sometimes, when I got so depressed that I broke down in tears, I called on the anger to blast me out of my sadness. To focus me on what I had to do: get back at the man—the men?—who had victimized me.

* * *

To prove how Jordan's article had held us up to ridicule, the lawyers advised us to hire a clipping service. We were flooded with articles. The wave of sarcasm, of derision, spread out across the country and bounced back. "I'm writing this column," wrote a man named Mike Lupica, who worked for the *New York Daily News,* "to announce that I won't be taking Cyndy Garvey to the prom this year."

> This has nothing at all to do with the excess of y's in her first name, annoying as they are. My decision about the prom goes deeper than that. It is all tied up to the fact that Cyndy Garvey has become a nuisance, the kind of semi-celebrity spawned by all the gossip columns in all the newspapers and magazines in the world.

Lupica accused me of whining, of using the article to attract publicity, of being ungrateful to Steve for getting me my job on television. He had some advice for me.

> . . . if you are any kind of wife, any kind of caring person, you do not air out the details of your marriage in the windowpanes of Beverly Hills. Unless you are taking a shot at serious celebrity.

And finally, he concluded:

> *Inside Sports* should have headed this story "Wyfe Dearest." Cyndy Garvey says in it that she can chew gum and talk. We are only assured of the latter.

"Wait a minute, Mr. Masterson," said Judge Kelleher, impatiently. "I don't understand. You say that Mr. Jordan took a quote from one place, put it together with a quote from another place, and made it look like one continuous quote? You mean that some things Mrs. Garvey said at her home are included in the section headed 'The Hotel'?"

"Let me explain, your honor!" *Newsweek*'s lawyer, just a few feet away from me, jumped to his feet and argued that these techniques were perfectly proper.

It was mid-January, 1981. We were in the judge's chambers, in the courthouse in downtown Los Angeles. Reams of briefs, arguments, and counter-arguments had been filed. Now the lawyers were arguing whether all of Jordan's notes and taped comments should be released to our side. Jordan, with his lineup of lawyers, sat on the other side of the courtroom. Again and again, Masterson, reading from the article, claimed that something I'd never said or meant was obviously a perfect expression of my feelings. Although Gary Bostwick had told me not to —although he'd told me I shouldn't even go to the hearings—I shook my head in disgust at his claims. Sitting next to me, Gary kicked my shins to get me to stop. He was right, as usual. I couldn't let my anger get the better of me. I noticed the judge, a distinguished-looking gray-haired man, peering at me curiously over his glasses.

We won. In his ruling, Judge Kelleher ordered Jordan to produce all the tapes, notes, and rough drafts he had withheld, in order to reveal Jordan's state of mind when he was writing the article.

Masterson turned dead white when the ruling was issued. "We've got 'em, Cyndy!" said Gary, to me. I hoped so, I told him. All I felt was a great tiredness. How long would this take? I wondered. Then I drove home to make dinner for my children.

None of the legal gains had any effect on the bad publicity or the scornful stares I was getting—or maybe, by that time just thought I was getting—in public. Under John Severino's edict, nobody at the station mentioned my problems. Gradually, the items in the local papers began to die down.

A few weeks later, Marvin Hamlisch called again from New York. This time I returned his call.

"I'm really sorry I upset you that morning," he said. I told him that I hadn't been feeling well, that it wasn't his fault.

"Well, listen," he said. "I'm coming out there next week on business. Can we have lunch?"

"Sure," I said. We met in an Italian restaurant in Beverly Hills. I ordered a bowl of soup, but just stared at it. I couldn't eat. My stomach hurt too much.

"You don't eat? What's the matter with you?" he said, half jokingly, half seriously.

I told him about my ulcer, about the Tagamet I was taking. He waved his hand. No problem. "Oh, I know about Tagamet," he said, and proceeded to tell me all about *his* ulcer. All the specialists he saw; all the forbidden foods he sneaked into his meals. He was funny, witty, self-deprecating. He had no desire to talk about baseball, the article, the lawsuit. Instead, to my pleasure, we talked about his life. About New York. Broadway. Music. Another world.

For an hour or so, he lifted me out of my troubles. Out of Los Angeles entirely; it was like a little trip to Manhattan—a literate, charming, fairy-tale Manhattan. He talked about *They're Playing Our Song,* his musical, that was just closing. He told me about the movies he was planning to score. About the new musical, on the life of Jean Seberg, he was planning. About his life in New York. "Tell me what it's like to live in New York," I asked, eagerly. He did.

Lincoln Center. The West Side. Cabs. Theater. Crowds. Traffic. Privacy. Anonymity.

"It sounds wonderful," I said. Yes, I thought. But it sounded thousands—no, millions—of miles away.

In late winter, the other side turned over Jordan's taped notes to us. We saw immediately why they had fought so hard against doing this. The notes, said my lawyers, were devastating to Jordan's case. They proved exactly, infuriatingly, what I had long suspected: that Jordan, without letting the reader know, had injected his own biases and hang-ups into the story.

Jordan had recorded strange, rambling reflections into his tape machine when neither Steve nor I was present. Or he and Susan would dissect us, with the recorder running, while they were in their hotel room or in their car. These so-called notes seemed to have had as much weight, when he was writing the story, as our actual interviews.

In some ways, I saw, the article was more about Jordan and Susan and his poor wife than it was about me and Steve. Susan, his notes showed, was the "New York actress," the "guest" at the studio who had "whispered to someone" that my "regional look" wouldn't "play in New York." My "gentleman companion" at the Polo Lounge was, of course, Pat Jordan.

Reading the new transcripts—and peering into his dark, distorted view of me—was worse than reading the article. At least, I thought, I had the chance to fight back against what he had published. Against these secret prejudices, I was helpless. And to think that I had trusted him! I was a child, a fool. And he had fooled me completely, pathetically.

There were slurs, fantasies, and sexual innuendos—some too filthy to repeat here—on my house, on my marriage, on me, on Steve.

But nobody will see this dirt, I realized. They'll only see the article. Only the gossip items, the placards.

"This stuff is devastating," said my lawyer. "I think they'll settle now."

"No, not now." I said. I wanted a trial. I wanted Jordan to pay.

But there was no trial. As our suit inched forward toward the courtroom, the case became even more of an obsession, a sickness. I talked to the lawyers by day—and worried, cried, and burned with anger at night.

No surprise: Steve seemed only minimally interested in what was happening. And after taking care of the girls and the show, I didn't have the energy left to try to get him involved. In fact, I found I didn't have the energy to talk to him any more. I'd stopped filling in the spaces in our conversations. I was too tired.

Even the semblance of our marriage was unraveling. I was making dinner one evening when the phone rang. Steve, on one of his rare nights home, answered it. "Uh-huh. Uh-huh," he said. He handed me the receiver. "It's for you," he said flatly.

"Hello?" It was Marvin Hamlisch, from New York. "I called to see how you're doing. I've been worried about you," he said.

That was nice of him, I thought, but—why? I couldn't quite figure out why Marvin Hamlisch, this man I'd barely met, whom I'd had several pleasant conversations with, was calling me. Why this single man—in his New York penthouse—was phoning me, elbow-deep in spaghetti sauce, in my Calabasas kitchen. My husband was sitting nearby, reading the newspaper. I felt odd, uncomfortable, talking to Marvin. I turned to Steve and threw up my hands in bafflement. He looked back at me blankly.

Cradling the phone on my shoulder, stirring the sauce, I gave him a short update on the libel case. He began to tell me what he was doing.

"Uh, listen, Marvin," I said, cutting him off. "It's great that you called, but I'm busy making dinner for Steve and the kids."

"Oh, okay!" he said, contritely. He apologized for intruding. "I'll call another time," he said. I hung up the phone and looked at Steve. He was still reading.

"It's Marvin Hamlisch," said Steve, holding out the phone. It was a week or so later; I shook my head and waved my hands, signaling to Steve that no, I didn't want to take the call from him.

"Here she is. One second," said Steve.

What? My husband was actually encouraging me to talk to this man—after I had told him I didn't want to? Why hadn't he turned the call away? What, exactly, was he telling me?

Well, all right then, I thought. In a burst of anger, I grabbed the phone. "Yes, Marvin. What's happening?" I said. I began to talk to him. And as I talked, I stared daggers at Steve. He did not look up.

I was coming home from work when I saw the truck. It was parked outside our house and it was filled with lights and camera equipment. As I walked in the door, I heard Steve's voice—his "interview voice," laughing and joking —and a woman's.

I peered into the front room. Steve was being interviewed by a young woman. There were lights set up all around the room. A photographer was snapping pictures.

"Excuse me, Steve, what's going on here?" I said.

"Just a moment," he said to the woman. Steve got up and joined me in the hall.

"What are you doing?" I asked, softly. I was conscious of the reporter, just a few feet away, trying to catch our conversation.

"I'm giving an interview to *Playboy*," he said.

His words took a second to register; he'd never mentioned anything like this to me. I couldn't believe what I was hearing. After all that had happened to us, after all the lies and innuendos about our sex life, our marriage, he was giving an interview to *Playboy* magazine?

"Are you crazy?" I whispered. "Are you out of your mind?"

He drew himself up, defensively. "It's not what you think," he said. "You're not in it. It's all about me."

Then the reporter, tape recorder in hand, was standing there with us. She stuck out her free hand. "Cyndy! I've heard all about you!"

"Listen," I said to her. "I don't want to be any part of this interview."

"Oh, you can be part of it! We'll set the ground rules!" she said.

"Sorry. No," I said, abruptly. I went upstairs, changed, dressed the girls, and took them to their dance classes. Two and a half hours later, when I came home, Steve and the woman were still talking, as if nothing whatever had happened.

I was beyond anger. I was finished with politeness, with any concern with niceness, with my "image." "All right, that's it," I said, brusquely, to the reporter. "The interview is over. Please get out of my house. Now."

"Okay!" said Steve, jumping up. "We'll finish up at the ballpark," he assured the woman, in his infuriating everything-is-just-fine voice.

I ran upstairs. At long last, it was perfectly clear to me. There was no hope of changing Steve. We led two completely separate lives. His career, his publicity—any publicity—was much more important to him than his family or our privacy.

I put the girls to bed, and cried. When I came back down, both the reporter and all the equipment were gone. And so, of course, was Steve.

That was a major blow. Maybe the final one. After the *Playboy* incident, I realized that Steve's actions, his feelings, had almost nothing to do with me. There seemed to be no point in trying to adjust my life to his.

Marvin Hamlisch kept calling. Perhaps I was wrong, or simply too tired to think straight, but I couldn't come up with a reason to stop him. He called in the evenings, usually around nine-thirty my time, on nights when—he told me later—he saw from the baseball schedule that Steve wouldn't be home.

He was a friend, during a terrible time when I had no friends. He was interested, concerned. He listened sympathetically to my accounts of the libel case; he asked about the girls; he told me what he was doing, the routine of his life in New York. I conjured up an almost magical image of his city—a city where nobody knew me, a city I could move to and simply disappear from view. I listened eagerly as he told me about his work, his friends, his music—and later, about his family, his upbringing in Brooklyn, so different from mine. I began to like Marvin —as a confidant, a healing voice on the phone. More than that.

In early spring Marvin flew out to Los Angeles on business, and while he was in town he came on the show. We went out to lunch together afterward.

"You know, Cynthia," he said. "I like you very much. So what's going on with you and Steve? Are you two still together?"

"I don't know, Marvin. We've been going through some hard times lately. I honestly, truly don't know."

Then he did a surprising thing. He looked me straight in the eye, and said, "Listen. I'm leaving for New York tonight. Before that, I have some business in the Valley. I'd like to come over to your house this afternoon. I'd like to meet Steve Garvey. God knows I talk to him on the phone enough! I'd like to ask him myself."

"You what?"

"Sure. Why not? What's the worst thing that could happen?"

I shook my head. His plan sounded bizarre. Marvin asking Steve about me? What good would that do? What possible connection could they make? What would Steve Garvey tell Marvin Hamlisch—this pale, bespectacled New Yorker—that he wouldn't tell me?

But Marvin smiled wryly, and kept insisting it would be useful. And as futile as it sounded, there was no real reason for me to turn him down. Certainly, satisfying Marvin's curiosity about Steve couldn't make things worse than they already were.

I called Steve's office, told the secretary that Marvin wanted to meet him, and arranged for him to be home.

Marvin showed up right on time. He winked at me as he stood in the doorway. "Good to meet you," said Steve, in his shorts and tennis shirt, shaking hands with Marvin, in his dark suit, tie, and glasses. The contrast was strange. But even so, I felt a weird foreboding. Some private male ritual, something I didn't understand, was going on between the two men. Marvin and Steve went to the den to talk. I went into the bedroom to play with the girls.

Marvin and Steve talked for two hours. When they came out, Marvin looked drained. Troubled. He didn't say anything. He just kissed me on the cheek, got into his car, and drove off to the airport.

"Well? What did you two talk about all that time?" I said to Steve.

"We talked about you," said Steve.

"Yes?"

And then Steve ended our marriage.

"I think you should go with him," he said.

Time stopped. I couldn't believe what I was hearing.

"What?" I said. Go with him? I thought. With Marvin? How? Why?

"Go with him. I think he would be better for you."

Finally, it sunk in. *He was giving me away.*

This was too much. Too insensitive, too cold-blooded, even for Steve. And yet, he'd done it. I was numb. Beyond anger.

I forced the words out. "Do you realize what you've just done, Steve?" I said. "Do you realize what you've done? You've just given me away. You've just given away your family. And not only that, you've given everything to a man I hardly know. Marvin is just a friend. He's not my lover. He's not my husband.

"You're my husband, Steve. *You* are."

He just stared. My words had no effect on him. He turned away, like so many times before, and left the house. That night he moved his things to the spare bedroom. It was over, I realized. All over. All the fight had gone out of me.

Shortly thereafter, I told the lawyers to settle our libel case. *Newsweek* issued an apology and gave us a cash settlement. It was an anticlimax. Amid the wreckage of our marriage, our victory—announced in tiny articles in the back pages of the newspapers—did nothing to ease my depression.

Steve and I settled down to our new life—he in his side of the house, me in mine. I realized, sadly, that our lives weren't that much different from before.

I tried to concentrate on the show. But it was no use. For the first time, I found myself acting, rather than reacting, my part. Regis' jokes were no longer funny. I had no stomach for trading barbs with him. Time to smile, Cynthia, I said in the space between wisecracks. My mind wandered during my interviews. I found myself lagging a beat behind the guests. Even the station executives were now telling me I looked too thin; Sunday was dabbing on more and more makeup to disguise my hollow cheeks and the dark circles under my eyes.

Steve's *Playboy* interview came out. In it, he was quoted as saying he'd been considering having an affair for "a couple of years. Anything is possible." Could this be possible? No, I realized. It didn't really matter. It was as carefully calculated a quote as he had ever put out.

The sarcastic newspaper columns, which had never really stopped, got some new fuel. I began to dread going out in public more and more. Alone at night, sometimes I would dream of escaping, getting out, of moving to a place where I wouldn't be recognized. Where I could start over.

New York, I thought. Not for Marvin, though it would be nice to see him. To escape from my tormentors. To run away from the newspapers, from baseball, from the baseball fans. From the shame of my make-believe marriage. From the nightmare of the past few years. For a fresh start.

* * *

In July, I told Frank Kelly that I would be leaving. That they should look for a replacement. He seemed surprised.

The girls were too young to understand all that was going on; I told them that we were moving to New York; that although he wasn't going with us their daddy loved them very much; that I would be looking for a home for the three of us there.

In September, I left both the show and my home. But of course I hadn't really escaped. By January, after my unsuccessful job search, I was back in Los Angeles.

Back to clean out the house. Back to discover Steve's secret life. Back to rage against his mistress and to bury myself in the beach house. Back to pain and despair and loneliness. Back to sleepless nights and too many sleeping pills. Back to throw myself into the black hole.

CHAPTER 24

I must have lost consciousness as they were carrying me into the ambulance. I don't remember arriving at the hospital—or what treatment they gave me when I got there. Only dim images: an IV machine hooked up to my arm. My brother Chris telling me the girls were fine, then sitting next to my bed for a while. A doctor, a stranger, leaning over me, shaking his head sadly, and saying, "You've lost too much weight."

They released me anyway, after just a few days. I went back to the beach house, pulled myself upstairs, and got into bed. I was weak, exhausted, not even strong enough for anger or despair. My mind, after all its struggling, was a blank. Even my demons, I realized faintly, were leaving me alone. I was too pathetic a victim to bother with.

Some zombie-like instinct—Pride? Shame? Force of habit?—got me out of bed once or twice a day. I fed and washed myself, then crawled back upstairs and stared at the ceiling. After a few days, our family doctor, Dr. Herbst, showed up at the front door. I could see the shock on his face. He examined me, gave me a prescription for vitamins, and sat down on the bed.

Of course, I thought. Just like on television.

"You can't go on like this, Cyndy," he said. "You're very ill. Your blood pressure is way down, your potassium level is low, and if you don't do something about it you'll give yourself a heart attack.

"You're a young woman with two beautiful children. You've got your whole life, your whole career, ahead of you."

He wrote a name and number on a slip of paper. "I want you to call this woman," he said. "I know her. She's good. She can help you." Then he put it on my night table, next to the phone.

I lay in bed for the next two weeks. As I got a little stronger, as my mind began to function somewhat, I waited for the demons to come back. But blessedly, they didn't. Maybe something has changed? I wondered. If they can just leave me alone for a while.

If they can just leave me alone.

One day, I found myself staring into the mirror. Oh my God. I was gaunt, like death. The skin was stretched across my face, a gray mask. I could see my ribs, the bones in my neck, standing out. My hair was breaking off at the roots. My nails were cracking. My hands were shaking like an old woman's.

"You're done. Finished," I said to myself. But then, surprisingly, from somewhere deep inside came another voice.

"You've got children to raise," it said. Oh my God. "You've got two children to raise. They're depending on you. They need you." I braced myself for the backlash, for the despair, for the hopeless feeling I knew was coming next.

There was nothing. Nothing! I risked saying it out loud. "I've got children to raise," I said to the sick woman in the mirror. I loved them so much. I couldn't let them down.

Was it true? I thought. Had I almost died, gone away, and left them all alone? The thought of what would have happened to them made me shudder, then cry.

I had children to raise. I used that thought, only that one thought, to keep the feelings of despair at bay. Over and over, I forced myself to concentrate on it. To keep my mind occupied, to fill up the emptiness. To hold onto my sanity. To keep myself together. While I raised my children.

Fighting down the nausea, I made myself eat several real meals in a row. I could feel a trickle of strength returning. The next day, I called the phone number my doctor had given me.

I got dressed, put on some makeup, and drove to my parents' house. Krisha and Whitney were there with my mother.

"Come on, girls. We're going home."

Concentrate, Cynthia. The girls were glad to have me back; they covered me with hugs and kisses. The next few days, filled with getting them up, and dressed, and to and from school, were the best in a long while. I saw myself, as if from a great height, taking care of my children, loving and raising them, under sunny skies in a nice house by the sea. If it weren't for the great, tearing hole in my insides, I thought, the picture might even be a happy one.

"Why have you come to see me?" asked the therapist.

She was the name on my doctor's notepad. I'd driven thirty miles to West Los Angeles, to a barely furnished office: chair, chair, couch, small bookcase. Barbara was a psychiatrist. She was tall, very tall. About ten years older than me. Short dark hair. Glasses. Intelligent-looking. Intense.

"I—I almost died." I said. She nodded.

"Go on."

I talked, hesitantly at first, and then, looking into Barbara's patient face, more freely. Going backward and forward through time, I told her about my nightmare. I sat on one of the chairs, facing her, told her about the overdose, the men with the ambulance, my stay in the hospital. My encounter with Steve's mistress. My rage, my

despair. My months in the beach house. The loneliness.
The accusing stares of the people on the street.

My marriage. Steve. The years of trying to reach him.
The anger at discovering his secret life. The betrayal of
my so-called friends.

The searing in my stomach. The nausea. The weight
loss. The rage. The helplessness. Then the hopelessness.
Then I had nothing more to say.

"Yes," said Barbara, finally. "I can see what has been
happening with you." Then she reached for her appointment book and began turning the pages.

We met twice a week, two hours at a time, on Tuesdays
and Thursdays. Ten in the morning until noon. The sessions were my lifeline; stepping-stones across the hours,
days, weeks. I drove the girls to school, then took the
long, twisting, Coast Highway into town. Sometimes,
driving into the city, going through the tunnel onto the
Santa Monica Freeway, I realized my mind had been
wandering. I couldn't remember going over any of the
narrow, dangerous road I'd just traveled. It frightened
me.

The next few sessions were much like the first. I told
Barbara again and again, compulsively, about the disappointments, the betrayal, the guilt—the demons. She concentrated on my physical self.

Don't let the bad feelings keep you from eating, she
said; she also prescribed a mild sedative to let me sleep on
bad nights. I took the vitamins, also; every three weeks, I
went to Dr. Herbst's office for an examination. Gradually, I gained a little weight. I felt stronger: strong
enough, sometimes, to talk about the awful, insoluble
problems I carried around with me, everywhere.

"I don't know who I am, Barbara. That's the worst
part. Who am I supposed to be?"

Tentatively at first, then urgently, I told Barbara about
Cyndy and Cynthia. About the split. About the years I'd
spent trying to become Cyndy to please Steve. About the

people who attacked me when Cyndy couldn't keep it up. About my efforts to kill off Cyndy. And, worst of all, about Cynthia's failures, my failures, as a person. A woman. A wife.

"Don't you see, Barbara? It's Cynthia that people don't like. It was Cynthia that Steve didn't know what to do with. It was Cynthia who stayed awake at night. It was Cynthia who took the sleeping pills. It was Cynthia who tried to kill herself."

Barbara shook her head. "It's Cynthia who's the healthy one," she said.

I realize now that my real therapy started at that moment. During the afternoons, after they came home from school, my children's needs kept me busy. Together. During the daytime, fighting the anxiety and despair, I took care of myself.

Barbara was hard on me. She made me tell her the secret story of my life. She listened, thought, interpreted. Pointed out the destructive patterns, brought them out in the open. Made me look at them, even when it was painful.

My father's violence. My mother's compliance. Steve's coldness. My fantasy of reaching Steve. Creating a real family for us, building a life for us—without him. As we talked, the connections between my father and Steve, always just below the surface, floated into view. "They're both strong, silent, uncommunicative men—aren't they, Cynthia?" said Barbara.

"Yes, but Steve isn't violent. He doesn't yell at anyone," I protested.

"No, he's not physically violent," said Barbara. "But there are other ways to abuse someone. By withholding affection. By being emotionally absent."

Emotionally absent. Yes. I thought about Steve, and my father, as I walked along the beach in the afternoons. On schooldays, when I didn't have a session with Barbara, I took long walks, thinking.

The similarities between the two were so obvious. So ridiculously, painfully obvious. The silences. *The uniform.* The job that took him away from home. Always away from home. But—I'd *known* about my father. I'd figured him out, shouted back, got him to stop hitting me. When I was just thirteen, still a child.

And yet I'd fallen in love with Steve. Maybe I still loved him. I'd chosen a man who was so much like my father. I'd *seen* what had happened to my mother. Was I falling into the same patterns? Was I repeating her life?

I walked for miles and miles, head down, talking to no one. But there were no answers. Could there ever be?

Steve lived up the coast, I knew, in a rented house with his girlfriend. In my mail, some days, came more evidence of his affair: phone bills, department store bills, airline ticket bills. I passed them on to the accountant, trying to keep my emotions under control. I was getting a little stronger, I realized. I needed to keep my strength, to keep myself together, for the children. And then, far enough away from them, in the relative safety of Barbara's office, I raged.

I raged against Steve, my father, Pat Jordan. I yelled and screamed and cursed and cried. I felt the hurt and hate flow through me, and I laid it all at Barbara's feet. She was my therapist, my counselor. She was a woman. She *had* to understand.

I shouted and cried and pleaded for answers. I wallowed in anger and self-pity until my voice was hoarse and my face ran wet with tears. But Barbara let me go on. She'd sit calmly in her chair, unruffled, and make no attempt to stop me. Then, when my tirades wound down, she'd speak, calmly but firmly, about the patterns of my life. About my lack of self-respect. About my misplaced trust in people who hadn't earned it.

Then the sessions would come to an end. I'd drive home, back to the beach house. And take yet another long walk. And I thought of what Barbara had told me.

All of it. Over and over. Her words hurt, but I knew she was right. It hurt more to think about what was coming up. But I knew what I had to face. And, amazingly, I was feeling a faint hope that someday, somehow, I would get through this long nightmare.

CHAPTER 25

"Cynthia, you came from a dysfunctional home. You are a classic victim of physical and emotional child abuse."

Barbara sat back in her chair and waited for my reaction. We were several months into my therapy. I knew this moment was coming; that this was the root cause of my broken life. The thought of looking at my childhood again frightened me. I'd flinched from it before, I knew. I'd been too scared of what I'd seen. But now—here, in front of Barbara, whom I couldn't fool—I'd have to finish what I'd started. It would be impossible to pull away.

Still, I tried. "Oh yes, I know that," I said, nervously. I felt my mouth twisting into a sort of smile. My voice took on a sing-song rhythm. I talked very fast.

"Oh sure," I said. "There was a *lot* wrong in my childhood. My father was very quick-tempered. *Very* quick-tempered. We moved *a lot*. I was always the outsider. It was sad. But you know, it wasn't the worst it could have been. There wasn't any *sexual* abuse. And we weren't really hurt physically *all* that badly. Maybe sometimes we deserved it. We were bad sometimes. My mother and father went through some rough times themselves. They *always* kept us fed and clothed. I'm sure it wasn't all that different from . . ."

"Stop," said Barbara.

". . . all that different from . . . other . . ."

"Please stop, Cynthia," she said. Stop? I thought, stunned. I forced myself to fight back the panic, fall silent, and look at her calm, intelligent face.

"I understand what you're telling me," she said. "But I want you to try something. For the next ten minutes, I want you to just sit here without talking. I want you to think back. Think back to when you were a little girl. Think back to all the times you can remember when your father hugged you, or kissed you, or even touched you."

Then she got up and left the room.

All the times my father had hugged me? I knew the answer to that. I sat silently, helplessly, and connected with what I knew, deep inside, had always been there. A huge, gaping hole. A secret reservoir of pain, of loss, of longing.

For ten minutes, I cried. When Barbara came back in, she handed me a tissue.

"He—he never hugged me," I cried.

"Yes. I understand," said Barbara. Her face was the saddest I'd ever seen it.

Once again, painfully, we went back through my childhood. This time, no evasions. This time, under Barbara's prodding and guidance, we went deeper: not only into the violence, but to the shame and fear and anger. About protecting my brothers; about trying to prevent my father's tirades; about blaming myself when, despite all my efforts, he exploded.

More long walks. I thought about what Barbara had said—and, through the sadness and anger it stirred up, tried to trace the long-term effects of my unhappy childhood. Sometimes, under control, I made a connection. Other times, submerged in emotion, I lost the thread.

One day, lost in anger at Steve, I decided I would show Barbara just what a monster he was. While the girls were in school, I gathered the evidence of Steve's cruelty. The bills, the names. The dates. The evidence. I gathered up my pile of paper and brought it in with me to Barbara's office. At the beginning of the next session I marched in and thrust it into her hands.

"See? See what he did to me?"

I sat across from her, burning. Barbara picked up the papers, calmly looked at a few, then set them aside.

"Yes," she said, after a few seconds. Then she looked at me with a little smile.

"These are all very nice. Can I throw them away now?"

Throw them away? I was stunned. For some reason, I nodded. She got up, took the papers, and quickly dropped them into the wastebasket.

Through the marriage—again—we went. But this time, Barbara wouldn't let me concentrate on my anger, on Steve. Instead, she made me look back at all of my doubts, all the stop signs I'd gone through in my efforts to make the relationship "work." All the allowances I'd made, all the encouragement I'd given my husband to continue things exactly as they were.

"You stayed too long," said Barbara, one day.

Yes, I realized sadly. Cyndy had stayed too long.

One day, on the spur of the moment, I decided to swim again. Just like in college, just like I remembered. I drove over to Pepperdine University and bought a pass for their big outdoor pool. I swam long, slow laps. Just a few at first, then for fifteen minutes. Then thirty minutes. Then forty-five. Up and back, following the thick black line on the bottom of the pool. I emptied my mind as I swam, concentrating only on my breathing, my stroke. In the evenings after my swimming sessions, I felt tired, but pleasantly so. Surprisingly, the fatigue didn't leave an opening for the anger and depression to take over. I slept better than at any time I could remember.

* * *

"You're too isolated," said Barbara. "You're too alone in that house. I think it would be good for you to go out—as Cynthia—and meet some new people."

The idea filled me with anxiety, but I decided to give it a chance. One night, for the first time, I went to a parents' meeting at the girls' school.

"Hello, Cyndy," said a woman my age, coming over to me. She introduced herself, told me whose mother she was, asked me where I lived and what I was doing these days.

"I'm home with my girls," I said. She nodded and smiled, perfectly normally. I braced myself for questions about Steve, about baseball. But there were none. We chatted pleasantly for a while about our children. And that was the start of our friendship.

I became part of a group of women. A group of mothers. There were five of us, some working, some not. There was a flight attendant, a teacher, a businesswoman, a housewife, a lawyer. Their names were Darlene Reid, Patty Dufay, Lee Clarke, and Pat O'Meara. They were wonderful to me. And I soaked up their friendship.

Our world revolved around our children. We talked about them when we were together. We drove them individually, and in bunches, to the beach, to the park, to lessons. They played and slept over in all our houses; a constant caravan of cars and toys and station wagons. We met in our houses, in coffee shops, to discuss our worries and problems. Baby-sitters. The new sewer system the county was putting in.

Normal worries. Normal problems. My new friends never dealt with me as a celebrity, as a baseball hero's wife—as, wonderfully, anyone different from them.

They never asked about my life with Steve until, slowly and gradually, I began to tell them. Yes, they said, they'd heard that I'd had a hard time. Some of them had been divorced themselves. They knew what I was going through. They listened to me. I listened to them. With

some trepidation, I told them my name was really
Cynthia. They thought that was interesting; to my surprise, they gave no signs that it seemed pretentious or
strange to them at all. They began to call me by my real
name.

They gathered around me. In public, when strangers
started to look at me curiously, they pointedly engaged
me in private conversation, turning me away from their
gaze. In a low-key way, they made sure I was taking care
of myself, that I had someone to talk to if I needed to.
"You're looking better this week, Cynthia," they said.

They were true friends. Where had they been before?
Why had I kept them out of my life? Oh, but I knew that.
It was all very sad—but what I had to do now was be
thankful they were here at last.

One afternoon, around that time, a strange thing happened. The phone rang—it was one of the Dodger wives
calling. I hadn't talked to her since my breakdown, and
very rarely in the couple of years before that.

"I've been wanting to call you for a long time," she
said, nervously. "How are you doing?"

"I'm better," I said.

We made some awkward small talk for a few minutes,
until it became apparent why she was calling. She had,
she said, known about Steve's infidelity for a long time.
She felt guilty for not telling me before. But now she
wanted to fill me in on the details.

"All right," I said, stunned. "Go ahead."

Standing up, I held the receiver to my ear. She reeled
off names, dates, places. And yet I remained oddly cool.
Detached. Why was she telling me this now? And, more
important, why wasn't I eagerly soaking up this vital evidence? A few months ago, I would have lapped it up. It
would have fueled my fires; maybe I would have
screamed at her for keeping the secret from me for so
long. And now? What she was saying seemed unimpor-

tant. Obvious. I didn't even reach for a pencil to take the information down.

Her words were a dull blur; I was concentrating, instead, on my interesting response. She went on for fifteen, twenty minutes.

". . . and anyway, Cyndy, I just thought you should know this."

"Well, thank you," I said firmly, not wanting to prolong the conversation, and I hung up. I never spoke to her again, and I never used the information.

I began to realize, as summer turned to fall, that I was thinking about Steve Garvey less and less. I had little contact with his accountant or his lawyer. I heard from him only rarely, on the infrequent occasions when he picked up Krisha and Whitney for an afternoon. I usually stayed inside the house when he met the girls on the front steps.

I realized, too, that the glances of people in the street weren't as intimidating as before. Earlier that summer, I had avoided any eye contact; worn dark glasses in public all the time. Now I walked briskly through the stores, conducted my business, and went home. There was still an occasional dirty look or "Where's Steve?" from a stranger—but fewer than I had feared there would be. Maybe, I thought, the world was ready to separate me from my husband. Maybe it had decided to leave me alone.

My days were full. I had my sessions with Barbara, the time I was spending with my girls and with my friends. I also spent many hours thinking about the new ideas I was trying to absorb. It left little time for anger.

Maybe I could . . . move on? The idea alternately excited and terrified me. I thought about it constantly. By giving up Steve, by giving up my flawed ideas, I had freed myself to build a new life. But what life was that? My freedom was also a huge hole, a blank space. What could I fill it with? Where should I go?

"What am I good for?" I asked Barbara.

"Well, think back," she said. "What did you do well? What made you happy? What did you dream about in the past?"

Studying. Reading. Going to medical school, becoming a doctor. But now I was in my thirties, with two girls to raise alone. "I can't do that any more," I told Barbara, sadly. "That dream is dead."

"Dead?" She smiled, shook her head.

I thought again. The obvious answer was working on television. Like my old job on "A.M." The research, the conversations, the relationships with the women there had sustained me through the hard times. Yet there was a problem.

"Working on television was Cyndy's job," I said. "That's who they wanted. That's who they thought they were hiring."

Barbara pounced on my answer.

"Yes!" she said. "That's right! They thought they were hiring Cyndy. But we know they were wrong. Deep down, it was really Cynthia doing the job. It was her mind, her character, that brought it off. Cyndy's part was just fluff. Window dressing.

"And now that you know that, you can fight for your real self. Your responsibility now, wherever you go, is to make sure you don't let Cynthia get submerged again.

"Why should a television show be any exception?"

I didn't believe her at first. I told her about the male ABC executives: their emphasis on my appearance; their comments and "suggestions."

"You let Cyndy respond to them the last time," said Barbara flatly.

Gradually, as I got stronger, I began to half believe I could give it a try. I timidly brought up the subject to my new friends. I couldn't, I told them, bear to start over in Los Angeles. But perhaps somewhere else? They were enthusiastic about my idea. But—how wonderful!—they were sad about the prospect of my moving away.

Finally, the worst of the anxiety simply faded away. I began to realize, at odd moments during the day, that I was spending more time thinking about the future than sifting through the past.

One morning in late fall, I stood in front of the mirror and looked at myself carefully. I hadn't done that in a while. I had gained back some weight, I realized with some surprise. My face was fuller, not as pinched. My hair was growing normally again. The dark circles were gone from under my eyes.

"Would you like to leave the beach and live somewhere else?" I asked Krisha that evening over dinner.

She looked up at me, worriedly. "Only if it's all three of us," she said.

"Of *course* all three of us, silly," I said.

"Then okay, Mommy," she said, happily, and went back to concentrating on getting her food onto her fork.

I thought, My beautiful, innocent, unspoiled little girls. My treasures. My best reasons for living.

The next day, only a little anxious, I called my agent. He was glad to hear from me, he said. I told him I was healthy and ready to go back to work.

CHAPTER 26

"Hey!"
        "Hey, Cyndy Garvey!"
        "Hey, Cyndy, ovah heah!"
"Hey, Cyndy! Whaddya do ta Steve Garvey?"
"Whydja leave him?"
"Yeah! How could ya screw him ovah like that?"

The construction workers, warming themselves by a fire in a trash can, whistled and taunted me as I went by them on the sidewalk. They were working on a big apartment building going up at Sixty-sixth Street and Columbus. It was just two blocks from the television station. Keep walking, Cynthia, I thought. I pushed back the anxiety. Nobody else on the street, walking briskly to work through the cold winter morning, was taking any notice of either them or me. You can ignore them, too, Cynthia. In a couple of minutes I was inside my own warm building, across the street from Lincoln Center. It was January, 1983. It was my first day on my new job.

I was hosting "The Morning Show," the New York City counterpart of my old show. It was aired on WABC, Channel 7, a sister station to KABC.

The way back to television had been surprisingly easy. That fall, I'd begun flying to New York to meet with station managers and network executives. A man named Bill Fyffe, the general manager of WABC—whom I'd met on my job-hunting the year before—greeted me warmly. Perhaps it was the fact that his morning program was getting very low ratings. Perhaps, I thought hopefully, he liked meeting Cynthia.

I sat across from him in his office and looked him straight in the eye. I talked briefly about how eager I was to go back to work. He talked vaguely, tantalizingly, about revamping the program.

"I can give you a good show out here, Bill," I said.

Bill commented that my hair wasn't as blond as he remembered it. The bleached part had grown out during the past six months. The proper Cyndy response, I thought, would be to agree to rebleach it. "No, that's my real hair color, Bill," I said.

It seemed to me, sitting in his office, that he liked my new attitude. He asked me if I would fill in as a substitute so they could take a look at me. I told him that would be fine. That fall and early winter, I flew to New York several times to sit in. Some of my old friends from KABC were now working there; the job was as challenging and exhilarating as I remembered it.

During the holidays, my agent called me at home. I was making dinner for the girls. "They're very interested in hiring you, Cyndy," he said. "The only problem they have, they say, is that they're having trouble finding a man, a male co-host, to pair off with you."

I thought for a second. "You know Regis Philbin. Why not get somebody like him?" I said.

"Regis Philbin?" said the agent, a little surprised. After I'd left "A.M. Los Angeles," Regis had left KABC and tried to launch a nationally syndicated talk show. It had gotten low ratings and been canceled. Now, I knew, he was looking for work. The job in New York would be ideal for him. But John Severino, our old boss, had also moved to WABC.

One evening, at ten o'clock, my phone rang.

"Hey! You've been to ABC in New York," said a cocky man's voice. "What's it like out there?"

It had been months and months since I'd heard that voice. At first, it didn't register.

"Who is this?" I said.

"Regis," he said, impatiently. "Hey! I'm thinking about going there and taking on their morning show."

"That's great, Regis," I said. We talked for a little while longer; he joked and kidded me gently. Neither of us brought up what we'd been doing the past year—it was as if I'd just seen him yesterday.

The next day my agent called me. "They're considering you and Regis to fill the spot," he said.

"That's good. That's fine. Work on it," I told him. A few weeks later, I signed my contract.

I was happier than I'd been in a long time. I had a good job in a city I'd always wanted to live in. And, most importantly, I wasn't dependent on Steve's money any more.

"Work hard in New York to let the Cynthia inside you become stronger," said Barbara, at the end of our last session together. She told me that I could always call if I needed her. She stood up and hugged me. I cried.

The first three months, until the girls were finished with school, I hired an English woman to move into the beach house and take care of the girls on weekdays. I called them every evening before going to sleep. Each Friday, after the show, I checked out of my hotel and flew back to Los Angeles. On the weekends, the girls were mine. I returned to New York on the Sunday afternoon plane. It was an exhausting schedule.

The show went well. Two bright young producers, borrowed from the network, set up the new "look" and format of our program. For several weeks Regis and I and the production team met daily to plan the show. Regis, as usual, joked and grumped his way through the process. When something displeased him, he buried his head in his hands in mock distress. At the end of the planning sessions he'd pull me aside—as if I'd secretly been agreeing with him—and whisper conspiratorially, "Don't worry, Cyndy. When these guys leave, we'll change it back to the way it should be."

As with most of what Regis said, I couldn't tell whether he was joking or not. I couldn't understand why he wanted to stir up trouble.

In truth, I thought the new format was just fine. Our opening segment was different than in Los Angeles; instead of placing us on a couch, with me sitting off to Regis' left, we sat on high stools, separate, facing the camera. This time, we were centered in the camera shot. That gave the audience the message that we were indeed co-hosts; the plan was to split the interviews down the middle.

It was easy for me to put Cynthia, not Cyndy, on the air. I watched my words and body language; I faced the camera, not Regis, when it was appropriate; I didn't automatically laugh at Regis' jokes, especially if I was the butt of them. If he made fun of me for asking a guest a serious question, I turned my back to him and didn't respond.

At the start, I had enough clout to influence the selection of guests: I tended to leave most of the show-business celebrities to Regis—he loved to talk to them—while I talked to the authors, the feminist writers and politicians, the health-care experts. Once again, I was surrounded by a group of bright, incredibly hardworking young women producers. In fact, I noticed that the whole station—which operated at a faster pace than "laid-back" KABC—seemed to run on the efforts of dozens of hardworking women. And we were climbing to number one in our time slot.

When I began work at WABC, I called Steve's lawyer to tell him that I was moving the girls to New York City. The lawyer called me back. Steve, he said, had no objection.

I found, rented, and furnished a cozy, two-bedroom

apartment on the Upper East Side. One lovely spring weekend, I packed up the girls' things, locked the beach house door behind me, and put us all on the plane. I had my girls with me again. We were a family.

Krisha and Whitney, my California children, took to Manhattan wonderfully. They loved the new colors, the new sounds, even the crowded sidewalks and parks. I taught Krisha how to raise her little arm and hail a cab for us. She quickly figured out the streets in our immediate neighborhood; she was proud when she learned how to read the red, green, and yellow lights to cross the street.

"Mommy! We're going outside!" she said. She'd take me for a walk: I hovered, full of love and anxiety, two or three steps behind her.

Our days slipped into a frantic, happy routine. My alarm rang at five-thirty in the morning, and I'd get up, brew some coffee, make the girls' breakfast, and read the morning papers until six-thirty. Then I'd wake up the girls, get all three of us fed and dressed and equipped with the proper pencils and papers and books and notebooks, and into the cab that arrived at our door each morning at seven-thirty.

I took the girls to their new school at Eighty-eighth and Central Park West—along with all the other business-suited women and men on their way to work. Then I hopped back into the cab and rode downtown to the station. At two-thirty in the afternoon, after the show and the production meeting were over, I stood outside the school door, talking with the other mothers, my new friends, and waiting for our children to spill out the door. Then, if the weather was nice, we'd all walk home.

The girls' dinner was at five-thirty. If I was going out that evening, the baby-sitter—a nice girl named Yvonne —would arrive. If not, we'd all settle down to do our homework together. There was a lot to do every weekday night. I was a single mother. We were a normal New York family. It was all I could have wished for.

* * *

I started seeing Marvin Hamlisch again. He lived within walking distance of our apartment; sometimes, after a day of working on his music at his house, he'd come over and have dinner with me and the girls. On Fridays and weekends, Marvin and I would go out to eat at a neighborhood restaurant or, occasionally, see a movie or a play. As he had in Los Angeles, Marvin sometimes came on the show. One week, when Regis was off, he co-hosted with me a couple of days.

Naturally, Regis tried to work Marvin into his on-air routines—substituting his name for Steve's in the same old wisecracks.

"Hey!" he said, with his mischievous-little-boy grin, "You were out on the town with Marvin Hamlisch again last night! Mr. Manhattan himself! What'd you two do last night, huh?"

No giggles. No blushes. Not this time. "Never mind that, Regis," I said, grinning back at him, looking him straight in the eye. "Where were *you?*" The crew laughed, and Regis backed off. I could see he was a little annoyed.

What Regis didn't realize was that, while I enjoyed my time with Marvin very much, my real love affair was with New York. With my new life. With a city, with people who thought of me as just a vaguely familiar face, as a person who worked on television—if any of them thought about me at all.

The men at the construction site, probably because they were led by a Dodger fan, heckled me almost every morning. That was annoying. Even Regis saw that. "Hey, guys, knock it off!" he yelled one day when we both walked past together. They didn't knock it off. But they were equally rude, I soon discovered, to most of the other women who passed by, also.

There was some press coverage of my new job at WABC, but nobody wrote any columns saying I was a disgrace to baseball or womanhood. If they did, it wasn't in any publication I or anyone I knew was reading. No Steve Garvey fans rang my apartment doorbell. Nobody stopped me on the street and asked me how Steve was doing. Nobody stopped me on the street, period.

They had better things to do. The people rushed past, wrapped up in their own lives, in a hurry. To some, I suppose, New York City might have seemed a cold and impersonal place. To me, the public anonymity, the feeling of being, at long last, left alone, was a precious gift.

I made the most of it. I joined the school's parents' association, and soon was in the same lovely circle of gossip and committees and coffee shops and sleep-overs that I'd had in Malibu. I joined the local chapter of NOW. I found a support group for adult victims of child abuse, which I attended, like most of the members, on a regular basis.

On weekends, the girls and I explored New York. We went all over together. To the little stores and banks and cleaners in our neighborhood, where they treated me with the same crusty, grudging familiarity they treated everybody. To the museums and the department stores and the hot dog stands, where we stood in line impatiently like everybody else. To Central Park, where the girls ran and played and fed the pigeons and roller-skated.

That was the year when *everyone* roller-skated. One afternoon, a tall, skinny man in his twenties, wearing T-shirt and shorts and knee pads, smiling wildly, skated straight toward the bench I was sitting on, and looped to a stop directly in front of me.

"Cyndy Garvey!" he shouted.

I thought of the crazy woman at Dodger Stadium. I flinched nervously, looked for Krisha and Whitney, playing near the Alice in Wonderland statue, and began to stand up to grab my children and get away from him.

He leaned forward and, still smiling, winked conspiratorially. "Don't worry," he said. "I'm from Los Angeles. But I won't blow your cover."

The scene was so ridiculous that, in spite of my fears, I began to laugh. "Well, thanks a lot. I'd appreciate it," I said. He bowed, shook my hand, and skated away.

Not everything was perfect. When we were negotiating my contract, I'd asked to be billed with my real name, Cynthia. Both Bill Fyffe and my agent looked at me like I was crazy. "But everybody out there knows you as Cyndy Garvey," they said. "Why confuse them unnecessarily?"

I didn't take the argument any further. But I wondered. I wonder even now. Should I have insisted? Should I have opened my heart to these men, in the business of selling me to the public, and explained my reasons? Would they have changed their minds even if I had? I don't know.

So I was Cyndy Garvey on television. Worse, I was still Cyndy to John Severino, who'd moved up in the network hierarchy and was in New York also—not directly involved with my show, but a powerful man nonetheless. At a big ABC party for the network affiliates, which all the Channel 7 on-air people had to attend, Severino asked me, in his usual macho manner, to dance with him. The thought of doing so repelled me. I fought down the feeling.

This is business, I thought. Nothing personal. Not the place or time to tell him what I thought of him. Thinking of all the changes I'd made since I'd last seen him, I got through the dance, through the evening.

Riding home alone in a taxi, I went over the encounter in my mind. If I hadn't said what I'd thought, at least I hadn't pretended to be someone I wasn't. I got out of the cab, said goodnight to the doorman, and went upstairs. Yvonne gathered up her schoolbooks and went home. I looked in on the girls, sleeping peacefully. I kissed them, closed the door quietly behind me, and went into my bedroom.

In my bed, books and notes for the next show by my side, I felt better.

I shook my head, picked up my reading, and began to work.

A quite wonderful thing happened shortly afterward. I was leaving the station, a little earlier than usual. It was a fine summer afternoon, and I decided to walk at least partway uptown. I'd have to run the gauntlet of the construction workers, but by then I barely noticed them.

As I approached their leader, a sweaty, beefy guy in a T-shirt and yellow hard-hat, he yelled, "Hey, Cyndy!"— and, a hot dog in his hand, loped toward me.

I fought down the instinct to turn and run.

"Yes. What?" I said.

He was smiling, thank God. "We been watching you for a long time now. We seen you come and go. And my wife watches you on TV."

"Yes?" I said. What could he do to me, I thought, out here on Columbus Avenue? He wiped his big hand on his pants and held it out for me to shake. "We come to the conclusion that Steve Garvey made a big mistake."

"Oh yeah?" I said, softening. I shook his hand.

"Well," I said, "at least, until you figured that out, you didn't drop a brick on my head."

From that day on, they stopped taunting me. No more comments about Steve. "Hey, Cyndy! How ya doin'?" they yelled when I walked past. I waved back, and, if I wasn't late, stopped and talked to them for a few minutes. They bought me hot dogs from the pushcart on the corner. I ate them. I signed autographs for their nieces and nephews.

There were, however, limits to our new friendship. Once, when their school term was over, I brought the girls to work with me. The men introduced themselves to Krisha and Whitney.

"Hey! You wanna go up to the top? The view's nice. We can take you, no sweat," said one of the guys. I looked up, *way* up, at the rickety iron cage attached to the tall framework of girders. I swallowed, hard. The girls giggled, then grabbed my legs in mock fright.

The thought petrified *me.* "Uh, no thanks," I said, laughing nervously, beginning to walk away.

"If ya change your mind," he said cheerfully, calling after me, "we'll still be here."

CHAPTER 27

John Severino began calling me. He called often, from his office to mine. He wanted, he said, to get together with me outside the station.

"Just for lunch," he said. Then for drinks. For dinner. Just the two of us. It would be like old times. It would be fun.

"I don't think so, John," I said.

I wanted as little as possible to do with him. Unfortunately, I wasn't brave enough to tell him that. My Cyndy side, I realized sadly, had not disappeared completely. Far from it. Awkwardly, embarrassingly, I turned him down again and again. I told him that no, sorry, I was just too busy.

Finally, worn down by his persistence, I agreed to meet him for lunch. We met in a fancy midtown restaurant, the kind in which broadcast executives liked to entertain their clients. Several diners craned their necks to look at us. He seemed pleased to be seen with me.

I was very uncomfortable. It was obvious that he planned to pick up his relationship with Cyndy where he had left off in Los Angeles. He told me about his recent accomplishments at and big plans for Channel 7. He gossiped about some of the other "personalities" at the station; he bent over close to me and touched my arm for emphasis.

He was still treating me, I saw with startling clarity, as he would a child. As someone absolutely powerless, someone whose status flowed from him alone. I was determined not to respond with fear or coyness. I kept myself prim and closed and upright. At first, he didn't notice.

I asked about his wife. She's fine, he said. And then he told me about his new apartment, one that he'd rented in town just for himself, and invited me over to look at it with him.

It's starting all over again, I thought—but this time, I suddenly realized, this man sees me slightly differently. I'm not connected to Steve. I'm not living with America's Hero any more. Now, he probably thinks that I'm even more beholden to him.

"John, I don't think that's a good idea," I said, as coolly as possible.

"Oh, come on!" he laughed. He was laughing at me. "There's no harm in it."

"No," I repeated. "I'm really not interested."

That was all I said. He stared at me incredulously, then a look of anger crossed his face. I've made an enemy, I thought.

We finished our meal quickly after that, left the restaurant, and went our separate ways. He didn't call my office any more.

It was shortly after that lunch that my status on the show began to change. At first, I was puzzled as to what was really happening.

My problems at work began gradually, subtly. Then, toward the end, they escalated. After a few months of high ratings the show's original producers, their job of creating the new format finished, left. Two new producers, less experienced young men, came on board.

Within a few weeks, Regis' influence began to grow. "I know how to make this show work," Regis would say, as we all sat around the conference table, planning the next day's show. It was common knowledge around the station that Regis, the old master of the local talk-show format, had started to socialize with the new producers; he'd decided to take them under his wing.

Nothing was wrong with that. But a peculiar thing began happening. Occasionally—maybe once a week—an interview I'd been assigned would vanish overnight. In the controlled panic before 9 A.M., I'd learn that my guest had canceled out, or that we'd run into time problems, or that the producers had decided the "mix" was wrong. Well, of course, they assured me, those things happened. Then they began to happen more often. Then after a while, I could sit offstage and read the newspaper between the infrequent segments I got to do.

After a month or two, I caught on. One of the production assistants, a young woman, told me confidentially that, after the scheduled meetings I attended broke up, Regis and the producers would have their own, private meetings. There they'd "adjust" the interview assignments.

"That's where all those 'cancelations' are coming from, Cyndy," she said.

I understood now what was happening. I also understood that it was my responsibility to fight back. In the meetings—ignoring Regis' wisecracks and asides—I stood up and, rearranging the cards on the storyboard, assigned myself interviews, and told everyone concerned that I wouldn't put up with any more "accidental" changes. Everyone was shocked that I would even think that. They solemnly agreed that they had no intention of cutting me out. For a while, that seemed to be true. The balance on the show shifted back to fifty-fifty.

Regis fought back hard—this time, on the air. Just as he had in Los Angeles, he began to turn his back on me when I was talking; to sigh or fidget or make faces when I had something serious to say. When I'd finish, he'd wait a few beats, letting my words hang in the air, before jumping back in on an entirely different topic.

While I was doing an interview, he'd stand off-camera in my eyeline, staring blankly at me or mugging to the crew or the studio audience. He also started making jokes about Marvin, about my private life, again. But now I refused to laugh.

"Regis is making fun of you on the air," said Marvin, who watched the show when he could. "He does it when you're talking, when you're not aware of it.

"You know," he said, sadly, "you really don't belong there."

The women at the station, the production assistants and the secretaries, now winced at Regis' antics and looked at me sympathetically.

"Why aren't you laughing at Regis' jokes?" asked Bill Fyffe in a meeting he'd arranged. I explained as best I could that Regis was insulting me.

"Oh, come on, Cyndy. Nobody's trying to take advantage of you. Part of your job is to laugh with Regis. To support him. This is a team effort. You're a part of the team. Everybody works together."

His words rang hollow. But they were familiar. It wasn't until I left his office that I figured it out. It was baseball talk, I realized. It was Steve and the Dodgers. It was indeed a conversation from Steve's world.

And . . . from Cyndy's world, too! Right then, right there in the corridor, the awful truth hit me. It was *Cyndy* they'd hired, not Cynthia. They *wanted* the girl they'd seen in Los Angeles. Only now I knew that I really wasn't Cyndy. That trying to be her had made me sick. That Cyndy was not available. That I had no choice but to give them—no, to be—the woman I really was.

The word came down from management that I should change my look—that I should darken my lipstick and lighten my hair. I ignored any suggestions in that direction.

"A big fan of yours wants to say hello to you, Cyndy," said Regis, mischievously, sitting on the stool next to me during our opening segment. "He'd *love* to give you a big kiss."

"Who is it?" I asked suspiciously. I had been looking at Regis, toward the center of the set, during this exchange. At that moment, I noticed Regis' eyes looking beyond me at something in the wings. Then I became conscious of someone approaching from behind. From my blind side.

I turned quickly toward the noise. Standing there, just a few feet away from me, was a huge, nearly naked man. An insanely grinning professional wrestler, grossly overweight, his body glistening with oil.

All this registered in a split second. Before I could react physically, the man grabbed me, lifted me, wrapped his arms around me, and kissed me directly on the mouth. Somewhere, far away, I could hear the crew members gasp. Then he put me down and backed away.

I was too stunned, too humiliated to speak. There was silence on the set. Dead air. "Make a joke about it," said Cyndy, in my ear. I ignored her, and said nothing.

Still standing in the same spot, I looked down at the front of my dress. It was completely covered with oil from the man's body. Ruined. There was only one thing to do. While Regis began joking nervously, frantically, to the camera, I disconnected my microphone, walked offstage to my dressing room, and changed clothes. When I was changed and ready to continue, I walked back onto the set and resumed my seat.

That afternoon, the executive producer called me into his office. This was live television, he said. The show, he told me, thrived on "spontaneity." Whatever happened in the future, I should *never* react like that again.

Perhaps I should have quit that day. But I'm glad I didn't. It was left to a friend, a wonderful woman at ABC whom I cannot name, to prod me into, finally, standing up for Cynthia.

It was the end of my first year at Channel 7. This woman, who had access to the financial affairs of the station, risked her job for me. She gave me a Xeroxed copy of Regis' contract. I read it at home, while the girls played with their toys alongside me. It was long, and crammed with legalese, but it wasn't hard to figure out. Regis, my co-host—the man whom I'd suggested the station hire, the man who shared the same agent with me—was making three times my salary. Yes, of course Regis had more experience. But the inequity was too much.

And then Cyndy was sitting there with me: I felt shamed, humiliated. What had I done wrong? Perhaps . . . I had not pleased the men in power. Perhaps I should just go along, and hope they would reward me later.

Perhaps I was making too much noise. A nag. A bitch. No.

I shuddered, and remembered my months in the beach house. My sessions with Barbara. I looked at my daughters—so happy, so bright, so beautiful. What would they think of me—what lesson would they learn?—if I gave in, now, to this? But I also realized, with a pang of terror, how tenuous, how *new* Cynthia really was.

Suddenly, it all seemed clear. How important it was that I defend myself—and how unimportant, by comparison, was my job or career or "reputation."

I put the girls to bed. I read Regis' contract again, and put it in my briefcase. What would happen to me now? I thought. To the three of us? I was under no illusions that I was Superwoman. That these men would melt underneath my new resolve. But I knew what I had to do.

CHAPTER 28

The next day I called my agent, told him what I'd found out, and directed him to talk to Bill Fyffe about my contract.

"I don't have to make what Regis is making," I said. "I just want my salary adjusted. I just want it to be more equal. The show is way up in the ratings and I am a *co*-host." He told me he would talk to the station management and get back to me.

The station refused to schedule a negotiating meeting. They offered me a small bonus instead of a raise. Their offer, they said, was final. At my instruction, my agent kept asking for a meeting. The tension level at work picked up considerably; I had little or no contact with the executives now.

On Thursday, May 17, Bill Fyffe knocked on my door and came into my office. It was 11 A.M.; I'd just taped a full show and a set of promo spots.

"Whatever happens now," said Bill, "I hope we can remain friends."

"What do you mean, Bill?"

"Well, I don't want you to come back tomorrow. You won't be working here until further notification."

"Don't do this, Bill," I said. "Please. Don't do this."

He said nothing; just turned and walked out. I called my agent and told him what had happened. "Don't worry, Cyndy," he said. "They can't fire you. You've got a contract. You haven't done anything wrong."

I called John Severino and his secretary instructed me to contact his lawyers if I had a question. That night, I called Regis at home. I asked him what was happening. He told me he had no idea what was going on. "Just stay out of this, Regis," I said. "If you can't help me, just stay out of this."

The next day, Friday, Regis did the show alone. He read a statement on the air: Because of "contractual disputes," it said, Cyndy Garvey "has been given the day off."

On Monday, there was no mention of me on the air. And Regis had a temporary co-host. It was Joy Philbin, Regis' wife.

I never appeared on "The Morning Show" again. There was a flurry of letters between my agent and station management; at first, ABC threatened to fire me outright. I hired a lawyer. The network executives made their next move. They declared that instead of being fired, I was "suspended": that is, while my contract with them was in force, I was off their show until further notice. I would receive my normal salary—for doing nothing—but until my contract with ABC ran out, one year hence, I was prohibited from appearing on any other show or looking for television work elsewhere.

I was in limbo. Professional limbo. Occasionally, throughout that year, my agent would get hints from ABC management that they were thinking of hiring me back; that they were just waiting for "things to blow over." But, inevitably, the rumors would come to nothing. And as the months passed, the issue faded from almost everyone's consciousness.

"Why aren't you on TV?" asked the people in the street, at the local stores, at the functions Marvin and I attended together.

"I heard you had left New York."

"Are you sick?"

I explained to them, on the advice of my attorney and agent, that I was fine, that ABC and I were simply working out a simple contract dispute. They shrugged, smiled sympathetically, and turned their minds to other matters.

In truth, my priorities were changing, too. At first, the pain of losing my work was deep. But after a while, the distress faded. To my surprise, I felt no great disappointment at being off the air, out of public view. I watched the show at home occasionally; I could see, hard lesson that it was, whom they really wanted in the first place. After I was gone, a succession of attractive young women co-hosts filled my chair; they smiled and laughed and were the butt of Regis' jokes. I saw my old self—my old Cyndy self—in all of them. They seemed happy in that role. I hoped they truly were. I knew also that I would never be that person again.

By this time, thankfully, Cyndy was too small a part of me.

I was a full-time mother now. I spent precious time with Krisha and Whitney. They were growing, growing. We talked for hours—about their world, mine, and ours. I dealt with my lawyers in Los Angeles and worked out my divorce.

I continued to date Marvin. My relationship with him deepened. He was as unlike Steve as a man could be: a complicated, introspective artist with an almost unlimited capacity for sensitivity—and despair.

Late that fall, Marvin asked the girls and me to move in with him. I gladly agreed. We shared expenses; he welcomed us into his life. He remodeled one of his bedrooms into a room for Krisha and Whitney. He helped them with their homework, took them on walks and trips, and showered love and presents on them.

Sadly, though, it did not work out. Our worlds did not mesh. Marvin was and is a driven man, an artist consumed by his work. When he was in a good mood, which was often, he was a supportive friend and lover to me and a loving companion for my children. In his dark moods —which, when his work was going badly, lasted for days and weeks—he was moody, unpredictable, unreachable. I felt doubly guilty: for disturbing Marvin, and for making my children cope with this difficult, adult situation. In May of 1985, at the end of my "suspension" year, Marvin and I discussed the problem, and decided that it would be best for all of us if the girls and I moved out. Two days before my contract was to expire, I got a call from Bill Fyffe at WABC. He would like to meet me for lunch tomorrow, he said, to talk about my future. He made reservations at the Top of the Sixes, a restaurant in a skyscraper on Fifth Avenue.

I dressed carefully, hailed a cab in front of my apartment, and arrived at the restaurant fifteen minutes early. Our appointed time came and went. I sat alone at the table for a half-hour more, then went home and called Bill at the station.

"What happened, Bill?" I said. "Where were you?"

"Well, Cyndy," he said, "I reconsidered. I just didn't think it would be in our best interest."

The next day, ABC notified my agent that they were not renewing my contract. My divorce from Steve was final the same week. A few days after that, my brother Chris called me from California. My mother had had a heart attack.

CHAPTER 29

"It was a bad one, Cynthia," said Chris, his voice strained and sad. "The doctors don't know what's going to happen."

We were packed and on the plane to Los Angeles the next day. Marvin owned a house in Los Angeles, and he kindly, unhesitatingly, lent it to us so I could take care of my mother.

Mom was in the hospital for a month. I rushed over from the airport to see her. She was in Intensive Care, barely conscious, looking frighteningly small and frail. I sat by her bedside, terrified that her damaged heart would give out. I felt helpless, desperate, frustrated that there was nothing I could do for her but worry. Each day, I arranged baby-sitters for the girls and drove my rented car to the hospital. After a week or so, thankfully, the doctors said she was out of danger.

She was moved to a regular room. Now, as I sat next to her, she slept. Occasionally, she'd wake up and smile weakly at me. I'd take her hand and smile back as she drifted off again.

The hours, the days passed. I studied her face, her hands, the gentle rising and falling of her chest. My mind drifted back to my childhood, to all the years we'd been together. To how beautiful she'd been. How kind, how gentle.

To the good times when my father was away. To the fear, to the violence when he was home. To my disappointment that she never protected me against his cruelty.

To the gulf between us. Yes, that was the real problem, the awful fact: that I'd never really understood her. That we'd never really talked as mother and daughter. Shared secrets. Solved problems. As I did with my own two girls. As we did, so wonderfully, every day.

We'd missed all that, I realized. It was all gone. Too late. For all the love we felt for each other, there was an impenetrable wall between us.

The sadness, the sense of loss, was almost unbearable. As she slept, I cried.

"Dad, you must leave her alone now. She's very sick. You can't yell at her. You've got to stop now. She'll die."

I pleaded with my father. He looked back at me blankly over the coffee shop table. I'd screwed up my courage and taken him to lunch to tell him this. He seemed older, grayer, than the last time I'd seen him. Maybe he would listen to me this time.

Maybe. He said nothing when I finished, but neither did he explode in rage at my suggestion. I hoped desperately that my words had had some effect; indeed, Chris told me later that Dad's attitude toward my mother had softened—at least for the time being.

Afraid my presence would set him off, I tried to avoid him as much as possible. When my mother left the hospital, I spent as much time with her as I could, making sure she got her rest and avoided doing heavy housework. I brought the girls over as often as I could; they enjoyed each other immensely. I could also see that they loved being back in Los Angeles.

Under the warm sun, in the open air, Krisha and Whitney were thriving. They went to the beach, swam, ran in the sand, met and hugged all their old friends, made new ones. Their skin was tanned, their hair long and free. I could see them growing every day.

To my surprise, I found myself enjoying being back in Los Angeles. My old friends, too, welcomed me back. "Oh, so you were gone for a while?" they joked; it was as if, indeed, I had never left. We met regularly, just like before. We helped each other take care of our children. They listened sympathetically to my problems, and I to theirs.

After a few months, even though my mother was substantially recovered, I realized we would not be going back to New York. I knew my intense relationship with Marvin was over, although he was still a treasured friend. He visited us frequently when he had business on the West Coast. I asked the girls how they would feel about staying in California. They were ecstatic.

I found a nice house, up the hill from the beach, and moved us into it. For the first time in a long time, the world held few immediate terrors for me. I could sit and think about the future; reassess my life and try to analyze my mistakes. Before I could get on with living, though, there was still one big problem I had to solve.

It was just a day like any other day. It was a beautiful, cool afternoon. I was doing my errands, Krisha in tow. We walked into the dry cleaner's, a store I'd done business in for years.

I picked up my cleaning, paid Judy, the owner, gave a small package to Krisha, and, thinking about our next stop, walked distractedly toward the door.

"Cyndy! You forgot your change!" Judy called out after me.

"Oops!" laughed Krisha. I turned around to go back— and almost ran into a man, a new customer, who was standing there staring at me.

"You're Cyndy Garvey?" he said, gruffly.

"Yes?" I said.

"Oh, so *you're* the bitch who left Steve Garvey."

Shocked speechless, my arms full, I could only watch the man turn around and leave the store. He got into his car and drove away. Then I realized, to my horror, that Krisha had seen everything.

I turned and looked at her. Her face was sad. Sad for me. But after a second she smiled, shrugged, and turned her face, her eyes, into a question mark. This is stupid, Mom, her eyes said to me. What are you going to do about it?

What was I going to do about it? How could I stop living down Cyndy's reputation—and stop the onslaught on my dignity and self-respect? Most of the world still treated me as Cyndy—because, to them, I *was* Cyndy. If I wanted to be treated as Cynthia, I had to find some way to let them know I existed.

A newspaper or television interview wouldn't help. The story was complicated, too complicated. There would be no way to explain myself in such a small space —and besides, they'd probably demand that Cyndy, not Cynthia, show up anyway.

I thought of writing a book. In the first person. My story. I told this idea to a friend of mine, an actor, who said he knew a man, a writer, who could help me.

Andy Meisler, he told me, was a journalist. He specialized in covering television; he'd also collaborated with several television personalities in writing magazine articles under their byline.

We met in a restaurant near his home. Andy was a few years younger than I was; he was married, he said, to a successful attorney. "Katie makes much more money than I do—thank God," he said, cheerfully.

I liked him. He seemed interested in my story: he'd long known, he said, that public image and reality had little relation to each other. He assured me that this would be in my book. He would use his writing skills to get my thoughts down on paper, but I would have total control over every word.

We agreed to start working together. He came to my house two or three times a week, I made coffee, and we sat together around the kitchen table as he asked me about my life. He was very friendly and open about his own life, but, after only a few sessions, I realized something was wrong. Despite his assurances, I couldn't help but think of Pat Jordan when I talked to him. Was this *Inside Sports* all over again? Would my weaknesses, would my secrets, be used against me? Was I being led into a trap? Would the world consider me a crybaby, a complainer, an ingrate?

No. I couldn't let that happen again. Even when Andy pressed me, questioned me gently about the same areas over and over, I censored my thoughts. I skipped lightly over my childhood, steering away his questions about my father and mother. I concentrated on my public life—baseball, the television. Regis. The station executives. ABC.

After six months we had half a book. But deep down, I knew it wasn't very good. I gave it to a trusted friend, a professional woman, to read. After she had finished, she made an appointment to meet me for lunch. When I met her at the table, she had the manuscript beside her. She had a strange expression on her face.

She hates it, I thought. My story, Cynthia's story, is not worth telling.

"Well, what do you think?" I asked. I braced myself for her criticism.

"Cynthia," she said, her eyes beginning to moisten. "This book made me very sad. But I don't quite know why. Something's not right. Something rings false."

She hesitated, then leaned forward and spoke in a low, urgent voice. "You don't come out and say it, but . . . reading between the lines . . . I may be wrong, of course . . ."

She paused again, and took a deep breath.

"Cynthia," she said, "I think you were an abused child."

CHAPTER 30

I began to cry uncontrollably. Across the table, my friend cried, too. She put her hand on mine. Inside of me, a dam broke. I knew—awfully, finally—that my childhood was not a secret that could be kept. It was too much a part of me. It was visible to anyone who cared to look hard enough. I would have to acknowledge and deal with it. Every day. Today.

I went home and re-read the chapters we had written. They were filled, I now saw, with evasions and denial and, above all, anger. The anger shocked and sickened me. It lay there just below the surface, poisoning everything I wrote about.

I hadn't realized I was so angry. I thought I had run away from it, pushed it all aside. I was wrong, wrong. I was still its prisoner.

And then, with a startling clarity, I saw my true story spread out before me. For just a crystal-clear, anger-free second, I glimpsed it: I wasn't a victim. No. I had no one person to blame for my troubles—not my father, not Steve, not Regis or John Severino, not anyone.

I had been affected by forces—my father's own childhood and frustrations, Steve's fame, the media—that, for most of my life, neither I nor anyone around me had ever really understood. My real story—the one I could be proud of, the one I would have to write, the one that might be helpful to others—was how I, like millions of women and men before me, had struggled with the legacy of child abuse, of lack of identity and self-esteem. How I, just like all the other lucky ones, had managed to confront the past, face the problem, and make a new beginning.

A new beginning! A new beginning with my children. Two beautiful, happy girls, raised with love and hope and understanding. In a home that was free of fear and silence. In a home filled with love and laughter.

I had broken the cycle of child abuse. Yes. That was my proudest achievement. That would be the message of my book. But first I had work to do. I had to go back, sift through the pain—and, fighting back the anger and blame, trace the forces that had shaped my life.

Could I do it? Was I really strong enough to go back again? That afternoon, like all afternoons, I picked Krisha and Whitney up at their school. They hugged me and kissed me and told me all about their day. No holding back. No secrets.

It was then that I realized, with a rush of pure joy, that I was being given another chance. To relive my childhood, happily. Not through them, but with them.

It is an opportunity, I now know, available to anyone who's been abused as a child. And, I'm just as certain, it is the responsibility of all of us who've been abused to break the silence. To pass this wonderful message on. And in time, perhaps, to even work out our differences with our parents. That would be the best we could work for.

The next day, I called Andy at his home. We talked for a long time. I told him my feelings about the book, and asked him if he would help me write the one I had just envisioned. He said he would be proud to join me. And we began again.

EPILOGUE

November, 1988: Steve Garvey became engaged to Rebecka Mendenhall, an Atlanta-based TV news producer whom he had been dating for two and a half years.

January 15, 1989: Steve Garvey was named as the father of a newborn baby girl by Cheryl Ann Moulton, a San Diego woman he had dated briefly.

January 18, 1989: Steve Garvey married Candace Thomas, a Los Angeles-area woman—with two daughters from a previous marriage—whom he has known for several months.

March 2, 1989: Rebecka Mendenhall, who had earlier told Steve Garvey that she, too, was pregnant with his child, filed a suit charging him with paternity and breach of promise. He told the media that he and his new wife are born-again Christians, and that he will "assume responsibility" for the children if they are proven to be his.

March 13, 1989: It was revealed in a *People* magazine article that Steve Garvey had been dating Judith Ross, his longtime girlfriend, at the same time he had been seeing Rebecka Mendenhall. He told reporters that he

does not believe that recent events will prevent him from
pursuing a political career.

March 13, 1989: A Superior Court judge in Los Angeles
issued an order that Steve Garvey undergo psychiatric
counseling before seeing his two daughters, Krisha and
Whitney Garvey.

Early this year, when this book was in its final editing
stages, my ex-husband's problems became public knowledge. These revelations did not surprise me. Nor did they
bring me any pleasure or feeling of vindication. In fact, it
was exactly the opposite: they brought back feelings of
anger and shame that I thought I had buried long ago.

The past several months have not been easy ones.

For my girls and me, the sad news began to break on
New Year's weekend. Krisha and Whitney had gone skiing with their father. Krisha called me at home, as we
had planned.

"Mommy! Mommy! Daddy's getting married!" she
said excitedly. She told me about her father's plans to
marry Rebecka Mendenhall in April.

The next time I saw Steve was several weeks later. He
was in the bleachers at Krisha's school gymnasium.
Krisha's volleyball team was playing a match. He was
sitting beside a young blond woman. The woman was not
Rebecka Mendenhall. It was Candace Thomas.

I had arrived late. When I first spotted my daughter
she was crying; her father's behavior had confused and
scared her. She left the game and ran to me. She wanted
Candace to leave. I asked her to and on the second request, she did.

Two weeks later Steve asked the girls to spend the
weekend skiing with him. They could not, because they
were taking high school placement exams. That weekend
he married Candace Thomas. The girls were to have been
surprise guests at his wedding. A week later the women

he had broken off with went public, and our lives were caught up once again in Steve's problems.

Most painful of all, of course, is watching my children try to deal with all of this. They are twelve and fourteen —too young to bear the consequences of their father's actions. And yet now they must. The newspapers report every new development in their father's tangled affairs; the television programs they watch are full of crude jokes about him. They liked Rebecka Mendenhall. They are sad about what has happened to her. They are confused about their father's public comments; about his references to religious guidance. They read the startling news in *People* magazine that their Christmas present from Steve was identical to the ones he had given his three girlfriends. They were, understandably, devastated.

They must also decide how to adjust to the fact that they have four new stepsisters and half-sisters. What kind of relationship will they have with them? With their stepmother? With their father?

These are questions I agonize over every day. I discuss them with Krisha and Whitney whenever necessary. I try to keep the lines of communication open.

While all this is being resolved, I'm going to protect my daughters as best as I can. Steve and I have been in court the last few weeks. After I requested it, the judge issued an order that prevents Steve from taking the girls out in public for publicity purposes. And she mandated psychiatric counseling for him.

As for the future: although the news about Steve Garvey will quickly fade from the headlines, it will not fade from our lives. When the jokes and the humiliation were at their height, my first impulse was to reassume my maiden name—and give it to my daughters. But I have changed my mind. Their last name is Garvey. My last name is Garvey. I don't want my daughters to be ashamed of carrying the name they were born with. I want them to be happy and proud—and to grow up to be strong women. Maybe someday they'll understand. Maybe when they're older they will resolve their unfinished business with their father.

Cynthia Garvey
April, 1989